GOOD HOUSEKEEPING

COMPLETE BOOK OF

PRESERVING

GOOD HOUSEKEEPING
COMPLETE BOOK OF
PRESERVING

EBURY PRESS
LONDON

Published in association with

First published by Ebury Press
an imprint of The Random Century Group
Random Century House
20 Vauxhall Bridge Road
London SW1V 2SA

British Library Cataloguing-in-Publication Data

"Good Housekeeping" complete book of preserving.
– (Good Housekeeping)
I. Good Housekeeping II. Series
641.4
ISBN 0–7126–4718–X

Editor: Helen Southall
Cookery Editor: Janet Smith
Designed by: Bridgewater Design Limited
Photographer: James Murphy
Stylist: Ian Hands
Home Economist: Allyson Birch
Additional Photography: Charlie Stebbings and Martin Brigdale
Illustrations: John Woodcock, Vana Haggarty and Danny McBride

Typeset in Bembo by Textype Typesetters, Cambridge
Printed and bound in Great Britain by Butler & Tanner Ltd, Frome and London

Contents

Introduction . . . . page 6

Jams and Conserves 8

Jellies 33

Marmalades 49

Butters, Cheeses and Curds 64

Pickles 76

Chutneys and Relishes 100

Sauces, Ketchups, Vinegars and Oils 121

Bottling and Fruits in Alcohol 129

Salting, Storing, Drying, Curing and Smoking 149

Drinks and Liqueurs 161

Candying and Crystallising 177

Mincemeats 185

Short-term and Other Preserves 192

Microwave Preserves 208

Index 221

Introduction

A fresh-tasting, tangy marmalade or fruit-packed conserve, thickly spread on hot, buttered toast, is a delicious way to start the day. No ploughman's lunch, cold meat platter or pork pie is complete without a good helping of chutney or a spoonful of pickle. In spite of the vast assortment of commercially-prepared preserves now available, none can compare with those made at home.

The making of preserves was once an important and regular feature of life; every household had a cupboard stacked with jars full of preserved foods. Nowadays, the increasing availability of fresh foods all year round, and of commercially-prepared preserves, means that the art of home preserving is sadly neglected.

In this book we hope to reintroduce you to those age-old skills which were once so lovingly practised. Here you will find all the classics: jams, jellies, pickles and chutneys, along with lots of new ideas for herb oils and vinegars, drinks, liqueurs, sauces and relishes, plus information on home bottling, salting, storing and drying.

Why Preserve?

The object of preserving is to take fresh foods in prime condition and to store or prepare them in such a way that they remain in this condition for long periods of time.

In the days before refrigeration and easily obtainable canned, dried and frozen foods, it was vital to be able to preserve fresh foods to feed the family when food was scarce. In country areas, each family kept a pig to fatten up during the summer and slaughter at the beginning of winter. Some meat was eaten fresh but the bulk of it had to be preserved in various ways so that it would last throughout the winter. Fresh fruits and vegetables were made into preserves both to prevent wastage and to enable people to enjoy their flavour when they were not available.

Although the necessity for preserving does not exist in quite the same way today, one of the most important benefits is still that of saving money. Jams, jellies and marmalades are best made when fruits are plentiful, cheap and in perfect condition.

Despite their high cost, the quality of commercially-produced preserves is rarely as good as that of home-made preserves. For example, fruits and vegetables can lose more of their nutritive value during commercial processing. Making preserves at home enables you to experiment with unusual combinations of flavours and to enjoy the satisfaction of serving foods that are the produce of your own kitchen. An added bonus is that some preserves, such as candied or crystallised fruits, make very acceptable gifts when decoratively packed.

How Preserving Works

Foods contain enzymes which are responsible for their growth, development and eventual breaking down and rotting. The action of these enzymes is what causes the cut surface of a piece of fruit to turn brown, for example, and allows for the growth of micro-organisms in the form of bacteria, yeasts and moulds. Bacteria in foods can lead to food poisoning, yeasts cause foods to ferment, and moulds spoil the appearance and flavour of foods. Moulds themselves are not harmful, but are often an indication of the presence of bacteria.

Traditional forms of preserving aim to keep out and prevent the growth of micro-organisms and so maintain the food in prime condition. The first methods of preservation were probably the result of experimentation and a fair amount of luck, but nowadays we know how and why these methods worked. They made use of natural facilities – sun, wind, smoke and salt.

Drying It was discovered that when foods were spread out in the sun or hung in the wind to dry, they did not perish. This is because micro-organisms can only survive where there is moisture and the drying effects of sunshine and wind prevent the growth of micro-organisms. Nowadays, fruits, vegetables and herbs can easily be dried at home in a very cool oven, airing cupboard or some other warm place. Of course, it is always important to store dried foods carefully to prevent the re-absorption of moisture.

Smoking When houses had huge fireplaces and chimneys, meat and fish could be hung in the chimneys until well dried out and 'smoked'. Again, it was the drying process that prevented the growth of bacteria. The flavour of the smoked foods would depend on the type of wood burned in the fire. Nowadays, such facilities for smoking are hard to find and smoking is rarely done in the home. It can also be dangerous if not carried out properly and if the growth of bacteria is not completely eliminated. Commercially-smoked foods are of good quality, if rather expensive, and some, such as smoked salmon, may even be preferred to the fresh variety. Because of the facilities needed, the risk of food poisoning and the availability of commercially-produced smoked foods, we do not recommend smoking as a method of home preserving today.

Salting In early days, sea salt was obtained by evaporation and rubbed into fish, meat and vegetables. The salt drew moisture out of the food and prevented the growth of micro-organisms. The salting of meat, however, is another method of preservation that can be dangerous if not carried out correctly. As fresh meat is now available all year round and can be preserved in other safer and more efficient ways, such as by freezing, we have not included instructions for salting or curing meat in this book. Small fish, such as anchovies or sprats, and vegetables, such as beans, can, however, be salted in the home without too much trouble (see pages 150–159).

These original methods of preservation were used long before it was discovered that sugar, vinegar, alcohol and temperature could also play a part.

Sugar A high concentration of sugar prevents the growth of micro-organisms and it is the sugar, combined with cooking to a high temperature, that preserves the fruits in jams, jellies, marmalades, conserves, butters and cheeses. Sugar also acts as the preservative when bottling fruits in a sugar syrup. Again, however, it is necessary to heat the filled bottles to a high temperature in order to sterilise the contents and hermetically seal the bottles to prevent further attack from micro-organisms.

Vinegar and alcohol Vinegar and alcohol also prevent the growth of micro-organisms. Vinegar is used for pickling fruits and vegetables, and in chutneys, sauces and relishes; alcohol is used to preserve fruits.

Sterilisation Extremely high temperatures stop enzyme activity and prevent growth of micro-organisms. Sauces, ketchups and bottled fruits and vegetables all need to be sterilised by heat. This has to be done after the bottles have been filled and covered so that the sterilising process can form a seal to keep out micro-organisms in the air. Milk is commercially sterilised by heat treatment during the pasteurisation process and some milk is heated to a higher temperature ('long-life' or UHT – ultra-high temperature) and can be kept for long periods of time without being refrigerated.

Refrigeration and freezing The discovery that low temperatures slow down or stop enzyme activity in foods has made a major difference to life in the home. Nowadays, almost every household has a refrigerator and many also own a freezer. Foods are kept at a sufficiently low temperature to stop the action of enzymes.

Although freezing is a method of home preserving, it is not one of the traditional home skills, so we have not included instructions for freezing in this book.

Jams and Conserves

Jam is basically a cooked mixture of fruit and sugar. The high concentration of sugar used in jam-making prevents the growth of micro-organisms and allows the jam to be kept for many months.

Conserves are whole, sometimes chopped, fruits suspended in a thick syrup. In most cases, to make a conserve, the fruit is layered with an equal quantity of sugar and left for 24 hours to extract the juices, before boiling for a short time, preserving the fruit with the minimum of cooking. Fruits which make good conserves are strawberries, raspberries and loganberries. The fruits retain a flavour which is very much closer to the original taste of the fruit. Conserves make the most acceptable gifts or excellent desserts when served with cream, fromage frais or Greek yogurt.

Equipment

Some special utensils and tools, though by no means essential, make making jams and conserves easier.

Preserving pans   Jams and conserves can be made in any heavy-based saucepan large enough to ensure that the contents come only halfway up the side once the sugar has been added. Proper preserving pans do make life easier, however, as their sloping sides help the jam to maintain a 'fast rolling boil' without boiling over. This is essential for a good set. Choose a preserving pan made from stainless steel, tin-lined copper or lined aluminium (see page 77). It should have a fairly thick base to prevent the jam burning, and should be wide enough to allow the jam to boil rapidly without splashing all over the hob. The best size for you will depend on how much jam you want to make at one time.

Old-style preserving pans made from unlined copper or brass can be used for jams, providing they are perfectly clean, but it is unwise to use very old pans that are damaged or impossible to clean thoroughly. Any discoloration or tarnish should be removed with a patent cleaner and the pan should be thoroughly washed before use. Jams made in copper or brass pans will contain less vitamin C than those made in aluminium or stainless steel pans. No preserve should be left standing in any unlined metal preserving pan.

If you haven't got a preserving pan, use a large heavy-based saucepan, remembering that, since most saucepans are not as wide as a preserving pan, you may need to allow a longer simmering and boiling period for the fruit.

Jam jars   You will need a good supply of jars, which should be free from cracks, chips or other flaws. Jars holding 450 g or 1 kg (1 or 2 lb) are the most useful sizes as you can buy covers for these sizes. Wash them well in warm soapy water and rinse thoroughly in clean, warm water. Dry off the jars in a cool oven, at 140°C (275°F) mark 1, and use while hot so that they do not crack when filled with boiling jam. You will need waxed discs, cellophane covers, rubber bands and labels for covering and labelling the jars. Packets containing all these are available from most stationery shops, cookshops and some chemists.

Other equipment

1. A large, long-handled wooden spoon for stirring the preserve.

2. A slotted spoon is useful for skimming off any scum or fruit stones from the surface of the preserve.

3. A sugar thermometer, though not essential, is very helpful when testing for a set (see page 11).

4. A funnel with a wide tube for filling jars is useful. Failing this, use a heatproof jug or large cup.

5. A cherry stoner saves time and prevents hands becoming stained with cherry juice.

6. Any sieve used in jam-making should be made of nylon, not metal, which may discolour the fruit.

Choosing the Fruit

Fruit should be sound and just ripe. It is better to use slightly under- rather than over-ripe fruit as the pectin is most readily available at this stage.

Pectin and acid content of fruit The preserve will only set if there are sufficient quantities of pectin, acid and sugar present. Some fruits are rich in pectin and acid and give a good set, while others do not contain so much (see chart below).

Pectin Content of Fruits and Vegetables used in Preserving		
Good	*Medium*	*Poor*
Cooking apples	Dessert apples	Bananas
Crab-apples	Apricots	Carrots
Cranberries	Bilberries	Cherries
Currants	Blackberries	Elderberries
(red and black)	Cranberries	Figs
Damsons	Greengages	Grapes
Gooseberries	Loganberries	Japonicas
Lemons	Mulberries	Marrows
Limes	Plums	Medlars
Seville oranges	Raspberries	Melons
Plums		Nectarines
(some varieties)		Peaches
Quinces		Pineapple
		Rhubarb
		Strawberries

Testing for pectin content If you are not sure of the setting qualities of the fruit you are using, the following test can be carried out: When the fruit has been cooked until soft and before you add the sugar (see page 11), take 5 ml (1 tsp) juice, as free as possible from seeds and skin, put it in a glass and, when cool, add 15 ml (1 tbsp) methylated spirits. Shake the glass and then leave for 1 minute. If the mixture forms a jelly-like clot, the fruit has a good pectin content. If it does not form a single, firm clot, the pectin content is low and some form of extra pectin will be needed.

Fruits that lack acid and pectin require the addition of a fruit or fruit juice that is rich in these substances. Lemon juice is most often used for this purpose, since it aids the set and often brings out the flavour of the fruit. Allow 30 ml (2 tbsp) lemon juice to 1.8 kg (4 lb) of a fruit with poor setting properties. Alternatively, use Sugar with Pectin (see

page 11) or some home-made pectin extract (see below) or add another pectin-rich fruit, making a mixed fruit jam. Yet another method is to use a commercially-bottled pectin according to the manufacturer's instructions.

Sometimes an acid only is added, such as citric or tartaric acid. These contain no pectin but help to extract the natural pectin from the tissues of the fruit and improve the flavour of fruits lacking in acid. Allow 2.5 ml (½ tsp) to 1.8 kg (4 lb) of a fruit with poor setting properties.

Home-made pectin extract Apple pectin extract can be made from any sour cooking apples or crab-apples as well as from apple peelings and cores and windfalls. Wash 900 g (2 lb) fruit and chop it roughly, without peeling or coring. Cover with 600–900 ml (1–1½ pints) water and stew gently for about 45 minutes, until well pulped. Strain through a jelly bag or muslin cloth (see page 34). Carry out the pectin test (see left) to ensure that the extract has a high pectin content. Allow 150–300 ml (¼–½ pint) of this extract to 1.8 kg (4 lb) fruit that is low in pectin. Pectin extract can be made from redcurrants or gooseberries in the same way.

Sugar

The presence of sugar in jam is very important as it acts as a preservative and affects the setting quality. The exact amount of sugar to be used depends on the pectin strength of the fruit, so always use the amount specified in a recipe. Too little sugar will result in a poor set and the jam may go mouldy on storing. Too much sugar will produce a dark and sticky jam, the flavour will be lost and it may crystallise. Granulated sugar is suitable and the most economical for jam-making, but when lump sugar or preserving crystals are used, less scum is formed and the preserve needs less stirring to prevent burning, since these sugars do not settle in a dense layer on the bottom of the pan. The finished preserve will also be slightly clearer and brighter. Caster sugar or brown sugar can also be used, but brown sugar produces much darker jam with a changed flavour.

Sugar with Pectin is a blend of granulated sugar, natural apple pectin and tartaric acid and is very useful when making jams and conserves with fruits low in pectin. When using Sugar with Pectin, the best results are achieved if you follow these tips:

1. If using less than one packet of sugar, empty the whole packet into a bowl and stir it to distribute the pectin, before adding the amount required to the fruit.

2. Do not use more than two packets of sugar at any one time.

3. Heat the preserve to a full rolling boil. The quoted boiling times apply after the boiling point has been reached. A full rolling boil cannot be stirred down.

4. The usual boiling time for jam is 4 minutes.

Jams can also be made with fructose, a refined sugar produced from fruit and vegetables; as it is metabolised differently from ordinary sugar, diabetics may use it as a substitute, within reason.

There is no completely satisfactory substitute for sugar in jam-making. If honey or treacle is used, its flavour is usually distinctly noticeable and the jam will not set easily. Glucose and glycerine do not have the same sweetening power as cane sugar. If one of these alternatives must be used, not more than half the amount of sugar specified in a recipe should be replaced.

You can make your own reduced-sugar jams similar to those you can buy. Do not reduce the sugar content by more than 20 per cent or the jam will be runny. As it does not keep well, make it in small batches and store in the refrigerator (for up to 6 weeks) or a cool place (for 3–4 weeks).

Preparing and Cooking the Fruit

Pick over the fruit, prepare it according to variety, and wash it quickly. Put the fruit into a preserving pan or large, strong saucepan, add water as directed in the recipe and then simmer gently until it is quite tender. The time will vary according to the fruit – tough-skinned fruit, such as gooseberries, blackcurrants or plums, will take 30–45 minutes. This simmering process releases the pectin and acid. If extra acid or pectin is needed, it should be added at this stage (see page 10). Adequate reduction of the fruit before adding the sugar is necessary for a good set. The sugar should only be added when the fruit has been sufficiently softened and reduced as sugar has a hardening effect on the fruit and, once added, the fruit will not soften.

Remove the pan from the heat and add the sugar, stirring well until dissolved. (The sugar will dissolve more easily if warmed in the oven before it is added.) Add a knob of butter to reduce foaming, then return the pan to the heat and boil rapidly, stirring constantly, until the jam sets when tested (see below).

Testing for a Set

There are several ways of testing a preserve for setting point, some of which are less accurate than others or require special equipment. The methods given here are the easiest to carry out and most accurate.

Temperature test   This is the most accurate method of testing for a set. Stir the jam and put in a sugar thermometer. Continue cooking and, when the temperature reaches 105°C (221°F), a set should be obtained. Some fruits may need a degree lower or higher than this, so it is a good idea to combine this test with one of the following.

Saucer test   Put a very little of the jam on a cold saucer or plate, allow it to cool, then push a finger gently through the jam. If the surface of the jam wrinkles, setting point has been reached. (The pan should be removed from the heat during the test or the jam may be over-boiled.

Flake test   Lift some jam out of the pan on a wooden spoon, let it cool a little and then allow it to drop back into the pan. If it has been boiled long enough, drops of jam will run together along the edge of the spoon and form flakes which will break off sharply.

Potting, Covering and Storing

The jars used for jam must be clean and free from flaws and they must be warmed before the jam is put in them (see page 9). As soon as a set has been reached, remove the pan from the heat, remove any scum with a slotted spoon and pot the jam, filling right to the tops. Exceptions are strawberry and other whole-fruit jams – these should be allowed to cool for about 15 minutes before being potted, to prevent the fruit rising in the jars. Wipe the outside and rims of the pots and cover the jam, while still very hot, with a waxed disc, waxed-side down, making sure it lies flat. Either cover immediately with a dampened cellophane round, securing with a rubber band or string, or leave the jam until quite cold before doing this. For long-term storage, cover the jam with a screw-top as well, but do not cover the pots when the jam is warm, as moisture from the warm jam will collect inside the lid and, without enough heat from the jam to kill the moulds, the preserve may go mouldy. Label the jar and store in a cool, dry, dark place.

Most preserves keep well for over a year if properly covered and stored, but their flavour deteriorates if they are kept for too long. The best idea, therefore, is to eat them within the year, thus making room in the store-cupboard for next year's batch of preserves.

Jam-making Problems

Mould This is most often caused by failure to cover the jam with a waxed disc while it is still very hot – this should be done immediately the jam is potted, or it may become infected with mould spores from the air. Alternatively, the pots may have been damp or cold when used, or insufficiently filled, or they may have been stored in a damp or warm place. Other possible causes are insufficient evaporation of water while the fruit is being 'broken down' by the preliminary cooking, and/or too short boiling after the sugar has been added. Jam with mould growing on its surface should not be eaten, even if the affected jam is removed, as the mould can produce toxins within the remaining jam. Throw away the whole jar if you find any mould on the top surface.

Bubbles in the jam Bubbles indicate fermentation, which is usually the result of too small a proportion of sugar in relation to fruit; accurate weighing of fruit and sugar is very important. This trouble can also occur, however, when jam is not reduced sufficiently, because this too affects the proportion of sugar in the preserve. Fermentation is harmless enough, but it is apt to spoil both flavour and colour. Fermented jam can be boiled up again but the boiling should only be continued for a short time if the preserve was not reduced enough in the first instance. It can then be re-potted and sealed in clean, preheated jars and used for cooking purposes.

Peel or fruit rising in the jam Strawberry jam is particularly susceptible to this trouble. It helps if the jam is allowed to cool for 15–20 minutes and then given a stir before potting (despite the fact that it is normally advisable to pot all preserves as hot as possible).

Crystallised jam This is usually caused by lack of sufficient acid. You should either use a fruit rich in acid, or make sure that acid is added to the fruit during the preliminary softening process (see page 10). Under- or over-boiling the jam after the sugar has been added can also cause crystallising, as it will upset the proportion of sugar in the finished jam.

Setting problems One cause is the use of over-ripe fruit in which the pectin has deteriorated. Another reason is under-boiling of the fruit, so that the pectin is not fully extracted; there may also be insufficient evaporation of the water before the sugar is added (this can be remedied by further boiling); or over-cooking after adding the sugar, for which there is no remedy.

To ensure a set with fruits deficient in pectin, such as strawberries, it is helpful to add an acid such as lemon juice or citric acid (see page 10); alternatively, mix with a pectin-rich fruit such as redcurrants, or a pectin extract (commercially made or prepared at home from apples – see page 10), or use Sugar with Pectin (see page 11).

Shrinkage of jam on storage   This is caused by inadequate covering, or failure to store the jam in a cool, dark, dry place.

Pressure Cooking Jams

Provided your cooker is one with a three-pressure gauge, it is a good idea to use it for preserving, as it saves quite a bit of time and the fruit retains its flavour and colour.

There are a few points to remember:

1. Always remove the trivet from the pressure pan.
2. Never fill the pan more than half-full.
3. Cook the fruit at medium (10 lb) pressure. If you have a cooker which is set to cook only at high (15 lb) pressure, you can send for alternative weights (available from the manufacturer) which will enable you to alter your cooker to cook at medium (10 lb) pressure. Cooking preserves at high (15 lb) pressure is not recommended because the pectin will be destroyed.

4. Reduce pressure at room temperature.
5. Only the preliminary cooking and softening of the fruit must be done under pressure – never cook a preserve under pressure after adding the sugar (and lemon juice, if used), but boil it up in an open pan.
6. You can adapt any ordinary jam recipe for cooking in a pressure cooker by using half the stated amount of water and doing the preliminary cooking of the fruit under pressure. These are the times required for different fruits (all at medium/ 10 lb pressure):

Apples	5 minutes
Blackberries and apples combined	7 minutes
Blackcurrants	3–4 minutes
Damsons, plums and other stone fruit	5 minutes
Gooseberries	3 minutes
Marrow	1–2 minutes
Pears (cooking)	7 minutes
Quinces	5 minutes

7. Soft fruits, such as raspberries and strawberries, need very little preliminary softening and are therefore not usually cooked in a pressure cooker.
8. When two fruits (eg. blackberries and apples) are combined, the cooking times may vary somewhat.

Strawberry Jam
~

MAKES ABOUT 1.8 KG (4 LB)

900 g (2 lb) strawberries, hulled and washed
1 kg (2.2 lb) Sugar with Pectin
juice of ¹/₂ lemon
~

Put the strawberries in a preserving pan with the sugar and lemon juice. Heat gently until the sugar has dissolved, stirring frequently.

2 Bring to the boil and boil steadily for about 4 minutes or until setting point is reached.

3 Remove from the heat and remove any scum with a slotted spoon. Leave to stand for 15–20 minutes.

4 Stir the jam gently and pot and cover in the usual way.

Raspberry Jam
~

MAKES ABOUT 3 KG (6¹/₂ LB)

1.8 kg (4 lb) raspberries, washed
1.8 kg (4 lb) sugar
a knob of butter
~

Put the fruit in a preserving pan and simmer very gently in its own juice for about 20 minutes, stirring carefully from time to time, until the fruit is really soft.

2 Remove the pan from the heat and add the sugar, stirring until dissolved, then add the butter and boil rapidly for about 30 minutes or until setting point is reached.

3 Remove any scum with a slotted spoon and pot and cover in the usual way.

VARIATION
Loganberry jam

Follow the above recipe, using loganberries instead of raspberries.

Light Set Raspberry Jam
~

MAKES ABOUT 2.3 KG (5 LB)

1.1 kg (2¹/₂ lb) raspberries, washed
1.4 kg (3 lb) sugar
~

Put the raspberries in a preserving pan and simmer very gently for about 10 minutes, stirring frequently, until the juice flows, then bring to the boil and boil gently for a further 10 minutes.

2 Meanwhile, warm the sugar in a heatproof bowl in the oven.

3 Stir the sugar into the fruit until it has dissolved. Bring the jam back to the boil and boil for 2 minutes.

4 Take the pan off the heat and remove any scum with a slotted spoon. Pot and cover in the usual way.

Summer Fruit Jam
~

MAKES ABOUT 550 G (1¹/₄ LB)

450 g (1 lb) strawberries, hulled and washed
100 g (4 oz) redcurrants, strings removed and washed
100 g (4 oz) raspberries, washed
275 g (10 oz) fructose
~

Put all the fruit in a bowl and sprinkle over 30 ml (2 tbsp) of the fructose. Cover and leave overnight in the refrigerator.

2 Transfer the fruit to a saucepan and add 50 ml (2 fl oz) water. Simmer gently until tender, then add the remaining fructose and stir until dissolved.

3 Bring to the boil and boil for 15–20 minutes or until setting point is reached. Remove any scum with a slotted spoon.

4 Leave the jam to cool for 5 minutes, then pot and cover in the usual way. Store in the refrigerator.

Raspberry and Gooseberry Jam
~

MAKES ABOUT 4.5 KG (10 LB)

1.4 kg (3 lb) gooseberries, topped, tailed and washed
1.4 kg (3 lb) raspberries, washed
2.7 kg (6 lb) sugar
a knob of butter

~

Put the gooseberries in a preserving pan with 600 ml (1 pint) water and heat very gently, mashing the fruit with a wooden spoon as it softens. Continue to cook for about 20 minutes or until well reduced.

2 Add the raspberries and cook until they are soft.

3 Remove the pan from the heat and add the sugar, stir until dissolved, then add the butter. Bring to the boil and boil rapidly for about 15 minutes or until setting point is reached.

4 Remove any scum with a slotted spoon, then pot and cover in the usual way.

Raspberry and Redcurrant Jam
~

MAKES ABOUT 2.3 KG (5 LB)

700 g (1½ lb) redcurrants, strings removed and washed
700 g (1½ lb) raspberries, washed
1.4 kg (3 lb) sugar
a knob of butter

~

Put the fruit in a preserving pan with 600 ml (1 pint) water. Simmer gently for about 20 minutes or until the fruit is really soft.

2 Remove from the heat, add the sugar and stir until dissolved. Add the butter, bring the jam to the boil and boil rapidly for about 10 minutes or until setting point is reached.

3 Remove any scum with a slotted spoon, then pot and cover in the usual way.

Note To reduce the amount of pips in this jam, cook the two fruits separately, each in 300 ml (½ pint) water, and sieve the redcurrants before adding them to the raspberries. The yield will then be slightly less.

Blueberry Bay Jam
~

MAKES ABOUT 2.3 KG (5 LB)

900 g (2 lb) blueberries, washed
90 ml (6 tbsp) lemon juice
3 bay leaves
1.1 kg (2½ lb) Sugar with Pectin
a knob of butter

~

Put the blueberries in a preserving pan with 150 ml (¼ pint) water, the lemon juice and the bay leaves. Simmer gently for 10–15 minutes or until the fruit is just beginning to pulp.

2 Remove the pan from the heat, add the sugar and stir gently until dissolved. Add the butter, bring to the boil and boil rapidly for 4 minutes or until setting point is reached.

3 Remove any scum with a slotted spoon, allow the jam to stand for 3–4 minutes, then remove the bay leaves. Pot and cover in the usual way.

Blackberry and Apple Jam
~

MAKES ABOUT 4.5 KG (10 LB)

1.8 kg (4 lb) blackberries, washed
700 g (1¹/₂ lb) sour cooking apples, peeled, cored and sliced
(prepared weight)
2.7 kg (6 lb) sugar
a knob of butter

~

*P*ut the blackberries in a large saucepan with 150 ml (¹/₄ pint) water and simmer gently until soft.

2 Put the apples in a preserving pan with 150 ml (¹/₄ pint) water and simmer gently until soft. Pulp with a wooden spoon or a potato masher.

3 Add the blackberries and sugar to the apple pulp, stirring until the sugar has dissolved, then add the butter, bring to the boil and boil rapidly, stirring frequently, for about 10 minutes or until setting point is reached.

4 Remove any scum with a slotted spoon, then pot and cover in the usual way.

Loganberry and Morello Cherry Jam
~

MAKES ABOUT 4.5 KG (10 LB)

1.4 kg (3 lb) Morello cherries, washed
1.4 kg (3 lb) loganberries, washed
juice of 2 lemons
2.7 kg (6 lb) sugar
a knob of butter

~

*S*tone the cherries, reserving some of the stones. Put the cherries and loganberries in a preserving pan with the lemon juice and 200 ml (7 fl oz) water.

2 Using a hammer, crack the reserved cherry stones and take out the kernels. Tie them in a piece of muslin and add to the pan.

3 Bring the fruit to the boil and simmer for about 30 minutes or until tender. Remove the muslin bag, squeezing well and allowing the juice to run back into the pan.

4 Remove the pan from the heat, add the sugar, stir until dissolved, then add the butter. Bring to the boil and boil rapidly for 15–25 minutes or until setting point is reached.

5 Remove any scum with a slotted spoon, then pot and cover in the usual way.

Mulberry and Apple Jam
~

MAKES ABOUT 2.3 KG (5 LB)

1.4 kg (3 lb) mulberries, washed
450 g (1 lb) cooking apples, peeled, cored and sliced (prepared weight)
1.6 kg (3¹/₂ lb) sugar
a knob of butter

~

*P*ut the mulberries in a preserving pan with 300 ml (¹/₂ pint) water and simmer gently for about 20 minutes or until soft and pulpy.

2 Put the apples in a saucepan with 300 ml (¹/₂ pint) water and simmer gently for about 20 minutes or until soft and pulpy.

3 Add the apples to the mulberries and stir in the sugar. Continue stirring until the sugar has dissolved, then add the butter and boil for about 10 minutes or until setting point is reached.

4 Remove any scum with a slotted spoon, then pot and cover in the usual way.

Bilberry Jam
~

MAKES ABOUT 2.5 KG (5½ LB)

1.1 kg (2½ lb) bilberries, washed
45 ml (3 tbsp) lemon juice
1.4 kg (3 lb) sugar
a knob of butter
227-ml (8-fl oz) bottle of commercial pectin

~

*P*ut the bilberries in a preserving pan with 150 ml (¼ pint) water and the lemon juice. Simmer gently for 10–15 minutes or until the fruit is soft and just beginning to pulp.

2 Remove the pan from the heat, add the sugar and stir until dissolved. Add the butter, bring to the boil and boil rapidly for 3 minutes.

3 Remove the pan from the heat, add the pectin, return to the heat and boil for a further minute.

4 Allow to cool slightly. Pot and cover in the usual way.

Uncooked Freezer Jam
~

MAKES ABOUT 3.2 KG (7 LB)

1.4 kg (3 lb) raspberries or strawberries, hulled
1.8 kg (4 lb) caster sugar
60 ml (4 tbsp) lemon juice
227-ml (8-fl oz) bottle of commercial pectin

~

*P*ut the fruit in a large bowl and very lightly crush with a fork.

2 Stir in the sugar and lemon juice and leave at room temperature, stirring occasionally, for about 1 hour or until the sugar has dissolved.

3 Gently stir in the pectin and continue stirring for a further 2 minutes.

4 Pour the jam into small plastic containers, leaving a little space at the top to allow for expansion. Cover and leave at room temperature for a further 24 hours.

5 Label the containers and freeze.

6 To serve, thaw at room temperature for about 1 hour.

Note This jam has a set similar to a conserve. It will keep for up to six months in a freezer.

Elderberry and Blackberry Jam
~

MAKES ABOUT 2.3 KG (5 LB)

*700 g (1½ lb) elderberries, stripped from their stalks and
washed (prepared weight)*
700 g (1½ lb) blackberries, washed
30 ml (2 tbsp) lemon juice
1.4 kg (3 lb) sugar

~

Put the fruits in a preserving pan with the lemon juice. Bring slowly to the boil, then simmer gently for about 20 minutes or until soft and pulpy. Press the fruit through a sieve, if a seedless jam is preferred.

2 Add the sugar and stir gently until dissolved. Bring to the boil and boil rapidly for about 10 minutes or until setting point is reached. Remove any scum with a slotted spoon, then pot and cover in the usual way.

Blackberry Jam
~

MAKES ABOUT 1.6 KG (3½ LB)

1 kg (2¼ lb) blackberries (not over-ripe), washed
juice of ½ lemon
1 kg (2.2 lb) Sugar with Pectin
a knob of butter

~

Put the blackberries in a preserving pan with the lemon juice and 100 ml (4 fl oz) water. Simmer very gently for about 30 minutes or until the blackberries are very soft and the contents of the pan are well reduced.

2 Remove the pan from the heat, add the sugar, stir until dissolved, then add the butter, bring to the boil and boil rapidly for 4 minutes or until setting point is reached.

3 Remove any scum with a slotted spoon, then pot and cover in the usual way.

Gooseberry and Apple Jam
~

MAKES ABOUT 2.3 KG (5 LB)

700 g (1½ lb) gooseberries (preferably red), topped, tailed and washed
900 g (2 lb) cooking apples, peeled, cored and chopped
1.6 kg (3½ lb) sugar
a knob of butter

~

Put the fruit in a preserving pan with 300 ml (½ pint) water. Bring to the boil and simmer gently for about 30 minutes or until the fruit is soft and pulpy.

2 Remove the pan from the heat, add the sugar and stir until it has dissolved. Add the butter, bring to the boil, stirring all the time, and continue to boil for 15 minutes or until setting point is reached.

3 Remove any scum with a slotted spoon, then pot and cover in the usual way.

Cranberry Jam
~

MAKES ABOUT 1.4 KG (3 LB)

900 g (2 lb) cranberries, washed
900 g (2 lb) sugar
a knob of butter

~

Put the fruit in a preserving pan with 200 ml (7 fl oz) water. Bring to the boil and simmer for 30–40 minutes or until the fruit is soft and the skins tender.

2 Remove the pan from the heat, add the sugar and stir carefully until dissolved. Add the butter, bring to the boil and boil rapidly for about 15 minutes or until setting point is reached.

3 Remove any scum with a slotted spoon, then pot and cover in the usual way.

Greengage Jam
~

MAKES ABOUT 4.5 KG (10 LB)

2.7 kg (6 lb) greengages, washed
2.7 kg (6 lb) sugar
a knob of butter

~

Put the greengages in a preserving pan with 600 ml (1 pint) water and simmer gently for about 30 minutes or until the fruit is really soft.

2 Remove the pan from the heat, add the sugar and stir until dissolved. Add the butter, bring to the boil and boil rapidly for about 15 minutes. Using a slotted spoon, lift out the stones as they rise to the surface. Continue boiling until setting point is reached.

3 Remove any scum with a slotted spoon, then pot and cover in the usual way.

Elderflower Gooseberry Jam
~

MAKES ABOUT 4.5 KG (10 LB)

20 elderflower heads, cut close to the stem and washed
2.7 kg (6 lb) gooseberries (slightly under-ripe), topped, tailed
and washed
2.7 kg (6 lb) sugar
a knob of butter
~

Tie the elderflowers in a piece of muslin. Put the gooseberries in a preserving pan with 1.1 litres (2 pints) water and the elderflower bundle. Simmer gently for about 30 minutes or until the fruit is really soft and reduced, mashing it to a pulp with a wooden spoon and stirring from time to time to prevent sticking.

2 Remove the pan from the heat, add the sugar and stir until dissolved, then add the butter. Bring to the boil and boil rapidly for about 10 minutes or until setting point is reached.

3 Remove any scum with a slotted spoon. Remove the muslin bag, then pot and cover in the usual way.

Damson Jam
~

MAKES ABOUT 4.5 KG (10 LB)

2.3 kg (5 lb) damsons, washed
2.7 kg (6 lb) sugar
a knob of butter
~

Put the damsons in a preserving pan with 900 ml (1½ pints) water and simmer gently for about 30 minutes or until the fruit is really soft and pulpy.

2 Remove the pan from the heat, add the sugar and stir until dissolved. Add the butter, bring to the boil and boil rapidly for about 10 minutes. Using a slotted spoon, lift out the stones as they rise to the surface.

3 Continue boiling until setting point is reached. Remove any scum with a slotted spoon, then pot and cover in the usual way.

Plum Jam
~

MAKES ABOUT 4.5 KG (10 LB)

2.7 kg (6 lb) plums, washed
2.7 kg (6 lb) sugar
a knob of butter
~

Put the plums in a preserving pan with 900 ml (1½ pints) water. Simmer gently for about 30 minutes or until the fruit is really soft and the contents of the pan are well reduced.

2 Remove the pan from the heat, add the sugar and stir until dissolved. Add the butter, bring to the boil and boil rapidly for 10–15 minutes or until setting point is reached.

3 Using a slotted spoon, remove the stones and any scum from the surface of the jam. Pot and cover the jam in the usual way.

Plum and Apple Jam
~

MAKES ABOUT 2.3 KG (5 LB)

900 g (2 lb) plums, washed, halved and stoned
900 g (2 lb) cooking apples, peeled, cored and sliced
1.4 kg (3 lb) sugar
a knob of butter

~

*P*ut the plums and apples in a preserving pan with 900 ml (1½ pints) water. Bring to the boil and boil for about 1 hour or until the fruit is tender and the contents of the pan have been reduced by half.

2 Remove the pan from the heat, add the sugar and stir until dissolved. Add the butter and boil rapidly for 10–15 minutes or until setting point is reached.

3 Remove any scum with a slotted spoon, then pot and cover in the usual way.

Somerset Apple Jam
~

MAKES ABOUT 2.3 KG (5 LB)

1.4 kg (3 lb) cooking apples, washed
100 g (4 oz) blackberries, washed (see Note)
300 ml (½ pint) cider
5 whole cloves
juice of 3 lemons
1.1 kg (2½ lb) sugar
a knob of butter

~

*S*lice the apples but do not peel or core them. Put them in a preserving pan with the blackberries, cider, cloves, lemon juice and 300 ml (½ pint) water. Simmer gently for 25–30 minutes or until the fruit is cooked to a pulp.

2 Remove the cloves from the fruit, then press the fruit through a sieve. Return the fruit pulp to the pan and add the sugar, stirring until dissolved. Add the butter, bring to

the boil and boil, stirring occasionally, for about 10 minutes or until setting point is reached.

3 Remove any scum with a slotted spoon, then pot and cover in the usual way.

Note The blackberries are included in this recipe mostly to improve the colour of the jam. Other berries, such as raspberries or cranberries could be used instead.

Apple Ginger Jam
~

MAKES 2.5–3.2 KG (5½–7 LB)

1.8 kg (4 lb) cooking apples
225 g (8 oz) preserved ginger, drained and chopped
45 ml (3 tbsp) ginger syrup from the jar
grated rind and juice of 3 lemons
1.4 kg (3 lb) sugar

~

*P*eel, core and slice the apples and tie the cores and peel in a piece of muslin. Put the apples and muslin bag in a preserving pan with 900 ml (1½ pints) water and simmer gently until the fruit is really soft and pulpy. Remove the muslin bag and mash the apples or press them through a nylon sieve.

2 Return the apple purée to the pan and add the ginger, ginger syrup, the rind and juice of the lemons and the sugar. Bring to the boil, stirring constantly, and boil rapidly for 10 minutes or until setting point is reached.

3 Remove any scum with a slotted spoon, then leave the jam to stand for 15 minutes before potting and covering in the usual way.

Note Windfall apples may be used in this recipe. The amount of ginger used can be varied according to taste.

Quince Jam
~

MAKES ABOUT 2.3 KG (5 LB)

900 g (2 lb) quinces, peeled, cored and sliced (prepared weight)
1.4 kg (3 lb) sugar
a knob of butter
~

Put the quinces in a preserving pan with 1 litre (1³/₄ pints) water and simmer very gently until the fruit is really soft and pulpy.

2 Remove the pan from the heat, add the sugar and stir until dissolved. Add the butter, bring to the boil and boil rapidly for 15–20 minutes or until setting point is reached.

3 Remove any scum with a slotted spoon, then pot and cover in the usual way.

Note If the quinces are really ripe, add the juice of 1 lemon with the sugar.

Quince and Marrow Jam
~

MAKES ABOUT 4.5 KG (10 LB)

900 g (2 lb) quinces, peeled, cored and sliced (prepared weight)
900 g (2 lb) marrow, peeled, seeded and diced (prepared weight)
60 ml (4 tbsp) lemon juice
2.7 kg (6 lb) sugar
a knob of butter
~

Put the quinces and marrow in a preserving pan with 900 ml (1¹/₂ pints) water and the lemon juice. Simmer gently for about 45 minutes or until pulpy.

2 Remove the pan from the heat and add the sugar, stirring until dissolved. Add the butter and boil rapidly for 10 minutes or until setting point is reached.

3 Remove any scum with a slotted spoon, then pot and cover in the usual way.

Peach Jam
~

MAKES ABOUT 2.7 KG (6 LB)

1.8 kg (4 lb) fresh peaches, skinned, stoned and chopped
juice of ¹/₂ lemon
1.4 kg (3 lb) Sugar with Pectin
a knob of butter
~

Put the peaches and lemon juice in a preserving pan with 450 ml (³/₄ pint) water. Bring to the boil and simmer for about 30 minutes or until the peaches are tender.

2 Remove the pan from the heat, add the sugar and stir until dissolved. Add the butter, bring to the boil and boil rapidly for 4 minutes or until setting point is reached.

3 Remove any scum with a slotted spoon, then allow the jam to cool slightly before potting and covering in the usual way.

Peach and Raspberry Jam
~

MAKES ABOUT 2.3 KG (5 LB)

900 g (2 lb) fresh peaches, skinned, stoned and chopped
(prepared weight)
900 g (2 lb) raspberries, washed
1.4 kg (3 lb) sugar
a knob of butter
~

Crack the peach stones with a nutcracker or hammer, take out the kernels and tie them in a piece of muslin. Put the fruit in a preserving pan with the muslin bag and 150 ml (1/4 pint) water. Bring to the boil and simmer gently for about 30 minutes or until the fruit is tender. Remove the muslin bag, squeezing well.

2 Remove the pan from the heat, add the sugar and stir until dissolved. Add the butter and boil for about 15 minutes or until setting point is reached.

3 Remove any scum with a slotted spoon, then pot and cover in the usual way.

Pear Jam
~

MAKES 900 G–1.1 KG (2–2½ LB)

1.4 kg (3 lb) cooking or firm eating pears
grated rind and juice of 2 lemons
1.1 kg (2½ lb) sugar
a knob of butter
half a 227-ml (8-fl oz) bottle of commercial pectin
~

Peel, core and chop the pears, reserving the peel and cores. Put the peel and cores in a saucepan with the lemon rind and 150 ml (1/4 pint) water and boil for 10 minutes.

2 Strain and pour the liquid into a preserving pan with the pear flesh and lemon juice. Simmer gently for 25–30 minutes or until the pears are tender.

3 Remove the pan from the heat, add the sugar and stir until dissolved. Add the butter, bring to the boil and boil for 5–10 minutes.

4 Remove the pan from the heat, add the pectin, then boil for a further minute. Remove any scum with a slotted spoon and allow the jam to cool slightly before potting and covering in the usual way.

Fresh Fig Jam
~

MAKES ABOUT 900 G (2 LB)

450 g (1 lb) fresh figs, washed and sliced
225 g (8 oz) cooking apples, peeled, cored and sliced
grated rind of 1 lemon
juice of 3 lemons
450 g (1 lb) sugar
a knob of butter
~

Put the fruit in a preserving pan with the lemon rind and juice. Simmer gently for about 30 minutes or until the fruit is quite tender.

2 Remove the pan from the heat, add the sugar and stir until dissolved. Add the butter, bring to the boil and boil rapidly for 10 minutes or until setting point is reached.

3 Remove any scum with a slotted spoon, then pot and cover in the usual way.

Spiced Fig Jam
~

MAKES ABOUT 3.6 KG (8 LB)

900 g (2 lb) dried figs, stalks removed
2.7 kg (6 lb) cooking apples, peeled, cored and roughly chopped
grated rind and juice of 3 lemons
2.5 ml (¹/₂ tsp) grated nutmeg
2.5 ml (¹/₂ tsp) ground cinnamon
1.25 ml (¹/₄ tsp) ground cloves
2.3 kg (5 lb) sugar
~

Put the figs and apples through a mincer or, if preferred, they can be finely chopped.

2 Put the minced fruit, lemon juice, grated lemon rind and spices in a preserving pan with 1.7 litres (3 pints) water. Bring to the boil and simmer until the fruit is tender and the contents of the pan reduced.

3 Remove the pan from the heat and add the sugar, stirring until dissolved. Bring to the boil and boil for 5 minutes or until setting point is reached.

4 Remove any scum with a slotted spoon, then pot and cover in the usual way.

Note If preferred, the fig seeds can be removed by rubbing the cooked fruit through a sieve before the sugar is added.

Apricot Jam
~

MAKES ABOUT 3 KG (6¹/₂ LB)

1.8 kg (4 lb) apricots, washed, halved and stoned (reserving
a few stones)
juice of 1 lemon
1.8 kg (4 lb) sugar
a knob of butter
~

Crack a few of the apricot stones with a weight, nutcracker or hammer, take out the kernels and blanch in boiling water for 1 minute, then drain.

2 Put the apricots, lemon juice, apricot kernels and 450 ml (³/₄ pint) water in a preserving pan and simmer for about 15 minutes or until they are soft and the contents of the pan are well reduced.

3 Take the pan off the heat and add the sugar, stirring until dissolved. Add the butter and boil rapidly for about 15 minutes or until setting point is reached.

4 Remove any scum with a slotted spoon, then pot and cover in the usual way.

Dried Apricot Jam
~

MAKES ABOUT 2.3 KG (5 LB)

450 g (1 lb) dried apricots
juice of 1 lemon
1.4 kg (3 lb) sugar
50 g (2 oz) blanched almonds, split
a knob of butter
~

Put the apricots in a bowl, cover with 1.8 litres (3 pints) water and leave to soak overnight.

2 Put the apricots in a preserving pan with the soaking water and lemon juice. Simmer for about 30 minutes or until soft, stirring from time to time.

3 Remove the pan from the heat and add the sugar and blanched almonds. Stir until the sugar has dissolved, then add the butter and boil rapidly for 20–25 minutes or until setting point is reached, stirring frequently to prevent sticking.

4 Remove any scum with a slotted spoon, then pot and cover in the usual way.

Prune Jam
~

MAKES ABOUT 2.7 KG (6 LB)

6 whole cloves
1 blade of mace
5 cm (2 inches) cinnamon stick
900 g (2 lb) prunes, washed and soaked overnight
juice of 2 lemons
900 g (2 lb) sugar
a knob of butter

~

Tie the spices in a piece of muslin. Drain the prunes and put them in a preserving pan with 1.1 litres (2 pints) fresh water, the lemon juice and muslin bag. Simmer gently for about 1 hour or until the prunes are very soft. Using a slotted spoon, remove the stones.

2 Remove the muslin bag, then take the pan off the heat and add the sugar, stirring until dissolved. Add the butter, then bring to the boil and boil rapidly for 10 minutes or until setting point is reached.

3 Remove any scum with a slotted spoon, then pot and cover in the usual way.

Black Cherry Jam
~

MAKES ABOUT 1.4 KG (3 LB)

900 g (2 lb) black cherries, washed and stoned
1 kg (2.2 lb) Sugar with Pectin
grated rind and juice of 2 oranges

~

Put the cherries in a preserving pan with the sugar, orange rind and orange juice. Heat gently until the sugar has dissolved, then simmer until the fruit is soft. Bring to the boil and boil rapidly for 4 minutes or until setting point is reached.

2 Remove any scum with a slotted spoon, then pot and cover in the usual way.

Cherry and Redcurrant Jam
~

MAKES ABOUT 2 KG (4¹/₂ LB)

900 g (2 lb) black cherries, washed and stoned
450 g (1 lb) redcurrants, strings removed and washed
1.4 kg (3 lb) sugar
a knob of butter

~

Put the fruit in a preserving pan with 150 ml (¹/₄ pint) water. Simmer gently for about 30 minutes or until the fruit is very soft.

2 Remove the pan from the heat, add the sugar and stir until dissolved. Add the butter and boil rapidly for about 15 minutes or until setting point is reached.

3 Remove any scum with a slotted spoon, then pot and cover in the usual way.

Cherry and Pineapple Jam
~

MAKES ABOUT 2.3 KG (5 LB)

*450 g (1 lb) fresh pineapple, peeled, cored and finely chopped
(prepared weight)
900 g (2 lb) Morello cherries, washed and stoned
juice of 1 lemon
1 kg (2.2 lb) Sugar with Pectin
a knob of butter*

~

Put the pineapple, cherries and lemon juice in a preserving pan. Simmer gently for about 45 minutes or until the fruit is tender.
2 Remove the pan from the heat and add the sugar, stirring until dissolved. Add the butter, bring to the boil and boil rapidly for 4 minutes or until setting point is reached.
3 Remove any scum with a slotted spoon, then pot and cover in the usual way.

Honey-Pineapple Jam
~

MAKES ABOUT 1.1 KG (2$\frac{1}{2}$ LB)

*1.4 kg (3 lb) ripe pineapple, peeled, cored and chopped
juice of 1 lemon
700 g (1$\frac{1}{2}$ lb) thick honey
half a 227-ml (8-fl oz) bottle of commercial pectin*

~

Crush the pineapple thoroughly with a rolling pin or masher and put in a preserving pan with the lemon juice and honey. Mix well, bring to the boil and simmer for 20 minutes, stirring occasionally.
2 Remove the pan from the heat and stir in the pectin. Bring to the boil for 1 minute and remove any scum with a slotted spoon. Pot and cover in the usual way.

Rose Petal Jam
~

MAKES ABOUT 450 G (1 LB)

*225 g (8 oz) deep red, heavily-scented rose blossoms, picked in
full bloom
450 g (1 lb) sugar
juice of 2 lemons*

~

Remove the petals from the rose blossoms and snip off the white bases of the petals.
2 Cut the petals into small pieces, but not too finely. Put in a bowl and add 225 g (8 oz) of the sugar. Cover and leave overnight. This will extract the scent and darken the petals.
3 Pour 1.1 litres (2 pints) water and the lemon juice into a saucepan and stir in the remaining sugar. Heat gently until the sugar has dissolved, but do not boil.
4 Stir the rose petals into the sugar syrup and simmer gently for 20 minutes. Bring to the boil and boil for about 5 minutes or until thick. (This jam is not brought to setting point.) Pot and cover in the usual way.

Cherry and Apple Jam
~

MAKES ABOUT 2.7 KG (6 LB)

900 g (2 lb) sour cooking apples, washed
1.8 kg (4 lb) Morello or Duke cherries, washed and stoned
juice of 1 lemon
1.6 kg (3½ lb) sugar
a knob of butter
~

Slice the apples without peeling or coring, put them in a large saucepan with 900 ml (1½ pints) water and simmer for 30–40 minutes or until they are well pulped.

2 Spoon the apple pulp into a jelly bag (see page 34) and leave to strain for several hours.

3 Put the apple extract, which should weigh about 275 g (10 oz), in a preserving pan with the cherries and lemon juice and simmer gently for about 30 minutes or until a large part of the moisture from the cherries has evaporated.

4 Remove the pan from the heat and add the sugar, stirring until dissolved. Add the butter, bring to the boil and boil for 10 minutes or until setting point is reached.

5 Remove any scum with a slotted spoon, then pot and cover in the usual way.

Melon and Ginger Jam
~

MAKES ABOUT 2.3 KG (5 LB)

1.8 kg (4 lb) honeydew melon, seeded, skinned and diced
(prepared weight)
1.8 kg (4 lb) sugar
25 g (1 oz) fresh root ginger
thinly pared rind and juice of 3 lemons
a knob of butter
~

Put the prepared melon in a bowl, sprinkle with about 450 g (1 lb) of the sugar and leave to stand overnight.

2 Crush or 'bruise' the ginger with a rolling pin or weight to release the flavour from the fibres and tie it in a piece of muslin with the lemon rind.

3 Put the muslin bag in a preserving pan with the melon and lemon juice. Simmer gently for 30 minutes, then remove the pan from the heat and add the remaining sugar, stirring until dissolved.

4 Add the butter and boil gently for about 30 minutes or until setting point is reached.

5 Remove the muslin bag and any scum with a slotted spoon, then pot and cover in the usual way.

Rhubarb and Ginger Jam
~

MAKES ABOUT 2 KG (4½ LB)

1.1 kg (2½ lb) rhubarb, trimmed and chopped (prepared weight)
1.1 kg (2½ lb) sugar
juice of 2 lemons
25 g (1 oz) fresh root ginger
100 g (4 oz) preserved or crystallised ginger, chopped
~

Put the rhubarb in a large bowl in alternate layers with the sugar and lemon juice. Cover and leave overnight.

2 Next day, crush or 'bruise' the root ginger slightly with a weight or rolling pin and tie in a piece of muslin.

3 Put the rhubarb mixture in a preserving pan with the muslin bag, bring to the boil and boil rapidly for 15 minutes. Remove the muslin bag, add the preserved or crystallised ginger and boil for a further 5 minutes, or until setting point is reached.

4 Remove any scum with a slotted spoon, then pot and cover in the usual way.

Marrow and Apricot Jam
~

MAKES ABOUT 2.3 KG (5 LB)

900 g (2 lb) marrow, peeled, seeded and cut into squares
(prepared weight)
225 g (8 oz) dried apricots, soaked overnight and drained
grated rind and juice of 2 lemons
1.4 kg (3 lb) sugar
~

Steam the marrow for about 15 minutes or until tender, then mash.

2 Put the apricots in a preserving pan with 900 ml (1½ pints) water and cook for about 30 minutes or until soft.

3 Add the marrow pulp to the apricots with the lemon rind, lemon juice and sugar. Heat gently until the sugar has dissolved, stirring to prevent sticking. Bring to the boil and boil rapidly for 15–20 minutes or until setting point is reached.

4 Remove any scum with a slotted spoon, then pot and cover in the usual way.

Rosy Tomato Jam
~

MAKES ABOUT 1.4 KG (3 LB)

5 lemons, washed and halved
900 g (2 lb) red tomatoes, skinned and quartered
900 g (2 lb) sugar
a knob of butter

~

Squeeze the juice from the lemons, reserving the pips. Remove the remaining flesh from the lemon halves and reserve. Strip the excess pith away from the lemon rind and cut the rind into thin strips.

2 Put the strips of rind in a saucepan, add 150 ml (¼ pint) water and simmer, covered, for 20 minutes.

3 Remove the cores and seeds from the tomato quarters and tie in a piece of muslin with the lemon pips and flesh. Shred the tomato flesh.

4 Measure the lemon juice, make it up to 1.7 litres (3 pints) with water and pour into a preserving pan. Add the tomato flesh with the softened lemon shreds, their cooking liquid and the muslin bag. Simmer gently for about 40 minutes or until tender.

5 Remove the muslin bag from the pan, squeezing it well and allowing the juice to run back into the pan.

6 Remove the pan from the heat, add the sugar and stir until dissolved. Add the butter and boil rapidly for 20 minutes or until setting point is reached.

7 Remove any scum with a slotted spoon, then pot and cover in the usual way.

Carrot Jam
~

MAKES ABOUT 1.8 KG (4 LB)

900 g (2 lb) large carrots, trimmed and peeled
3 lemons, washed
900 g (2 lb) sugar
25 g (1 oz) blanched almonds, split
15 ml (1 tbsp) brandy

~

Slice or chop the carrots. Grate the rind from the lemons and squeeze out the juice, reserving the pips. Roughly chop the lemon pith and tie tightly in a piece of muslin with the pips.

2 Put the carrots, grated lemon rind and juice, muslin bag and 1.1 litres (2 pints) water in a preserving pan and bring to the boil. Boil for about 1 hour or until the carrots are tender.

3 Remove the muslin bag from the pan. Drain the carrots and press them through a sieve or liquidise in a blender.

4 Return the pulp to a clean pan with the sugar. Heat gently, stirring, until the sugar has dissolved, then bring to the boil and boil rapidly for about 10 minutes or until setting point is reached.

5 Remove any scum with a slotted spoon. Stir the almonds into the jam with the brandy. Pot and cover in the usual way.

Note Preserved ginger may be used instead of almonds.

Bar-Le Duc
~

MAKES ABOUT 2.3 KG (5 LB)

*900 g (2 lb) black or redcurrants or a mixture, strings removed
and washed*
1.4 kg (3 lb) sugar
~

If time, gently prick each currant and place in a bowl with the sugar. Cover and leave overnight.

2 Transfer the fruit and sugar to a saucepan, bring slowly to the boil and boil for 3 minutes.

3 Remove the pan from the heat and leave for about 30 minutes, until a skin begins to form. Stir gently to distribute the fruit, then pot and cover in the usual way.

Kiwi Conserve
~

MAKES ABOUT 1.4 KG (3 LB)

900 g (2 lb) kiwi fruit, peeled
900 g (2 lb) sugar
~

Slice the fruit thickly and place in a bowl in layers with the sugar. Cover and leave for 24 hours.

2 Transfer the fruit to a saucepan and bring slowly to the boil, stirring until the sugar dissolves. Boil rapidly for 5 minutes. Leave to cool for 15 minutes, then pot and cover in the usual way.

Strawberry Conserve
~

MAKES ABOUT 1.4 KG (3 LB)

1.4 kg (3 lb) strawberries, hulled
1.4 kg (3 lb) sugar
~

Put the strawberries in a large bowl in layers with the sugar. Cover and leave for 24 hours.

2 Put the strawberries and sugar in a preserving pan and heat gently, stirring until the sugar dissolves. Bring to the boil and boil rapidly for 5 minutes.

3 Return the mixture to the bowl, cover and leave in a cool place for a further 2 days.

4 Return to the pan again and boil rapidly for 10 minutes. Leave to cool for 15 minutes, then pot and cover in the usual way.

Note Raspberries and loganberries can be conserved in the same way.

Raspberry Kirsch Conserve
~

MAKES ABOUT 900 G (2 LB)

450 g (1 lb) raspberries, washed
450 g (1 lb) sugar
15 ml (1 tbsp) kirsch
~

Put the raspberries and sugar in separate ovenproof dishes. Heat in the oven at 180°C (350°F) mark 4 for 15 minutes.

2 Turn the raspberries and sugar into a large bowl and stir for a few minutes. Leave to stand for 20 minutes. Repeat the stirring and standing three times.

3 Stir the kirsch into the conserve, then pot and cover in the usual way. Store in a cool, dark place for at least 3 months before using.

Harvest Preserve with Port
~

MAKES ABOUT 1.6 KG (3½ LB)

450 g (1 lb) each strawberries, raspberries and redcurrants
juice of 1 large orange
juice of 2–3 lemons
1.4 kg (3 lb) sugar
a knob of butter
60 ml (4 tbsp) port

~

*H*ull and rinse the strawberries and raspberries. String and wash the currants. Drain well.

2 Put the raspberries in a preserving pan with 150 ml (¼ pint) water, 150 ml (¼ pint) orange juice and 90 ml (6 tbsp) lemon juice. Simmer gently for 5–10 minutes or until very soft. Push through a nylon sieve to remove the seeds.

3 Return the raspberry purée to the rinsed-out pan and add the remaining fruit. Simmer for 5 minutes or until soft and pulpy.

4 Remove the pan from the heat and add the sugar, stirring until dissolved. Add the butter, bring to the boil and boil rapidly for 10–20 minutes or until setting point is reached.

5 Remove any scum with a slotted spoon. Leave to cool for 10 minutes, then stir in the port and pot and cover in the usual way.

Rhubarb and Ginger Conserve
~

MAKES ABOUT 2.3 KG (5 LB)

1.1 kg (2½ lb) rhubarb, trimmed, washed and cut into small
pieces
1.1 kg (2½ lb) Preserving Sugar
25 g (1 oz) fresh root ginger
100 g (4 oz) stem ginger, roughly chopped

~

*P*ut the rhubarb in a bowl in layers with the sugar. Cover and leave overnight.

2 Put the rhubarb and sugar in a preserving pan. Crush or 'bruise' the root ginger slightly, using a rolling pin or hammer, and tie in a piece of muslin. Add to the pan and bring slowly to the boil, stirring, until the sugar has dissolved. Boil rapidly for 15 minutes.

3 Add the stem ginger to the pan and boil for a further 5 minutes.

4 Remove the muslin bag and any scum with a slotted spoon, then pot and cover in the usual way.

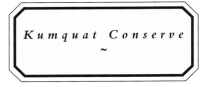

Kumquat Conserve
~

MAKES ABOUT 1.8 KG (4 LB)

900 g (2 lb) kumquats, washed
900 g (2 lb) sugar
90 ml (6 tbsp) brandy

~

*P*rick the kumquats all over with a needle. Place the fruit in a bowl in layers with the sugar. Cover and leave for 24 hours.

2 Transfer the fruit to a saucepan and bring to the boil slowly, stirring until the sugar has dissolved. Boil rapidly for 10 minutes.

3 Remove any pips that have risen to the surface and stir in the brandy. Leave to cool for 15 minutes, then pot and cover in the usual way.

Jellies

Jellies take longer to make than jams but are well worth the extra trouble. The equipment and method used for making jellies is similar to that used for jams (see page 9) but there are a few special, additional points.

The Fruit

Fruits giving a good set (that is with a high pectin content – see page 10) are best for jelly-making. Fruits with poor setting qualities can be combined with others with a higher pectin content or the jelly can be made with Sugar with Pectin (see page 11).

Jelly-making

Preparing the fruit Fruit for jelly-making needs very little preparation, though any damaged fruits should not be used. It is not necessary to peel or core fruit; just wash and roughly chop it. Any skin, core, stones or pips will be extracted when the pulp is strained.

Cooking the fruit The first stage of jelly-making is to cook the fruit in water. The amount of water needed depends on how juicy the fruit is. Hard fruits should be covered with water. The cooking must be very slow and thorough to extract as much juice as possible, so only simmer the fruit gently until very tender. This takes from 30 minutes – 1 hour, depending on the softness of the fruit. To save time, particularly when using hard fruits, this stage of jelly-making can be done in a pressure cooker (see opposite).

Straining off the juice After cooking, the fruit pulp is transferred to a jelly bag and left to drip until all the juice has been strained off. If you have not got a jelly bag, improvise with a large piece of muslin or a double thickness of fine cloth (such as a clean tea-towel or cotton sheet). Whatever you use should first be scalded in boiling water. Suspend the bag or cloth between the legs of an upturned chair or stool

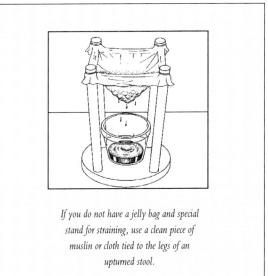

If you do not have a jelly bag and special stand for straining, use a clean piece of muslin or cloth tied to the legs of an upturned stool.

with a large bowl placed underneath to catch the dripping juice. Leave until the dripping has stopped (overnight if necessary) and don't be tempted to squeeze or poke the bag or the finished jelly will be cloudy.

Double extraction If a fruit that is very high in pectin is being used, a double extraction can be made to increase the final yield. After the first straining, the pulp should be cooked again in a little water and then strained again. The two juices are then combined.

Adding the sugar The next stage of jelly-making is to add the sugar to the juice. If necessary, the pectin test (see page 10) can be carried out beforehand. If the result is poor, put the juice in a pan, boil, then test again.

Measure the strained juice (known as the extract), put it in a preserving pan and add the sugar. 600 ml (1 pint) extract rich in pectin will set with 450 g (1 lb) sugar, and 600 ml (1 pint) juice with a medium pectin content will set with 350 g (12 oz) sugar. Granulated sugar is suitable, though lump sugar or preserving crystals are preferable as they will cause less scum and will result in a much clearer jelly. Stir the sugar into the juice, return the pan to the heat and warm gently, stirring until the sugar has dissolved. Bring to the boil and boil until setting point is reached, stirring occasionally. Test for setting point in the same way as for jam (see page 11). When setting point is reached (usually after boiling the jelly for about 10 minutes), remove any scum with a slotted spoon, then pot and cover the jelly as for jam (see page 12).

Yield

It is not practicable to state the exact yield in jelly recipes because the ripeness of the fruit and the time allowed for dripping both affect the quantity of juice obtained. As a rough guide, for each 450 g (1 lb) sugar added, a yield of about 700 g (1½ lb) will result.

Pressure Cooking Jellies

The fruit used for making jellies can also be softened in the pressure cooker.

1. Prepare the fruit. Place the fruit in the pressure cooker (without the trivet) and allow only half the amount of water stated in the recipe.

2. Cook at medium (10 lb) pressure, then reduce the pressure at room temperature. If you have a cooker which is set to cook only at high (15 lb) pressure, see page 13.

3. Mash the fruit well and strain.

Below are examples of the cooking times required for some fruits when cooked in a pressure cooker.

Apples	5 minutes
Blackberries and apples combined	9 minutes
Blackcurrants	4 minutes
Damsons, plums and other stone fruit	5 minutes
Gooseberries	3 minutes
Pears (cooking)	9 minutes
Quinces	7 minutes
Citrus fruits	25 minutes

Quince Jelly
~

1.8 kg (4 lb) quinces, washed and roughly chopped
grated rind and juice of 3 lemons
sugar
~

*P*ut the fruit in a preserving pan with 2.3 litres (4 pints) water and the lemon rind and juice. Simmer, covered, for 1 hour or until the fruit is tender. Stir from time to time to prevent sticking.

2 Spoon the fruit pulp into a jelly bag or cloth attached to the legs of an upturned stool, and leave to strain into a large bowl for at least 12 hours.

3 Return the pulp in the jelly bag to the pan and add 1.1 litres (2 pints) water. Bring to the boil, simmer gently for 30 minutes, then strain again through a jelly bag or cloth for at least 12 hours.

4 Discard the pulp remaining in the jelly bag. Combine the two lots of extract and measure.

5 Return the extract to the preserving pan with 450 g (1 lb) sugar for each 600 ml (1 pint) extract. Heat gently, stirring, until the sugar has dissolved, then boil rapidly for about 10 minutes or until setting point is reached.

6 Remove any scum with a slotted spoon, then pot and cover in the usual way.

Mint Jelly
~

2.3 kg (5 lb) cooking apples, such as Bramleys
a few large sprigs of fresh mint
1.1 litres (2 pints) distilled white vinegar
sugar
90–120 ml (6–8 tbsp) chopped fresh mint
a few drops of green food colouring (optional)

~

Remove any bruised or damaged portions from the apples and roughly chop them into thick chunks without peeling or coring.

2 Put the apples in a preserving pan with 1.1 litres (2 pints) water and the mint sprigs. Bring to the boil, then simmer gently for about 45 minutes or until soft and pulpy. Stir from time to time to prevent sticking. Add the vinegar and boil for a further 5 minutes.

3 Spoon the apple pulp into a jelly bag or cloth attached to the legs of an upturned stool, and leave to strain into a large bowl for at least 12 hours.

4 Discard the pulp remaining in the jelly bag. Measure the extract and return it to the preserving pan with 450 g (1 lb) sugar for each 600 ml (1 pint) extract.

5 Heat gently, stirring, until the sugar has dissolved, then boil rapidly for about 10 minutes or until setting point is reached.

6 Remove any scum with a slotted spoon, then stir in the chopped mint and add a few drops of green food colouring, if liked. Allow to cool slightly, stir well to distribute the mint, then pot and cover in the usual way.

VARIATIONS
Herb jellies

Other fresh herbs, such as rosemary, parsley, sage and thyme, can be used equally as well as mint. Serve these herb jellies with roast meats – rosemary jelly with lamb; parsley jelly with gammon; sage jelly with pork; and thyme jelly with poultry.

Rose Geranium Jelly

~

2.3 kg (5 lb) cooking apples
2 large handfuls of rose geranium leaves
1.1 litres (2 pints) malt vinegar
sugar
green food colouring (optional)

~

*R*emove any bruised or damaged portions from the apples and chop them roughly into thick chunks without peeling or coring.

2 Put the apples in a preserving pan with 1.1 litres (2 pints) water and the rose geranium leaves. Bring to the boil, then simmer for about 45 minutes or until soft and pulpy. Stir from time to time to prevent sticking. Add the vinegar and boil for a further 5 minutes.

3 Spoon the apple pulp into a jelly bag or cloth attached to the legs of an upturned stool. Allow the juice to strain into a large bowl for at least 12 hours.

4 Discard the pulp from the jelly bag. Measure the extract and return to the preserving pan with 450 g (1 lb) sugar for every 600 ml (1 pint) extract. Heat gently, stirring, until the sugar has dissolved, then boil rapidly, without stirring, for about 10 minutes or until setting point is reached.

5 Remove any scum with a slotted spoon. Add a few drops of colouring, if required, then pot and cover in the usual way.

Crab-apple Jelly
~

2.5 kg (5½ lb) crab-apples, washed
6 cloves
sugar

~

Cut the crab-apples into quarters without peeling or coring and put them in a preserving pan with the cloves and 1.7 litres (3 pints) water. Bring to the boil and simmer gently for about 1½ hours or until the fruit is soft and pulpy, adding a little more water if necessary. Stir from time to time to prevent sticking.

2 Spoon the fruit pulp into a jelly bag or cloth attached to the legs of an upturned stool, and leave to strain into a large bowl for at least 12 hours.

3 Discard the pulp remaining in the jelly bag. Measure the extract and return it to the pan with 450 g (1 lb) sugar for each 600 ml (1 pint) extract. Heat gently, stirring, until the sugar has dissolved, then boil rapidly for about 10 minutes or until setting point is reached.

4 Remove any scum with a slotted spoon, then pot and cover in the usual way.

Cranberry and Apple Jelly
~

1.4 kg (3 lb) cooking apples, washed
900 g (2 lb) cranberries, washed
sugar

~

Remove any bruised or damaged portions from the apples, then roughly chop them without peeling or coring.

2 Put the apples and cranberries in a preserving pan with sufficient water to cover and simmer gently for 45 minutes–1 hour or until the fruit is really soft and pulpy. Stir from time to time to prevent sticking.

3 Spoon the pulp into a jelly bag or cloth attached to the legs of an upturned stool, and leave to strain into a large bowl for at least 12 hours.

4 Discard the pulp remaining in the jelly bag. Measure the extract and return it to the preserving pan with 450 g (1 lb) sugar for each 600 ml (1 pint) extract. Bring slowly to the boil, stirring, until the sugar has dissolved, then boil rapidly for about 10 minutes or until setting point is reached.

5 Remove any scum with a slotted spoon, then pot and cover in the usual way.

Japonica Jelly
~

700 g (1½ lb) japonicas, washed and roughly chopped
30 ml (2 tbsp) lemon juice
sugar

~

Put the fruit in a preserving pan with the lemon juice and 1.7 litres (3 pints) water. Simmer gently for 45 minutes–1 hour or until the fruit is very soft and the contents of the pan are reduced by about one third. Stir from time to time to prevent sticking.

2 Spoon the fruit pulp into a jelly bag or cloth attached to the legs of an upturned stool, and leave to strain into a large bowl for at least 12 hours.

3 Discard the pulp remaining in the jelly bag. Measure the extract and return it to the preserving pan with 450 g (1 lb) sugar for each 600 ml (1 pint) extract.

4 Heat gently, stirring, until the sugar has dissolved, then bring to the boil and boil rapidly for about 10 minutes or until setting point is reached. Remove any scum with a slotted spoon, then pot and cover in the usual way.

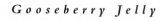

Grape Jelly
~

450 g (1 lb) black grapes, washed
450 g (1 lb) cooking apples, washed
juice of 1 lemon
sugar
~

$\mathcal{P}$ut the grapes in a preserving pan and lightly crush them with a potato masher. Remove any bruised or damaged portions from the apples, roughly chop them without peeling or coring and add them to the pan.

2 Add the lemon juice and 300 ml (½ pint) water to the pan and simmer gently for about 30 minutes or until the fruit is very soft and pulpy. Stir from time to time to prevent sticking.

3 Spoon the fruit pulp into a jelly bag or cloth attached to the legs of an upturned stool, and leave to strain into a large bowl for at least 12 hours.

4 Discard the pulp remaining in the jelly bag. Measure the extract and return it to the preserving pan with 450 g (1 lb) sugar for each 600 ml (1 pint) extract. Heat gently, stirring, until the sugar has dissolved, then boil rapidly for about 10 minutes or until setting point is reached.

5 Remove any scum with a slotted spoon, then pot and cover in the usual way.

Gooseberry Jelly
~

1.8 kg (4 lb) gooseberries, washed
sugar
~

$\mathcal{P}$ut the gooseberries in a preserving pan with sufficient water to cover. Bring to the boil, then simmer gently for 45 minutes–1 hour or until the fruit is really soft and pulpy. Stir from time to time to prevent sticking.

2 Spoon the fruit pulp into a jelly bag or cloth attached to the legs of an upturned stool, and leave to strain into a large bowl for at least 12 hours.

3 Discard the pulp remaining in the jelly bag. Measure the extract and return it to the preserving pan with 450 g (1 lb) sugar for each 600 ml (1 pint) extract. Heat gently, stirring, until the sugar has dissolved, then boil rapidly for about 15 minutes or until setting point is reached.

4 Remove any scum with a slotted spoon, then pot and cover in the usual way.

VARIATION
Gooseberry mint jelly

Cook the gooseberries with a few sprigs of mint and add finely chopped fresh mint to the jelly before potting.

VARIATION
Gooseberry and elderflower jelly

Tie two large elderflower heads in a piece of muslin. When the jelly has reached setting point, remove from the heat, add the muslin bag and stir around in the hot jelly for about 3 minutes. This will produce a good flavour that is not over-dominant. Remove the muslin bag and pot and cover the jelly in the usual way.

Currant and Apple Jelly

~

900 g (2 lb) red or blackcurrants, washed
900 g (2 lb) cooking apples, washed
sugar

~

There is no need to remove the stalks from the currants. Remove any bruised portions from the apples and slice them without peeling or coring.

2 Put the fruit in a preserving pan and add 1.4 litres (2½ pints) water. Simmer very gently for about 1 hour or until the fruit is thoroughly cooked and pulpy. Stir from time to time to prevent sticking.

3 Spoon the fruit pulp into a jelly bag or cloth attached to the legs of an upturned stool, and leave to strain into a large bowl for at least 12 hours.

4 Discard the pulp remaining in the jelly bag. Measure the extract and return it to the preserving pan with 450 g (1 lb) sugar for each 600 ml (1 pint) extract.

5 Heat gently, stirring, until the sugar has dissolved, then boil rapidly for 8–10 minutes or until setting point is reached. Remove any scum with a slotted spoon, then pot and cover in the usual way.

Currant and Port Jelly

~

1.4 kg (3 lb) red or blackcurrants
sugar
45 ml (3 tbsp) port

~

There is no need to remove the currants from their stalks. Put the currants in a preserving pan with 600 ml (1 pint) water and simmer gently for about 30 minutes or until the fruit is really soft and pulpy. Stir from time to time to prevent sticking.

2 Spoon the fruit pulp into a jelly bag or cloth attached to the legs of an upturned stool, and leave to strain into a large bowl for at least 12 hours.

3 Discard the pulp remaining in the jelly bag. Measure the extract and return it to the preserving pan with 450 g (1 lb) sugar for each 600 ml (1 pint) extract.

4 Heat gently, stirring, until the sugar has dissolved, then boil rapidly for about 15 minutes or until setting point is reached.

5 Stir in the port, remove any scum with a slotted spoon and pot and cover in the usual way.

Elderberry Jelly

~

900 g (2 lb) cooking apples, washed
900 g (2 lb) elderberries, washed
Sugar with Pectin

~

Remove any bruised or damaged portions from the apples and roughly chop them without peeling or coring. Put them in a saucepan with just enough water to cover and simmer gently for about 1 hour or until the fruit is very soft and pulpy.

2 Put the elderberries in another saucepan with just enough water to cover and simmer gently for about 1 hour or until the fruit is very soft and tender.

3 Combine the two lots of fruit pulp and spoon into a jelly bag or cloth attached to the legs of an upturned stool. Leave to strain into a large bowl for at least 12 hours.

4 Discard the pulp remaining in the jelly bag. Measure the extract and transfer it to a preserving pan with 350 g (12 oz) sugar for each 600 ml (1 pint) extract.

5 Heat gently, stirring, until the sugar has dissolved, then boil rapidly for 4 minutes or until setting point is reached. Remove any scum with a slotted spoon, then pot and cover in the usual way.

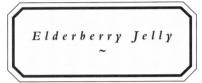

VARIATION
Bilberry jelly

If preferred, follow the above recipe, using bilberries instead of elderberries.

Rosehip Jelly
~

900 g (2 lb) cooking apples, washed
450 g (1 lb) ripe rosehips, washed
sugar

~

Remove any bruised or damaged portions from the apples, then roughly chop without coring or peeling.

2 Put the apples and rosehips in a preserving pan with just enough water to cover. Bring to the boil, then simmer gently for about 45 minutes or until the fruit is soft and pulpy. Stir from time to time to prevent the fruit sticking.

3 Spoon the fruit pulp into a jelly bag or cloth attached to the legs of an upturned stool, and leave to strain into a large bowl for at least 12 hours.

4 Discard the pulp remaining in the jelly bag. Measure the extract and return to the preserving pan with 450 g (1 lb) sugar for each 600 ml (1 pint) extract.

5 Heat gently, stirring, until the sugar has dissolved, then bring to the boil and boil rapidly for about 15 minutes or until setting point is reached. Remove any scum with a slotted spoon, then pot and cover in the usual way.

Rowanberry Jelly
~

1.4 kg (3 lb) firm, ripe rowanberries, washed
juice of 1 lemon
sugar

~

*P*ut the berries in a preserving pan with 600 ml (1 pint) water and the lemon juice. Bring to the boil, then simmer gently for 45 minutes–1 hour or until the fruit is very soft and pulpy, stirring occasionally.

2 Spoon the fruit pulp into a jelly bag or cloth attached to the legs of an upturned stool, and leave to strain into a large bowl for at least 12 hours.

3 Discard the pulp remaining in the jelly bag. Measure the extract and return to the preserving pan with 450 g (1 lb) sugar for each 600 ml (1 pint) extract.

4 Heat gently, stirring, until the sugar has dissolved, then bring to the boil and boil rapidly for about 10 minutes or until setting point is reached. Remove any scum with a slotted spoon, then pot and cover in the usual way.

Haw Jelly
~

1.4 kg (3 lb) haws
sugar
juice of 3 lemons

~

*P*ick off any leaves or stalks, then rinse and drain the haws. Put in a preserving pan with 1.4 litres (2½ pints) water and simmer for about 45 minutes or until tender, mashing the fruit from time to time.

2 Spoon the fruit pulp into a jelly bag or cloth attached to the legs of an upturned stool, and leave to strain into a large bowl for at least 12 hours.

3 Discard the pulp remaining in the jelly bag. Measure the extract and return to the preserving pan with 450 g (1 lb) sugar for each 600 ml (1 pint) extract. Stir in the lemon juice.

4 Heat gently, stirring, until the sugar has dissolved, then bring to the boil and boil rapidly for about 15 minutes or until setting point is reached. Remove any scum with a slotted spoon, then pot and cover in the usual way.

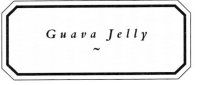

Guava Jelly
~

900 g (2 lb) guavas, washed and sliced
sugar
juice of 2 lemons

~

*P*ut the fruit in a preserving pan with 900 ml (1½ pints) water, bring to the boil and simmer gently for 30 minutes or until the fruit is really soft and pulpy. Stir from time to time to prevent sticking.

2 Spoon the fruit pulp into a jelly bag or cloth attached to the legs of an upturned stool, and leave to strain into a large bowl for at least 12 hours.

3 Discard the pulp remaining in the jelly bag. Measure the extract and return it to the preserving pan with 450 g (1 lb) sugar for each 600 ml (1 pint) extract. Add the lemon juice.

4 Heat gently, stirring, until the sugar has dissolved, then boil rapidly for about 15 minutes or until setting point is reached. Remove any scum with a slotted spoon, then pot and cover in the usual way.

Orange and Thyme Jelly
~

1.8 kg (4 lb) oranges, washed
450 g (1 lb) lemons, washed
120 ml (8 tbsp) chopped fresh thyme
sugar

~

*S*lice the oranges and lemons, then cut the slices into quarters. Put in a preserving pan with 60 ml (4 tbsp) chopped thyme and 2.8 litres (5 pints) water. Bring to the boil, then simmer gently for about 1¼ hours or until the fruit is soft. Stir from time to time to prevent sticking.

2 Spoon the fruit pulp into a jelly bag or cloth attached to the legs of an upturned stool, and leave to strain into a large bowl for at least 12 hours.

3 Discard the pulp remaining in the jelly bag. Measure the extract and return it to the preserving pan with 450 g (1 lb) sugar for each 600 ml (1 pint) extract.

4 Heat gently, stirring, until the sugar has dissolved, then bring to the boil and boil rapidly for about 15 minutes or until setting point is reached. Remove any scum with a slotted spoon, then stir in the remaining chopped thyme.

5 Allow the jelly to cool slightly, then stir well to distribute the thyme. Pot and cover in the usual way.

Orange and Apple Jelly
~

4 sweet oranges, washed
1.4 kg (3 lb) cooking apples, washed
sugar

~

*C*ut the oranges and apples into slices without peeling or coring the apples or removing the pith from the oranges.

2 Put the sliced fruit in a preserving pan with any juice that comes from the oranges, add 1.9 litres (3¼ pints) water and simmer very gently for 1¼ hours or until the fruit is thoroughly tender. (The skin of some oranges is rather tough and it may be necessary to cook for a longer time.)

3 Spoon the fruit pulp into a jelly bag or cloth attached to the legs of an upturned stool, and leave to strain into a large bowl for at least 12 hours.

4 Discard the pulp remaining in the jelly bag. Measure the extract and return to the preserving pan with 450 g (1 lb) sugar for each 600 ml (1 pint) extract.

5 Heat gently, stirring, until the sugar has dissolved, then bring to the boil and boil rapidly for 10 minutes or until setting point is reached. Remove any scum with a slotted spoon, then pot and cover in the usual way.

Quick Mint Jelly
~

300 ml (½ pint) distilled white vinegar
450 g (1 lb) sugar
50 g (2 oz) fresh mint
227-ml (8-fl oz) bottle of commercial pectin
2–3 drops of green food colouring (optional)

~

*P*ut the vinegar and sugar in a large saucepan with half the mint sprigs. Heat gently, stirring, until the sugar has dissolved.

2 Strain through a sieve to remove the mint, then return the vinegar syrup to the pan and bring to the boil. Boil for 1 minute, then stir in the pectin. Bring to the boil again and boil for 2 minutes.

3 Chop the remaining mint and stir into the pan with the food colouring, if using. Allow to cool slightly, then stir to distribute the mint. Pot and cover in the usual way.

Raspberry Jelly
~

1.8 kg (4 lb) raspberries, washed
sugar

~

Put the raspberries in a preserving pan and heat very gently until the juices flow, then simmer for about 1 hour or until they are quite soft and pulpy. Stir from time to time to prevent sticking.

2 Spoon the raspberry pulp into a jelly bag or cloth attached to the legs of an upturned stool, and leave to strain into a large bowl for at least 12 hours.

3 Discard the pulp remaining in the jelly bag. Measure the extract and return it to the pan with 450 g (1 lb) sugar for each 600 ml (1 pint) extract.

4 Heat gently, stirring, until the sugar has dissolved, then bring to the boil and boil rapidly for about 10 minutes or until setting point is reached. Remove any scum with a slotted spoon, then pot and cover in the usual way.

VARIATION
Loganberry jelly

If preferred, follow the above recipe, using loganberries instead of raspberries.

Sweet Cider Jelly
~

1.1 litres (2 pints) sweet apple cider
thinly pared rind of 2 oranges
15 ml (1 tbsp) chopped fresh rosemary
1.4 kg (3 lb) sugar
227-ml (8-fl oz) bottle of commercial pectin

~

Put the cider, orange rind and rosemary in a large saucepan. Bring slowly to the boil and reduce the heat.

2 Add the sugar to the pan and heat gently, stirring, until dissolved. Add the pectin and bring to a fast rolling boil. Boil hard for 1 minute. Strain through a nylon sieve, then pot and cover in the usual way.

Blackcurrant Jelly
~

1.8 kg (4 lb) blackcurrants, washed
sugar

~

There is no need to remove the blackcurrants from their stalks. Put the fruit in a preserving pan with 1.4 litres (2½ pints) water and simmer gently for about 1 hour or until the fruit is really soft and pulpy. Stir from time to time to prevent sticking.

2 Spoon the fruit pulp into a jelly bag or cloth attached to the legs of an upturned stool, and leave to strain into a large bowl for at least 12 hours.

3 Discard the pulp remaining in the jelly bag. Measure the extract and return it to the preserving pan with 450 g (1 lb) sugar for each 600 ml (1 pint) extract.

4 Heat gently, stirring, until the sugar has dissolved, then bring to the boil and boil rapidly for about 15 minutes or until setting point is reached. Remove any scum with a slotted spoon, then pot and cover in the usual way.

Blackberry or Bramble Jelly
~

900 g (2 lb) blackberries or brambles, washed
Sugar with Pectin

~

*P*ut the fruit in a preserving pan with 600 ml (1 pint) water. Bring to the boil and simmer gently for 30 minutes or until very tender.

2 Spoon the fruit pulp into a jelly bag or cloth attached to the legs of an upturned stool, and leave to strain into a large bowl for at least 12 hours.

3 Discard the pulp remaining in the jelly bag. Measure the extract and return it to the preserving pan with 450 g (1 lb) sugar for each 600 ml (1 pint) extract.

4 Heat gently, stirring, until the sugar has dissolved, then bring to the boil and boil rapidly for 1 minute or until setting point is reached. Remove any scum with a slotted spoon, then pot and cover in the usual way.

Redcurrant and Gooseberry Jelly
~

1.1 kg (2½ lb) gooseberries, washed
700 g (1½ lb) redcurrants, washed
sugar

~

*P*ut the fruit in a preserving pan with 900 ml (1½ pints) water. Simmer gently for 45 minutes–1 hour or until the fruit is thoroughly cooked.

2 Spoon the fruit pulp into a jelly bag or cloth attached to the legs of an upturned stool, and leave to strain into a large bowl for at least 12 hours.

3 Discard the pulp remaining in the jelly bag. Measure the extract and return to the preserving pan with 450 g (1 lb) sugar for each 600 ml (1 pint) extract.

4 Heat gently, stirring, until the sugar has dissolved, then bring to the boil and boil rapidly for 7–10 minutes or until setting point is reached. Remove any scum with a slotted spoon, then pot and cover in the usual way.

Redcurrant and Cinnamon Jelly
~

900 g (2 lb) redcurrants, washed
1 cinnamon stick
Sugar with Pectin
30 ml (2 tbsp) lemon juice

~

*P*ut the redcurrants in a preserving pan with 300 ml (½ pint) water and the cinnamon.

2 Bring slowly to the boil, mashing the fruit occasionally to break it up, then simmer gently for 30 minutes.

3 Spoon the fruit pulp into a jelly bag or cloth attached to the legs of an upturned stool, and leave to strain into a large bowl for at least 12 hours.

4 Discard the pulp remaining in the jelly bag. Measure the extract and return to the preserving pan with 450 g (1 lb) sugar for each 600 ml (1 pint) extract. Add the lemon juice.

5 Heat gently, stirring, until the sugar has dissolved, then bring to the boil and boil rapidly for 1 minute or until setting point is reached. Remove any scum with a slotted spoon, then pot and cover in the usual way.

VARIATION
Redcurrant mint jelly

Add a few sprigs of fresh mint when cooking the fruit and some finely chopped mint before potting the jelly.

Mulberry and Apple Jelly
~

1.1 kg (2½ lb) sour cooking apples, washed
1.4 kg (3 lb) mulberries, washed
juice of 2 lemons or 7.5 ml (1½ tsp) citric acid
sugar

~

*R*emove any bruised or damaged portions from the apples and roughly chop them without peeling or coring. Put the apples and mulberries in a preserving pan with 1.7 litres (3 pints) water and the lemon juice or acid. Simmer gently for about 1 hour, mashing from time to time, until the fruit is very soft and the contents of the pan have reduced considerably.

2 Spoon the fruit pulp into a jelly bag or cloth attached to the legs of an upturned stool, and leave to strain into a large bowl for at least 12 hours.

3 Discard the pulp remaining in the jelly bag. Measure the extract and return it to the preserving pan with 450 g (1 lb) sugar for each 600 ml (1 pint) extract.

4 Heat gently, stirring, until the sugar has dissolved, then bring to the boil and boil rapidly for about 10 minutes or until setting point is reached. Remove any scum with a slotted spoon, then pot and cover in the usual way.

Plum Jelly
~

900 g (2 lb) plums, washed, halved and stoned (reserving the stones)
1 kg (2.2 lb) Sugar with Pectin

~

*T*ie the plum stones in a piece of muslin. Put the plums and muslin bag in a preserving pan with 600 ml (1 pint) water. Bring to the boil and simmer until the fruit is very soft.

2 Spoon the fruit pulp into a jelly bag or cloth attached to the legs of an upturned stool, and leave to strain into a large bowl for at least 12 hours.

3 Discard the pulp remaining in the jelly bag. Measure the extract – there should be about 900 ml (1½ pints). Return to the preserving pan with the sugar.

4 Heat gently, stirring, until the sugar has dissolved, then bring to the boil and boil rapidly for 1 minute or until setting point is reached.

5 Remove any scum with a slotted spoon, then pot and cover in the usual way.

Four-Fruit Jelly
~

450 g (1 lb) redcurrants, washed
450 g (1 lb) raspberries, washed
450 g (1 lb) Morello or May Duke cherries, washed
450 g (1 lb) strawberries, washed
60 ml (4 tbsp) lemon juice
sugar

~

*I*t is not necessary to string the redcurrants. Put all the fruit in a preserving pan with the lemon juice and 600 ml (1 pint) water. Simmer gently for about 1 hour or until the fruit is really soft and pulpy. Stir from time to time to prevent sticking.

2 Spoon the fruit pulp into a jelly bag or cloth attached to the legs of an upturned stool, and leave to strain into a large bowl for at least 12 hours.

3 Discard the pulp remaining in the jelly bag. Measure the extract and return it to the preserving pan with 450 g (1 lb) sugar for each 600 ml (1 pint) extract.

4 Heat gently, stirring, until the sugar has dissolved, then bring to the boil and boil rapidly for about 10 minutes or until setting point is reached. Remove any scum with a slotted spoon, then pot and cover in the usual way.

Damson and Apple Jelly
~

2.7 kg (6 lb) cooking apples, washed
1.4 kg (3 lb) damsons, washed
sugar

~

Remove any bruised or damaged portions from the apples and roughly chop them into large chunks without peeling or coring. Put the apples and damsons in a preserving pan with 2.3 litres (4 pints) water and simmer gently for about 1 hour or until the fruit is really soft and pulpy. Stir from time to time to prevent sticking.

2 Spoon the fruit pulp into a jelly bag or cloth attached to the legs of an upturned stool, and leave to strain into a large bowl for at least 12 hours.

3 Discard the pulp remaining in the jelly bag. Measure the extract and return it to the preserving pan with 450 g (1 lb) sugar for each 600 ml (1 pint) extract.

4 Heat gently, stirring, until the sugar has dissolved, then bring to the boil and boil rapidly for about 10 minutes or until setting point is reached. Remove any scum with a slotted spoon, then pot and cover in the usual way.

Sloe Jelly
~

1.8 kg (4 lb) sloes, washed
sugar

~

Prick the sloes all over, using a darning needle. Put the sloes in a preserving pan, add a little water – hardly enough to cover – and bring to the boil. Simmer very gently for 1¹/₂–2 hours or until the fruit is very soft and pulpy. Stir the fruit from time to time to prevent sticking.

2 Spoon the fruit pulp into a jelly bag or cloth attached to the legs of an upturned stool, and leave to strain into a large bowl for at least 12 hours.

3 Discard the pulp remaining in the jelly bag. Measure the extract and return it to the preserving pan with 450 g (1 lb) sugar for each 600 ml (1 pint) extract.

4 Heat gently, stirring, until the sugar has dissolved, then bring to the boil and boil rapidly for about 10 minutes or until setting point is reached. Remove any scum with a slotted spoon, then pot and cover in the usual way.

Apple and Rose Petal Jelly
~

900 g (2 lb) cooking apples, washed
60 ml (4 tbsp) lemon juice
50 g (2 oz) dark red, scented rosebuds (about 12)
sugar
4–6 drops triple-strength rosewater

~

Roughly chop the apples without peeling or coring. Put the apples in a preserving pan with 600 ml (1 pint) water and the lemon juice. Simmer gently for about 30 minutes or until the fruit is pulpy.

2 Spoon the apple pulp into a jelly bag or cloth attached to the legs of an upturned stool, and leave to strain into a large bowl for at least 12 hours.

3 Meanwhile, separate the petals from the rosebuds, cut the white base from each petal and discard. Put the petals in a small saucepan with 150 ml (¹/₄ pint) water, cover and simmer for 15 minutes. Leave to infuse for 1 hour, then strain through a muslin cloth overnight. Separate and reserve a few rose petals to add to the jelly; discard the remainder.

4 Mix the two liquids together, measure them and put in a medium saucepan. For every 600 ml (1 pint) juice, add 350 g (12 oz) sugar. Heat gently, stirring, until the sugar has dissolved, then bring to the boil and boil rapidly for about 10 minutes or until setting point is reached. Remove any scum with a slotted spoon, then add the reserved rose petals and the rosewater. Pot and cover in the usual way.

Honey and Apple Jelly
~

1.1 kg (2½ lb) thin honey
300 ml (½ pint) pure apple juice
227-ml (8-fl oz) bottle of commercial pectin

~

Put the honey and apple juice in a large saucepan and bring rapidly to the boil. Add the pectin, stirring constantly, and bring back to the boil.

2 Continue boiling rapidly for 5 minutes, then take the pan off the heat. Remove any scum with a slotted spoon, then pot and cover in the usual way.

Grapefruit and Tangerine Jelly
~

2 grapefruit, washed and roughly chopped
3 tangerines, washed and roughly chopped
2 lemons, washed and roughly chopped
sugar

~

Put the fruit in a preserving pan with 3.1 litres (5½ pints) water and boil for 2 hours or until the fruit is soft and pulpy.

2 Spoon the fruit pulp into a jelly bag or cloth attached to the legs of an upturned stool, and leave to strain into a large bowl for at least 12 hours.

3 Return the pulp from the jelly bag to the preserving pan, cover with water and boil for 1 hour. Spoon into a jelly bag and strain again for 12 hours.

4 Discard the pulp remaining in the jelly bag. Combine and measure the two extracts and return to the preserving pan with 450 g (1 lb) sugar for each 600 ml (1 pint) extract.

5 Heat gently, stirring, until the sugar has dissolved, then bring to the boil and boil rapidly for about 10 minutes or until setting point is reached. Remove any scum with a slotted spoon, then pot and cover in the usual way.

Bitter Lime Jelly with Pernod
~

1.8 kg (4 lb) limes, washed and sliced
sugar
15 ml (1 tbsp) Pernod

~

Put the limes in a preserving pan with 3.4 litres (6 pints) water and simmer gently for 1 hour or until the fruit is soft.

2 Spoon the fruit into a jelly bag or cloth attached to the legs of an upturned stool, and leave to strain into a large bowl for at least 12 hours.

3 Discard the pulp remaining in the jelly bag. Measure the extract and return it to the preserving pan with 450 g (1 lb) sugar for each 600 ml (1 pint) extract.

4 Heat gently, stirring, until the sugar has dissolved, then bring to the boil and boil rapidly for 10–15 minutes or until setting point is reached. Stir in the Pernod. Remove any scum with a slotted spoon, then pot and cover in the usual way.

Note If a less acid jelly is preferred, add 1.25 ml (¼ tsp) bicarbonate of soda to the water when cooking the limes.

Marmalades

Marmalade is a preserve that is nearly always made from citrus fruits and is most commonly seen on the breakfast table. At one time, marmalade was made from a variety of fruits, but nowadays other fruits are only used in recipes which combine them with citrus fruits. The method and equipment used for making marmalade is very similar to that used for jam (see page 9) but with a few special points to remember.

The Fruit

Seville or bitter oranges make the best marmalades with a pleasing flavour and appearance. Sweet oranges make marmalade that is rather cloudy and the pith does not turn as translucent as that of Seville oranges. Sweet oranges are usually only used in combination with other citrus fruits.

The best time to make marmalade is in January and February when Seville oranges are available. Fortunately, it is possible to freeze Seville oranges. Freeze the oranges whole, but after a few months the pectin level will fall slightly. To compensate for this, add one-eighth more fruit to the recipe. See the method for making marmalade from whole oranges on page 51.

Making Marmalade

Preparing the fruit The peel of citrus fruits is tougher than that of most fruits used for jam-making and must therefore be evenly shredded, either by hand or in the slicer attachment of a food mixer, or in a food processor. You can choose the thickness of peel that you prefer. Do not use a coarse mincer to cut up the peel as it produces a paste-like marmalade. If you are making a very large quantity of marmalade, however, it may be a good idea to mince half the peel by machine and cut the remainder by hand.

There are several methods of preparing and softening the fruit, each resulting in a different type of marmalade, such as coarse-cut, thin-cut and fine-shred jelly marmalade. The method you choose for peeling and preparing the fruit depends on the recipe you are using and precise instructions are given.

It is sometimes suggested that the peel should be cut up and soaked in water overnight to help soften it. However, soaking is not essential and the long, first cooking stage is usually sufficient. Sometimes it may be more convenient to prepare the fruit one day and make the marmalade the next day, in which case the peel should be left in water overnight to prevent it drying out.

First cooking Cooking times required for marmalades are usually much longer than for jams – at least 1 hour and very often 2–3 hours. Consequently, larger quantities of water are needed to allow for evaporation. The purpose of the first cooking stage is to extract the pectin, reduce the contents of the pan by about half and to soften the peel. Once the sugar is added, the peel won't tenderise any further, so it is essential that it is soft and that the pith is almost opaque before any sugar is poured in. Failure to do this is one of the most common reasons for marmalade not setting. You can shorten the cooking time by using a pressure cooker (see page 51).

If you wish to double the recipe quantities, it may be necessary to adjust the cooking time and to use an extra large pan.

Extracting the pectin Much of the pectin in oranges is contained in the pips and membranes, and it is important that it is all extracted. Put all the pips, and any membrane that has come away from the peel during squeezing, in a clean piece of muslin. If you haven't got any muslin, improvise by using an old, large, clean handkerchief. Tie the muslin or handkerchief in a bundle with a long piece of string, then tie the string to the handle of the pan so that the bundle hangs down into the marmalade and can easily be removed after cooking. Cook this with the fruit for the first cooking, then take it out, squeezing it as much as possible and letting the pulpy juice run back into the pan. A good way to do this is to press the bag in a nylon sieve with the back of a wooden spoon. Discard the contents of the muslin bag.

Second cooking   The sugar is added at the beginning of the second cooking stage and stirred in until it dissolves. The marmalade is then boiled rapidly for 15–20 minutes or until setting point is reached. Prolonged boiling after the addition of sugar gives marmalade a dark colour. Test for a set in the same way as for jams (see page 11), then skim the marmalade with a slotted spoon to remove any scum.

We advise using granulated sugar for marmalade-making, unless you are planning to show your marmalade, in which case a clearer marmalade can be made using preserving sugar.

First, place the sugar in a bowl and warm gently in a low oven before adding to the fruit. This helps it to dissolve more quickly and also prevents the temperature of the fruit from falling drastically, which would increase the cooking/boiling time. Long boiling can impair the flavour.

Potting and covering   Marmalades should be potted and covered in the same way as jam (see page 12). Leave the marmalade to stand for 10–15 minutes, then stir to distribute the peel before potting.

Pressure Cooking Marmalade

Follow the instructions given for jam on page 13, but add only a quarter of the amount of water required in the recipe when the fruit is cooked under pressure. More water is added with the sugar. Cook citrus fruits for 20 minutes at medium (10 lb) pressure. (See recipe on page 55). Marmalades can also be cooked at high (15 lb) pressure as citrus fruits are rich in pectin. Check in your cooker manufacturer's handbook.

Seville Orange Marmalade
~

MAKES ABOUT 4.5 KG (10 LB)

1.4 kg (3 lb) Seville oranges, washed
juice of 2 lemons
2.7 kg (6 lb) sugar

~

Halve the oranges and squeeze out the juice and pips. Tie the pips, and any extra membrane that has come away during squeezing, in a piece of muslin.

2 Slice the orange peel thinly or thickly, as preferred, and put it in a preserving pan with the fruit juices, muslin bag and 3.4 litres (6 pints) water. Simmer gently for about 2 hours or until the peel is really soft and the liquid reduced by about half.

3 Remove the muslin bag, squeezing it well and allowing the juice to run back into the pan. Add the sugar.

4 Heat gently, stirring until the sugar has dissolved, then bring to the boil and boil rapidly for about 15 minutes or until setting point is reached. Remove any scum with a slotted spoon, then pot and cover in the usual way.

VARIATION
Seville orange marmalade (whole fruit method)

As an alternative method, place the whole washed fruit in a saucepan with 3.4 litres (6 pints) water. Cover and simmer gently for about 2 hours or until a fork will pierce the peel easily. Remove the fruit from the pan and leave to cool a little, then cut it up, thinly or thickly, with a knife and fork. Save the pips and tie them in a piece of muslin. Put the muslin bag in the liquid in the saucepan, add the lemon juice and boil for 5 minutes.

Weigh a preserving pan, put the fruit in it, add the liquid from the saucepan, discarding the muslin bag, and boil off the excess liquid until the contents weigh 2 kg (4½ lb). Add the sugar, stirring until it has dissolved, then bring to the boil and boil rapidly for about 15 minutes or

Above (left to right): Four Fruit Processor Marmalade
(page 58), Bitter Chunky Marmalade (page 54),
Seville Orange Marmalade (page 51), Ginger and
Grapefruit Jelly Marmalade (page 62)
Opposite: Bitter Chunky Marmalade (page 54)

until setting point is reached. Remove any scum with a slotted spoon, leave to stand for about 15 minutes, then stir gently to distribute the peel. Pot and cover in the usual way.

VARIATION
Whisky marmalade

Follow the recipe for Seville orange marmalade on page 51. When setting point is reached, remove any scum with a slotted spoon, then stir in 150 ml (¼ pint) whisky. Leave to stand for about 15 minutes, then stir to distribute the peel. Pot and cover in the usual way.

VARIATION
Dark chunky marmalade (1)

Follow the recipe for Seville orange marmalade on page 51. Cut the peel into thick slices. When the sugar is added, stir until it has dissolved, bring to the boil, then simmer gently for a further 1½ hours or until the colour of the marmalade has darkened and setting point is reached. Remove any scum, then pot and cover in the usual way.

VARIATION
Dark chunky marmalade (2)

Follow the recipe for Seville orange marmalade on page 51. Cut the peel into thick slices. Either replace the white sugar with the same quantity of demerara sugar, or stir in 30 ml (2 tbsp) black treacle with the white sugar.

Quick Seville Orange Marmalade
~

MAKES ABOUT 4.5 KG (10 LB)

900 g (2 lb) Seville oranges
2 kg (4.4 lb) Sugar with Pectin
~

Scrub the oranges, but do not peel. Cut up the oranges roughly, discarding the pips, then mince into a large bowl. Add 1.6 litres (2¾ pints) water and leave to soak overnight.

2 Transfer the contents of the bowl to a preserving pan. Bring to the boil, then simmer for 1 hour.

3 Add the sugar and heat gently, stirring, until it has dissolved, then bring to the boil and boil rapidly for 4 minutes or until setting point is reached.

4 Allow to stand for 5 minutes, stirring occasionally to distribute the peel, then pot and cover in the usual way.

Oxford Marmalade
~

MAKES ABOUT 4.5 KG (10 LB)

1.4 kg (3 lb) Seville oranges
2.7 kg (6 lb) sugar
~

Peel the oranges. Cut the peel into strips and the fruit into small pieces, reserving the pips. Put the pips into a small bowl. Put the strips of peel and chopped flesh into a large bowl.

2 Bring 3.4 litres (6 pints) water to the boil and pour 600 ml (1 pint) over the pips and the remainder over the orange peel and flesh. Cover and leave for several hours or overnight.

3 The next day, the pips will be covered with a soft transparent jelly which must be washed off into the orange peel and flesh. To do this, lift the pips out of the water with a slotted spoon and put them in a nylon sieve.

Pour the water the pips were soaking in over the pips into the large bowl. Repeat the process, using water from the large bowl. Discard the pips.

4 Transfer the orange peel, flesh and water to a preserving pan and boil until the peel is very soft – the longer this mixture boils the darker the marmalade will be. When the peel is quite soft, remove the pan from the heat and add the sugar, stirring until it has dissolved.

5 Bring to the boil again and boil very gently until the marmalade is as dark as you like it, then boil rapidly for about 15 minutes or until setting point is reached. Remove any scum with a slotted spoon, leave the marmalade to stand for 15 minutes, then stir to distribute the peel. Pot and cover in the usual way.

Bitter Chunky Marmalade
~

MAKES ABOUT 2.3 KG (5 LB)

3 large sweet (or Seville) oranges (about 900 g/2 lb)
2 large lemons (about 450 g/1 lb)
900 g (2 lb) sugar
900 g (2 lb) demerara sugar
15 ml (1 tbsp) black treacle
~

Wash the fruit well, then squeeze to obtain the juice. Remove excess membranes and reserve with the pips. Strain the juice.

2 Cut the citrus peel into short 3 mm (⅛ inch) thick strips. Put in a preserving pan with the fruit juices and 2.3 litres (4 pints) water. Tie the pips and any spare membranes in a piece of muslin and add to the pan.

3 Bring to the boil, then simmer gently for 2–3 hours or until the peel is very soft and the liquid reduced by half.

4 Remove the muslin bag, squeezing well to extract all the juices. Stir in the sugar and treacle. Heat gently, stirring, until all the sugar has completely dissolved.

5 Bring to the boil and boil rapidly for 10 minutes or until setting point is reached.

6 Remove any scum with a slotted spoon. Leave the marmalade to cool slightly, then stir to distribute the fruit evenly through the jelly. Pot and cover in the usual way.

Ginger Marmalade
~

MAKES ABOUT 4.5 KG (10 LB)

450 g (1 lb) Seville oranges, washed
1.4 kg (3 lb) cooking apples, peeled, cored and sliced
3 kg (6 ½ lb) sugar
225 g (8 oz) preserved ginger, diced
20 ml (4 tsp) ground ginger
~

Peel the oranges and shred the peel finely. Roughly chop the oranges, removing and reserving any tough membrane, pith, pips and juice. Tie the membrane, pith and pips in a piece of muslin.

2 Put the peel, chopped orange, juice, muslin bag and 2.8 litres (5 pints) water in a preserving pan and simmer for about 1½ hours or until the peel is soft and the contents of the pan reduced by half. Remove the muslin bag, squeezing well and allowing the juice to run back into the pan.

3 Put the apples in a saucepan with 150 ml (¼ pint) water and simmer gently until the fruit is soft and pulped. Combine the apples with the oranges in the preserving pan, add the sugar and stir until it has dissolved.

4 Add the preserved ginger and ground ginger, bring to the boil and boil rapidly for about 15 minutes or until setting point is reached. Remove any scum with a slotted spoon, leave the marmalade to stand for about 15 minutes, then stir to distribute the peel and ginger. Pot and cover in the usual way.

Pressure-Cooked Marmalade
~

MAKES ABOUT 4.5 KG (10 LB)

1.4 kg (3 lb) Seville oranges, washed
juice of 2 lemons
2.7 kg (6 lb) sugar
~

Halve the oranges and squeeze out the juice, reserving the pips and pulp. Tie the pips and pulp in a piece of muslin.

2 Slice the orange peel thinly and place in a pressure cooker with the fruit juices, 900 ml (1½ pints) water and the muslin bag.

3 Bring to medium (10 lb) pressure and cook for 20 minutes until the peel is soft. Leave the pan to cool at room temperature until the pressure is reduced.

4 Remove the muslin bag, squeezing it well and allowing the juice to run back into the cooker. Add 900 ml (1½ pints) water and the sugar and stir until the sugar has dissolved.

5 Bring to the boil and boil rapidly for 15 minutes or until setting point is reached. Remove any scum with a slotted spoon, leave the marmalade to stand for 15 minutes, then stir gently to distribute the peel. Pot and cover in the usual way.

Three Fruit and Ginger Marmalade
~

MAKES ABOUT 3.6 KG (8 LB)

4 Seville oranges, washed
2 sweet oranges, washed
2 lemons, washed
225 g (8 oz) preserved ginger
2.3 kg (5 lb) sugar
~

Pare the rinds from the fruit as thinly as possible, using a sharp knife or potato peeler, and cut the rind into thin shreds.

2 Squeeze the juice out of the fruit, reserving the pips. Tie the remaining pith and the pips in a piece of muslin. Cut the ginger into small strips.

3 Put the shredded rind, juice, ginger and muslin bag in a preserving pan and add 3.4 litres (6 pints) water. Simmer for 1½–2 hours or until tender.

4 Remove the muslin bag, squeezing well to remove as much juice as possible. Add the sugar and stir until it has dissolved.

5 Bring to the boil and boil rapidly for 10–15 minutes or until setting point is reached. Remove any scum with a slotted spoon, leave the marmalade to stand for about 15 minutes, then stir to distribute the peel. Pot and cover in the usual way.

Sweet Orange and Lemon Marmalade
~

MAKES ABOUT 1.8 KG (4 LB)

2 sweet oranges, washed and thinly sliced
3 lemons, washed and thinly sliced
900 g (2 lb) sugar
~

Remove all the pips from the fruit and tie them in a piece of muslin. Put the fruit and muslin bag in a preserving pan with 1.4 litres (2½ pints) water and simmer gently for about 1½ hours or until the contents of the pan have reduced by about half.

2 Remove the muslin bag, squeezing it well and allowing the juice to run back into the pan. Add the sugar and stir until dissolved.

3 Bring to the boil and boil rapidly for about 10 minutes or until setting point is reached. Remove any scum with a slotted spoon, leave the marmalade to stand for 15 minutes, then stir gently to distribute the peel. Pot and cover in the usual way.

Orange Shred Marmalade
~

MAKES ABOUT 2.3 KG (5 LB)

900 g (2 lb) Seville oranges, washed
juice of 2 lemons
1.4 kg (3 lb) sugar
~

*P*are off enough rind from the oranges, avoiding the pith, to weigh 100 g (4 oz). Cut the rind into thin strips.

2 Cut up the remaining fruit and put in a preserving pan with the lemon juice and 1.4 litres (2½ pints) water. Simmer for about 2 hours or until the fruit is really soft.

3 Put the shredded rind in a saucepan with 600 ml (1 pint) water, cover and simmer gently until this also is very soft. Drain off the liquid from the shreds and add them to the fruit in the other pan.

4 Pour the contents of the pan into a jelly bag or cloth attached to the legs of an upturned stool, and leave to strain into a large bowl for 15 minutes.

5 Return the pulp in the jelly bag to the preserving pan with 600 ml (1 pint) water. Simmer for a further 20 minutes, then pour into the jelly bag again and leave to strain for several hours.

6 Combine the two lots of extract and test for pectin (see page 10). If the liquid does not clot, reduce it slightly by rapid boiling, then test again.

7 Add the sugar and stir until it has dissolved. Add the orange peel shreds from the jelly bag and boil rapidly for about 15 minutes or until setting point is reached. Remove any scum with a slotted spoon, leave the marmalade to stand for about 15 minutes, then stir to distribute the peel. Pot and cover in the usual way.

VARIATION
Lemon shred marmalade

Follow the recipe above but substitute 900 g (2 lb) lemons for the oranges.

Lemon Marmalade
~

MAKES ABOUT 4.5 KG (10 LB)

1.4 kg (3 lb) ripe, juicy lemons, washed
2.7 kg (6 lb) sugar
~

*F*or this recipe, weigh the empty preserving pan before you start.

2 Halve the lemons and squeeze out the juice and pips. Cut each 'cap' of peel in half and, with a sharp knife, remove the membrane and some of the pith from the peel. Tie the membrane, pith and pips in a piece of muslin.

3 Slice the peel to the desired thickness and put it in a preserving pan with the juice, muslin bag and 3.4 litres (6 pints) water. Bring to the boil, then simmer gently for about 2 hours or until the peel is soft and the contents of the pan reduced by half.

4 Remove the muslin bag, squeezing out as much juice as possible. The contents of the pan should have reduced to 2 kg (4½ lb).

5 Add the sugar, stir until dissolved, then bring to the boil and boil rapidly for about 15 minutes or until setting point is reached. Remove any scum with a slotted spoon, leave the marmalade to stand for about 15 minutes, then stir to distribute the peel. Pot and cover in the usual way.

Lime Marmalade
~

MAKES ABOUT 2.3 KG (5 LB)

700 g (1½ lb) limes, washed
1.4 kg (3 lb) sugar
~

For this recipe, weigh the empty preserving pan or saucepan before you start.

2 Put the limes in a preserving pan or large saucepan and add 1.7 litres (3 pints) water. Cover with a tight-fitting lid and simmer for 1½–2 hours or until the fruit is very soft.

3 Remove the fruit from the pan with a slotted spoon and slice very thinly (using a knife and fork), discarding the pips and reserving any juice. Return the sliced fruit and juice to the pan and weigh it. If necessary, boil the mixture again until reduced to about 1.1 kg (2½ lb).

4 Add the sugar and stir until it has dissolved, then bring to the boil and boil rapidly for about 15 minutes or until setting point is reached. Remove any scum with a slotted spoon, leave the marmalade to stand for about 15 minutes, then stir gently to distribute the fruit. Pot and cover in the usual way.

Grapefruit Marmalade
~

MAKES ABOUT 2 KG (4½ LB)

2 large grapefruit (about 900 g/2 lb), washed
4–5 lemons (about 450 g/1 lb), washed
1.4 kg (3 lb) sugar
~

Pare the rinds from the grapefruit and lemons as thinly as possible, using a sharp knife or potato peeler, and shred finely. Remove the pith from the fruits and roughly cut up the flesh, removing and reserving any pips and saving the juice.

2 Tie the pith and pips in a piece of muslin and put the rind, fruit, juice and 1.7 litres (3 pints) water in a preserving pan with the muslin bag. Simmer gently for about 1½ hours or until the peel is very soft and the contents of the pan reduced by half.

3 Remove the muslin bag, squeezing it well and allowing the juice to run back into the pan. Add the sugar and stir until it has dissolved, then bring to the boil and boil rapidly for 15–20 minutes or until setting point is reached. Remove any scum with a slotted spoon, leave the marmalade to stand for about 15 minutes, then stir to distribute the peel. Pot and cover in the usual way.

Four Fruit Processor Marmalade
~

MAKES ABOUT 2.3 KG (5 LB)

1 grapefruit (about 350 g/12 oz)
2 large sweet oranges (about 700 g/1½ lb)
2 large lemons (about 450 g/1 lb)
350 g (12 oz) cooking apples
1.4 kg (3 lb) sugar
~

Wash all the fruit well. Quarter the citrus fruit and cut each quarter across into three pieces. Slice very thinly by hand with a sharp knife, or using the slicing disc of a food processor. Reserve the pips.

2 Peel, quarter and core the apples. Reserve the peel and thinly slice the flesh. Tie the pips, apple peel and cores in a piece of muslin.

3 Put all the sliced fruit in a preserving pan and add 2 litres (3½ pints) water and the muslin bag. Bring to the boil, then simmer gently for about 2 hours or until the peel is very soft and the contents of the pan reduced by half. Stir occasionally. Remove the muslin bag, squeezing it well and allowing the juice to run back into the pan.

4 Add the sugar to the pan, stirring until it has dissolved.

5 Bring to the boil and boil rapidly for 8–10 minutes or until setting point is reached. Remove any scum with a slotted spoon, leave the marmalade to stand for about 15 minutes, then stir to distribute the peel. Pot and cover in the usual way.

Diabetic Marmalade
~

MAKES ABOUT 1.8 KG (4 LB)

3 large oranges, washed
3 lemons, washed
900 g (2 lb) Sorbitol powder
227-ml (8-fl oz) bottle of commercial pectin
~

Pare the rinds from the oranges and lemons as thinly as possible, using a sharp knife or a potato peeler, and shred the rind very finely.

2 Halve the oranges and lemons and squeeze out the juice and pips. Tie the pips and pith in a piece of muslin.

3 Put the fruit juices, shredded rind, muslin bag and 1.1 litres (2 pints) water in a preserving pan, bring to the boil, then simmer gently for 1–1½ hours or until the rind is soft and the contents of the pan reduced by half.

4 Remove the muslin bag, squeezing it well and allowing the juice to run back into the pan. Add the Sorbitol powder and stir until it has dissolved, then bring to the boil and boil rapidly for 5 minutes.

5 Remove from the heat and stir in the pectin. Boil for a further minute, then take the pan off the heat and remove any scum with a slotted spoon. Leave the marmalade to cool for 15 minutes, then stir to distribute the peel. Pot and cover in the usual way. Small jars are recommended as the marmalade will not keep for long.

Lemon Rhubarb Marmalade
~

MAKES ABOUT 2.3 KG (5 LB)

2 lemons, washed
2 Seville oranges, washed
1.4 kg (3 lb) rhubarb, trimmed and washed
7 g (¼ oz) tartaric acid
1.4 kg (3 lb) sugar
~

Pare the rinds from the lemons and oranges as thinly as possible, using a sharp knife or potato peeler, and shred the rind very finely.

2 Halve the fruit and squeeze out the juice, discarding the pips. Cut the pith up fairly finely and tie in a piece of muslin. Put the muslin bag, fruit juice and shredded rind in a preserving pan with 600 ml (1 pint) water and leave to soak overnight.

3 Next day, bring the pan contents to the boil and simmer for 1–1½ hours or until the rind is soft and the contents of the pan reduced by half. Press the bag of pith occasionally to squeeze out as much pectin as possible.

4 Meanwhile, cut the rhubarb into neat pieces. Add to the pan with a further 300 ml (½ pint) water and the tartaric acid. Cook gently, stirring, until the fruit becomes a thick pulp.

5 Remove the muslin bag, squeezing it well and allowing the juice to run back into the pan. Add the sugar to the pan and stir until dissolved. Bring to the boil and boil for about 10 minutes or until setting point is reached. Remove any scum with a slotted spoon, then pot and cover in the usual way.

Overleaf: Tangerine Jelly Marmalade (page 62)

Tangerine Jelly
Marmalade JAN.

Ginger and Grapefruit Jelly Marmalade

~

MAKES ABOUT 1.8 KG (4 LB)

6 large grapefruit (about 1.8 kg/4 lb), washed
2.5 cm (1 inch) piece of fresh root ginger, peeled and thinly
sliced
sugar
stem ginger in syrup

~

Cut the grapefruit into quarters. Chop finely, using a sharp knife, or the slicing blade of a food processor.

2 Put the grapefruit and root ginger in a preserving pan and add 2.8 litres (5 pints) water. Bring to the boil, half cover and boil gently for about 1 hour or until the fruit is very soft and the contents of the pan reduced to a thick pulp (there should be little free liquid).

3 Spoon the contents of the pan into a jelly bag or cloth attached to the legs of an upturned stool, and leave to strain into a large bowl for at least 12 hours.

4 Discard the pulp remaining in the jelly bag. Measure the extract (there should be about 1.7 litres/3 pints) and return to the preserving pan.

5 Add 450 g (1 lb) sugar and 25 g (1 oz) finely shredded stem ginger for each 600 ml (1 pint) extract. Heat gently, stirring, until the sugar has dissolved.

6 Bring to the boil and boil rapidly for about 10 minutes or until setting point is reached. Remove any scum with a slotted spoon, leave the marmalade to stand for 10–15 minutes to allow the jelly to thicken sufficiently to suspend the ginger, then pot and cover in the usual way.

Tangerine Jelly Marmalade

~

MAKES ABOUT 2.3 KG (5 LB)

900 g (2 lb) tangerines, washed
1 large grapefruit, washed
1 lemon, washed
5 ml (1 tsp) citric acid
1.4 kg (3 lb) sugar

~

All together, the fruit should weigh about 1.3 kg (2¾ lb). Peel the tangerines and cut the peel into fine shreds. Tie the shreds in a piece of muslin.

2 Peel the grapefruit and lemon and cut the peel up finely. Roughly chop the flesh of all the fruit, reserving the juice, and put the flesh, juice and peel in a preserving pan with the muslin bag.

3 Add the citric acid and 2.8 litres (5 pints) water to the pan and simmer for about 2 hours or until the fruit is soft. Remove the muslin bag after 30 minutes, squeezing it well and allowing the juice to run back into the pan.

4 Untie the muslin bag, place the tangerine peel in a sieve, wash under cold water, then drain and reserve.

5 Spoon the pulped fruit into a jelly bag or cloth attached to the legs of an upturned stool, and leave to strain into a large bowl for about 2 hours.

6 Discard the pulp remaining in the jelly bag. Pour the extract into a clean preserving pan and add the sugar. Heat gently, stirring, until the sugar has dissolved. Bring to the boil, stir in the reserved tangerine peel and boil rapidly for 10 minutes or until setting point is reached. Remove any scum with a slotted spoon, leave the marmalade to stand for 15 minutes, then stir to distribute the shreds. Pot and cover in the usual way.

Windfall Marmalade
~

MAKES ABOUT 4 KG (9 LB)

900 g (2 lb) windfall apples
2 grapefruit, washed
4 lemons, washed
2.3 kg (5 lb) sugar

~

Peel, core and chop the apples, reserving the cores and peel. Pare the rind from the grapefruit and lemons as thinly as possible, using a sharp knife or potato peeler, and shred the rind finely.

2 Remove the pith from the fruits and roughly chop the flesh, removing and reserving any pips. Tie the citrus pith, pips, apple peel and cores in a piece of muslin.

3 Put all the fruit in a preserving pan with the shredded rind, muslin bag and 2.8 litres (5 pints) water. Bring to the boil, then simmer gently for about 2½ hours or until the peel is soft and the contents of the pan reduced by half.

4 Remove the muslin bag, squeezing well and allowing the juice to run back into the pan. Add the sugar to the pan, stir until it has dissolved, then bring to the boil and boil rapidly for 15–20 minutes or until setting point is reached. Remove any scum with a slotted spoon, leave the marmalade to stand for 15 minutes, then stir to distribute the peel. Pot and cover in the usual way.

Green Tomato Marmalade
~

MAKES ABOUT 2.3 KG (5 LB)

5 lemons, washed
900 g (2 lb) green tomatoes
1.6 kg (3½ lb) sugar

~

Halve the lemons and squeeze out the juice. Remove the remaining flesh from the lemon halves and reserve with the pips. Strip away the excess pith and cut the rind into thin strips. Place the rind in a saucepan, add 450 ml (¾ pint) water and simmer, covered, for 20 minutes or until soft.

2 Meanwhile, cut the tomatoes into quarters, remove the seeds and tie in a piece of muslin with the reserved lemon pips and lemon flesh. Shred the tomato flesh and put in a preserving pan.

3 Measure the lemon juice, make it up to 1.7 litres (3 pints) with water and add it to the pan with the muslin bag and the softened lemon shreds and liquid. Simmer all together for about 40 minutes or until the tomato is tender.

4 Remove the muslin bag, squeezing well and allowing the juice to run back into the pan. Add the sugar to the pan, stir until it has dissolved, then boil rapidly for about 15 minutes or until setting point is reached. Remove any scum with a slotted spoon, leave the marmalade to stand for about 15 minutes, then stir to distribute the peel. Pot and cover in the usual way.

Butters, Cheeses and Curds

Fruit butters, cheeses and curds are all traditional country preserves which are usually only made when there is a glut of fruit, as a large quantity of fruit produces only a comparatively small amount of finished preserve.

Butters and Cheeses

Fruit butters are soft and butter-like and can be used like jam. They do not keep very well so should only be made in small quantities and used up fairly quickly.

Cheeses are very thick preserves that are often served as an accompaniment to meat, poultry, game and cheese. The preserve is so thick that it can be potted in small moulds or jars and turned out whole when required. Cheeses store much better than butters and, in fact, improve on keeping.

The fruits most commonly used for making fruit butters and cheeses are apples, apricots, blackberries, gooseberries, damsons, medlars and quinces.

Preparation and cooking Fruit for butter- or cheese-making only needs picking over and washing, although larger fruits should be roughly chopped. Put the prepared fruit in a preserving pan or large saucepan with just enough water to cover, and simmer until really soft. Press the fruit pulp through a nylon sieve, using a wooden spoon so that the fruit does not discolour. Measure the pulp and allow the following amounts of sugar: For *butters*, allow 225–350 g (8–12 oz) sugar to each 600 ml (1 pint) pulp. For *cheeses*, allow 350–450 g (12 oz–1 lb) sugar to each 600 ml (1 pint) pulp.

Return the pulp to the pan, add the sugar and stir until dissolved. Boil gently until the required consistency is reached. Stir continuously to prevent the preserve sticking to the bottom of the pan as it cooks and thickens. Butters should be cooked until they are like thick cream. The finishing point is determined by consistency rather than by set or temperature – the cooled butter should be thick and almost set so that it may be spread like jam. Cheeses should be cooked until they are so thick that a spoon drawn across the bottom of the pan leaves a clean line through the preserve.

Potting For butters, prepare jars or small pots and cover as for jam (see page 12), or use caps and rings as for bottling (see page 130).

For cheeses, brush the inside of some small, prepared pots or jars (preferably straight-sided) or moulds with vegetable oil. This enables the preserve to be turned out. Pour in the cheese, cover as for jam (see page 12) and store for 3–4 months before using.

Curds

Made with eggs and butter as well as caster sugar and fruit, curds are not a true 'preserve' and should only be made in small quantities and eaten quickly. They will keep for up to a month in a cool cupboard or for up to 3 months in the refrigerator.

Cooking Cook curds very gently in the top of a double saucepan or in a heatproof bowl standing over a pan of simmering water, stirring all the time. The mixture should not be allowed to boil or it will curdle, and it should be cooked until it is thick enough to coat the back of a wooden spoon. Curds can also be made in the microwave (see page 213).

Potting and covering Strain the cooked curd through a fine sieve, to remove any lumps of egg white, before pouring into small jars. Fill the jars right to the top as the curd will thicken and shrink as it cools. Cover immediately as for jam (see page 12).

Lemon Curd
~

MAKES ABOUT 700 G (1¹/₂ LB)

grated rind and juice of 4 medium ripe, juicy lemons
4 eggs
100 g (4 oz) butter, cut in small pieces
350 g (12 oz) caster sugar
~

*P*lace all the ingredients in the top of a double saucepan or in a deep heatproof bowl standing over a pan of simmering water.

2 Stir until the sugar has dissolved and continue heating gently, without boiling, for about 20 minutes or until the curd is thick enough to coat the back of a wooden spoon.

3 Strain the curd into jars and cover in the usual way.

Note Home-made lemon curd should be made in small quantities as it only keeps for about 1 month. Store in a cool place.

VARIATION

The fresh lemon juice can be replaced with 180 ml (12 tbsp) bottled lemon juice. To give extra tang, the grated rind of a fresh lemon can be added, if liked.

VARIATION
Lime curd

Make as above using the grated rind and juice of five large ripe, juicy limes.

Honey Lemon Curd
~

MAKES ABOUT 900 G (2 LB)

grated rind and juice of 4 ripe, juicy lemons
5 eggs, beaten
100 g (4 oz) butter, cut in small pieces
225 g (8 oz) thick honey
50 g (2 oz) caster sugar
~

*P*ut all the ingredients in the top of a double saucepan or in a deep heatproof bowl standing over a pan of simmering water.

2 Heat gently, without boiling and stirring frequently, for 10–20 minutes or until the sugar has dissolved and the curd is thick enough to coat the back of a spoon.

3 Strain the curd into small pots and cover in the usual way. Stored in a cool place, preferably the refrigerator, this curd will keep for about 1 month.

Note You will need about 175 ml (6 fl oz) lemon juice, so squeeze another lemon if necessary.

Orange Curd
~

MAKES ABOUT 450 G (1 LB)

grated rind and juice of 2 large oranges
juice of ¹/₂ lemon
225 g (8 oz) caster sugar
100 g (4 oz) butter, cut in small pieces
3 egg yolks, beaten
~

*P*lace all the ingredients in the top of a double saucepan or in a deep heatproof bowl standing over a pan of simmering water.

2 Heat gently, stirring, for about 20 minutes or until the sugar has dissolved and the mixture has thickened enough to coat the back of a wooden spoon.

3 Strain, pot and cover the curd in the usual way.

Tangerine Curd
~

MAKES ABOUT 450 G (1 LB)

3 tangerines, washed
150 g (5 oz) caster sugar
100 g (4 oz) butter, cut in small pieces
3 egg yolks
~

Finely grate the rinds of two of the tangerines. Squeeze the juice from all the fruit and strain into the top of a double saucepan or a deep heatproof bowl standing over a pan of simmering water. Add the rind, sugar, butter and egg yolks.

2 Heat gently, stirring, for about 20 minutes or until the mixture thickens enough to coat the back of a wooden spoon.

3 Strain, pot and cover the curd in the usual way.

Three Fruit Curd
~

MAKES ABOUT 550 G (1¼ LB)

1 medium juicy grapefruit
1 medium juicy orange
2 thin-skinned lemons
50 g (2 oz) butter, cut in small pieces
4 eggs
150 g (5 oz) caster sugar
~

Finely grate the rinds of the grapefruit, orange and one lemon into the top of a double saucepan or a deep heatproof bowl standing over a pan of simmering water. Halve all the fruits and squeeze out the juice.

2 Add 75 ml (5 tbsp) grapefruit juice, 45 ml (3 tbsp) orange juice and 60 ml (4 tbsp) lemon juice to the grated rinds with the butter, eggs and sugar. Whisk lightly to break up the eggs.

3 Heat gently, stirring all the time, until the curd thickens enough to coat the back of a wooden spoon.

4 Strain the curd into small pots, taking care to fill them to the top. Cover as usual. Store in the refrigerator and use within 2 weeks.

Ugli Fruit Curd
~

MAKES ABOUT 450 G (1 LB)

1 small ugli fruit
1 lemon
3 eggs, beaten
75 g (3 oz) unsalted butter, cut in small pieces
caster sugar
~

Squeeze and strain the juice from the ugli fruit – you need about 150 ml (¼ pint). Finely grate the lemon rind and squeeze the juice from half the lemon only.

2 Place the lemon rind and fruit juices in the top of a double saucepan or in a deep heatproof bowl standing over a pan of simmering water. Add the eggs, butter and 25 g (1 oz) sugar. Heat gently, stirring frequently, until the mixture thickens enough to coat the back of a wooden spoon.

3 Taste the curd, adding more sugar if wished. Strain, pot and cover the curd in the usual way.

Overleaf: Blueberry Curd (page 70)

Blueberry Curd

~

MAKES ABOUT 450 G (1 LB)

225 g (8 oz) blueberries, washed
50 g (2 oz) butter, cut in small pieces
225 g (8 oz) caster sugar
3 eggs, size 3

~

Put the fruit and 15 ml (1 tbsp) water in a heavy-based saucepan, cover and cook gently until tender. Press through a fine sieve.

2 Return the fruit purée to the saucepan and add the butter and sugar. Heat gently, stirring frequently, to dissolve the sugar and melt the butter.

3 Beat the eggs together in a bowl, then strain into the hot mixture. Heat gently, stirring, until thick enough to coat the back of a wooden spoon.

4 Strain, pot and cover the curd in the usual way. Once opened, store in the refrigerator and use within 1 month.

Gooseberry and Elderflower Curd

~

MAKES ABOUT 1.4 KG (3 LB)

900 g (2 lb) gooseberries, washed
2 large elderflower heads, roughly chopped
50 g (2 oz) unsalted butter, cut in small pieces
4 eggs, beaten
450 g (1 lb) caster sugar

~

Put the gooseberries and chopped elderflowers together in a medium saucepan with 50 ml (2 fl oz) water. Bring to the boil, cover and simmer gently for 20–25 minutes or until very soft and pulpy. Remove from the heat and purée in a blender or food processor. Push through a nylon sieve.

2 Place the fruit purée in a large heatproof bowl over a pan of gently simmering water. Stir in the butter, eggs and sugar. Continue stirring for 25–30 minutes or until the sugar has dissolved and the mixture has thickened enough to leave a trail on the surface when the spoon is lifted. (It is not necessary to stir continually, but do it frequently, especially as the mixture gets hotter and thickens.)

3 Strain, pot and cover the curd in the usual way.

Raspberry Curd

~

MAKES ABOUT 700 G (1 ½ LB)

350 g (12 oz) raspberries, washed
225 g (8 oz) cooking apples, peeled, cored and chopped
grated rind and juice of 1 orange
4 eggs, beaten
100 g (4 oz) butter, cut in small pieces
350 g (12 oz) caster sugar

~

Put the raspberries, apples, orange rind and orange juice in a saucepan. Bring to the boil, then simmer for 20 minutes or until the fruit is soft.

2 Using a wooden spoon, press the fruit pulp through a nylon sieve into the top of a double saucepan or a deep heatproof bowl standing over a pan of simmering water. Add the eggs, butter and sugar.

3 Heat gently, stirring, until the sugar has dissolved and continue heating gently, stirring frequently, for 35–40 minutes or until the curd is thick enough to coat the back of a wooden spoon.

4 Strain, pot and cover the curd in the usual way.

Apricot and Orange Butter
~

MAKES ABOUT 1.4 KG (3 LB)

1.4 kg (3 lb) fresh apricots, skinned and stoned
grated rind and juice of 2 oranges
sugar

~

*P*lace the apricots, orange rind and orange juice in a saucepan and add just enough water to cover. Simmer gently for about 45 minutes or until the fruit is soft and pulpy.

2 Using a wooden spoon, press the fruit pulp through a nylon sieve. Measure the purée and return to the saucepan with 350 g (12 oz) sugar for each 600 ml (1 pint) purée.

3 Heat gently, stirring, until the sugar has dissolved, then bring to the boil and boil for 30–40 minutes, stirring frequently, until the mixture is thick and like jam in consistency.

4 Pot and cover the butter in the usual way.

Plum Butter
~

MAKES ABOUT 1.1 KG (2¹/₂ LB)

1.4 kg (2¹/₂ lb) plums, skinned and stoned
grated rind and juice of 1 lemon
sugar

~

*P*ut the plums, lemon rind and lemon juice in a large saucepan and add about 450 ml (³/₄ pint) water to cover. Simmer gently for 15–20 minutes or until the fruit is soft and pulpy.

2 Using a wooden spoon, press the fruit pulp through a nylon sieve and measure the pureé.

3 Return the purée to the pan and add 350 g (12 oz) sugar for each 600 ml (1 pint) purée.

4 Heat gently, stirring, until the sugar has dissolved, then bring to the boil and boil for 20–25 minutes, stirring frequently, until the mixture thickens and is like jam in consistency.

5 Pot and cover the butter in the usual way.

Black Butter
~

MAKES ABOUT 3.9 KG (8¹/₂ LB)

2.3 litres (4 pints) cider
900 g (2 lb) cooking apples, peeled, cored and sliced
1.8 kg (4 lb) eating apples, peeled, cored and sliced
grated rind and juice of 2 thin-skinned lemons
sugar
5 ml (1 tsp) ground cinnamon
5 ml (1 tsp) grated nutmeg

~

*P*our the cider into a large, heavy-based saucepan and boil rapidly until reduced by half.

2 Combine the apple slices and add half to the cider. Continue cooking and, when the apples are soft, add the remaining apples with the lemon rind and juice. Cook until well reduced and pulpy.

3 Measure the pulp and add 350 g (12 oz) sugar for each 600 ml (1 pint) pulp.

4 Add the spices and continue cooking, stirring frequently, until no free liquid remains. (Keep the heat low towards the end of the cooking time as the preserve tends to spit.)

5 Pot and cover the butter in the usual way.

Crunchy Harvest Butter
~

MAKES ABOUT 1.4 KG (3 LB)

*1.4 kg (3 lb) cooking apples, windfalls or crab-apples, washed
and chopped
sugar
25 g (1 oz) walnuts, finely chopped
45 ml (3 tbsp) crunchy natural wheatgerm*

~

*P*lace the apples in a saucepan, cover with water and simmer gently for 1 hour or until really soft and pulpy.

2 Using a wooden spoon, press the apple pulp through a nylon sieve and measure the purée.

3 Return the purée to the pan and add 350 g (12 oz) sugar for each 600 ml (1 pint) purée. Heat gently, stirring, until the sugar has dissolved, then bring to the boil and boil for 30–45 minutes, stirring frequently, until the mixture is thick and like jam in consistency.

4 Stir in the walnuts and wheatgerm and pot and cover the butter in the usual way.

Crab-apple Butter
~

MAKES ABOUT 1.4 KG (3 LB)

*1.4 kg (3 lb) crab-apples, washed
600 ml (1 pint) cider
2.5 ml (½ tsp) ground cinnamon
2.5 ml (½ tsp) ground cloves
sugar*

~

*C*ut the crab-apples into quarters without peeling. Put in a saucepan and add 600 ml (1 pint) water and the cider. Cover and cook until soft and pulpy.

2 Using a wooden spoon, push the fruit pulp through a nylon sieve and measure the purée.

3 Return the purée to the pan and add the spices and

350 g (12 oz) sugar for every 600 ml (1 pint) purée. Heat gently, stirring, until the sugar has dissolved, then bring to the boil and boil for 30–45 minutes, stirring frequently, until the mixture is thick and creamy in consistency.

4 Pot and cover the butter in the usual way.

Blackberry Cheese
~

MAKES ABOUT 900 G (2 LB)

*900 g (2 lb) blackberries, washed
450 g (1 lb) cooking apples, peeled, cored and diced
sugar*

~

*P*lace the blackberries and apples in a large saucepan or preserving pan with 600 ml (1 pint) water. Bring to the boil and simmer gently for about 30 minutes or until the blackberries are just tender.

2 Using a wooden spoon, press the fruit pulp through a nylon sieve and measure the purée. Return the purée to the pan and add 350 g (12 oz) sugar for each 600 ml (1 pint) purée.

3 Heat gently, stirring, until the sugar has dissolved, then bring to the boil and boil for about 30 minutes or until the mixture is so thick that the wooden spoon leaves a clean line through the mixture when drawn across the bottom of the pan.

4 Pot and cover the cheese in the usual way or, if preferred, prepare and fill a bowl or several small moulds (see page 65) from which the cheese can be turned out and served whole. Leave to set and cover as usual.

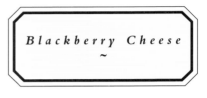

*Opposite (left to right): Cranberry Lemon Cheese
(page 74), Blackberry Cheese (above)*

Cranberry Lemon Cheese
~

MAKES ABOUT 1.4 KG (3 LB)

1 kg (2¹/₄ lb) cranberries, washed
thinly pared rind and juice of 2 lemons
sugar

~

Place the cranberries in a large heavy-based saucepan. Add the pared lemon rind, 45 ml (3 tbsp) lemon juice and 1.3 litres (2¹/₄ pints) water.

2 Bring slowly to the boil, then cover and simmer for about 30 minutes or until very soft.

3 Using a wooden spoon, press the berries and juices through a nylon sieve and measure the purée. Return the purée to the pan and add 350 g (12 oz) sugar for every 600 ml (1 pint) purée.

4 Heat gently, stirring, until the sugar has completely dissolved, then bring to the boil and boil, stirring frequently, for about 30 minutes or until a spoon drawn across the bottom of the pan leaves a clear line through the mixture. Take care as the preserve will spit as it reduces.

5 Pot and cover the cheese in the usual way or, if preferred, set in small dishes or moulds (see page 65).

Apple Cheese
~

MAKES ABOUT 1.4 KG (3 LB)

1.4 kg (3 lb) cooking apples, windfalls or crab-apples, washed
2.5 ml (¹/₂ tsp) ground cinnamon
1.25–2.5 ml (¹/₄ –¹/₂ tsp) ground cloves
sugar

~

Chop the apples without peeling or coring and put them in a large saucepan. Add just enough water to cover and simmer gently for about 1 hour or until the apples are very soft and pulpy.

2 Using a wooden spoon, press the apple pulp through a nylon sieve and measure the purée. Return the purée to the pan and add the spices and 450 g (1 lb) sugar for each 600 ml (1 pint) purée.

3 Heat gently, stirring, until the sugar has dissolved, then bring to the boil and boil gently, stirring frequently, for 30–45 minutes or until the mixture is so thick that the wooden spoon leaves a clean line through it when drawn across the bottom of the pan.

4 Pot and cover the cheese in the usual way or, if preferred, set in several small dishes or moulds (see page 65).

Quince Cheese
~

MAKES ABOUT 1.4 KG (3 LB)

1.4 kg (3 lb) quinces, washed
sugar

~

Chop the quinces without peeling or coring, put them in a large saucepan and add just enough water to cover. Simmer gently for about 30 minutes or until the fruit is very soft.

2 Using a wooden spoon, press the fruit pulp through a nylon sieve and measure the purée. Return the purée to the pan and add 450 g (1 lb) sugar for each 600 ml (1 pint) purée.

3 Heat gently, stirring, until the sugar has dissolved, then bring to the boil and boil gently, stirring frequently, for 30–40 minutes or until the mixture is so thick that the wooden spoon leaves a clean line through it when drawn across the bottom of the pan.

4 Pot and cover the cheese in the usual way or, if preferred, set in several small oiled dishes or moulds (see page 65).

Damson Cheese
~

MAKES ABOUT 1.4 KG (3 LB)

1.4 kg (3 lb) damsons, washed
sugar
~

Place the fruit in a saucepan, cover with water and simmer gently for 15–20 minutes or until the fruit is very soft. Scoop out the stones with a slotted spoon as they come to the surface.

2 Using a wooden spoon, press the fruit pulp through a nylon sieve and measure the purée.

3 Return the purée to the pan and add 350 g (12 oz) sugar for each 600 ml (1 pint) purée. Heat gently, stirring, until the sugar has dissolved, then bring to the boil and boil gently, stirring frequently, for 30–40 minutes or until the mixture is so thick that the wooden spoon leaves a clean line through the mixture when drawn across the bottom of the pan.

4 Pot and cover the cheese in the usual way or, if preferred, set in several small oiled dishes or moulds (see page 65).

VARIATION
Gooseberry cheese

Make as above, using 1.4 kg (3 lb) gooseberries and 150 ml (¼ pint) water.

VARIATION
Damson and blackberry cheese

Make as above, using 450 g (1 lb) damsons and 900 g (2 lb) blackberries.

Medlar Cheese
~

MAKES ABOUT 900 G (2 LB)

900 g (2 lb) medlars, washed
2 lemons
sugar
5 ml (1 tsp) ground mixed spice
~

Cut each medlar into four. Halve the lemons, squeeze out the juice and cut up the peel. Tie the peel in a piece of muslin with any pips.

2 Put the fruit, lemon juice and muslin bag in a saucepan, add 300 ml (½ pint) water and simmer gently until the medlars are tender. Remove the muslin bag.

3 Using a wooden spoon, press the fruit pulp through a nylon sieve and measure the purée. Return the purée to the pan and add 350 g (12 oz) sugar for each 600 ml (1 pint) purée. Stir in the spice.

4 Heat gently, stirring, until the sugar has dissolved, then bring to the boil and boil rapidly for about 5 minutes or until the mixture is so thick that the spoon leaves a clean line through it when drawn across the bottom of the pan.

5 Pot and cover the cheese in the usual way or, if preferred, set in several small oiled dishes or moulds (see page 65).

Pickles

Pickles make delicious accompaniments to a wide range of foods, including cold meats, cheese, baked potatoes, pies and antipasto. They can be either sweet or sharp, or an interesting blend of both, and are made by preserving raw or lightly cooked vegetables or fruit in clear, spiced vinegar. Only crisp, fresh fruits and vegetables should be pickled.

Equipment for Pickling

Pans To make pickles you need a good-sized pan made from enamel, stainless steel or lined aluminium. Recently there has been concern about a possible link between aluminium and Alzheimer's disease. At the time of going to press, research is still inconclusive but, for the time being, it would seem safer not to cook acidic fruits or preserves made with vinegar in unlined aluminium pans. Make sure that your pan is scrupulously clean, and if it is pitted, throw it away. It is not strictly necessary to use a preserving pan unless you are going to cook large quantities, but do remember to allow plenty of time and space for the liquid to evaporate. Do not use brass or copper preserving pans as the vinegar will corrode the metal, giving the pickle a disagreeable taste.

Pickle jars Large, wide-necked bottles are recommended for pickling, though smaller jam jars can be used. Jars with screw-tops with plastic-coated linings, such as those used for coffee jars and commercially-prepared pickles, are ideal. The number of jars needed for a specific quantity of pickles varies so much, depending on the size of the vegetables or fruit and how tightly they are packed, that it is not practicable to state exact numbers. Before filling with pickle, jars should be preheated in the oven.

Vinegar

Vinegar acts as the preserving agent in pickles and is a very important factor. It should be of the best quality, with an acetic acid content of at least 5 per cent. Most vinegars and all red or white wine vinegars on the market today have an acetic acid content of 5 per cent or over. The colour of vinegar is no indication of its strength; further distilling has the effect of rendering vinegar colourless. This 'white' vinegar gives a better appearance to light-coloured pickles, such as onions and cauliflower, but malt vinegar gives a rather better flavour. Wine vinegar and cider vinegar are more delicately flavoured but are more expensive; cider vinegar, with its apple base, is good for sweeter pickles, while the colour of red wine vinegar is best for pickled red cabbage or beetroot. Vinegar to be used for pickling is normally given extra flavour by being infused with herbs and spices.

Brining

When making sharp pickles, the vegetables are usually brined beforehand. This removes surplus water which would otherwise dilute the vinegar and render it too weak to act as a preservative to the vegetables. Ordinary table salt is quite suitable for brining.

Fruits for pickling do not require brining as they are usually lightly cooked before pickling and the surplus moisture evaporates during the cooking. Sweet pickles are mostly made of fruit as they contain more sugar.

Dry brining For cucumber, marrow, tomato and red cabbage. Prepare the vegetables according to the recipe and layer them in a bowl with salt, allowing 15 ml (1 tbsp) salt to each 450 g (1 lb) vegetables. Cover and leave overnight.

Wet brining For cauliflower, walnuts and onions. Prepare the vegetables according to the recipe and place in a large bowl. Cover with a brine solution, allowing 50 g (2 oz) salt dissolved in 600 ml (1 pint) water to each 450 g (1 lb) vegetables. Put a plate over the surface to ensure that the vegetables are kept under the liquid, cover and leave overnight.

Finishing

After brining, vegetables for pickling should be well rinsed in cold water, drained and then packed into jars to within 2.5 cm (1 inch) of the top. Pour spiced vinegar over, taking care to cover the vegetables well and to add at least 1 cm ($^1/_2$ inch) extra to allow for any evaporation which may take place. Leave a little space at the top of the jar to prevent the vinegar coming into contact with the cover. Cover immediately with a waxed disc, waxed side down. Place a cellophane disc over the top of the jar and screw a plastic top down over it. Avoid using metal screw-tops as they have a tendency to corrode and rust.

If the jars are not adequately covered, the vinegar will evaporate, the preserve will shrink and the top dry out.

When pickling crisp, sharp vegetables, such as cabbage or onion, the vinegar is poured over cold. For softer pickles, such as plums or walnuts, hot vinegar is used.

Storing

Store pickles in a cool, dry, dark place and leave to mature for 2–3 months before eating. The exception is red cabbage, which loses its crispness after 2–3 weeks.

Pickled Mushrooms and Shallots

~

50 g (2 oz) salt
450 g (1 lb) shallots or small button onions
600 ml (1 pint) white distilled vinegar
2 sprigs fresh tarragon or 10 ml (2 tsp) dried
12 peppercorns
450 g (1 lb) small button mushrooms

~

Mix the salt with 600 ml (1 pint) water and pour over the unpeeled shallots. Cover and leave for 24 hours.

2 Bring the vinegar to the boil with the herbs and peppercorns, pour into a bowl and leave to cool.

3 Drain and peel the shallots, then rinse and dry. Trim and wipe the mushrooms.

4 Strain the vinegar into a saucepan and bring to the boil. Add the vegetables and boil for 1 minute.

5 Spoon the vegetables into jars and cover with vinegar. Seal the jars in the usual way.

Pickled Beetroot
~

beetroot

salt

water

spiced vinegar (see page 127)

~

Weigh the beetroot and wash them carefully, taking care not to damage the skins. Wrap the beets in foil and bake in the oven at 180°C (350°F) mark 4 for 2–3 hours, depending on size, or until tender.

2 Alternatively, mix up a brine solution, allowing 50 g (2 oz) salt dissolved in 600 ml (1 pint) water for each 450 g (1 lb) beets. Put the beets in a large saucepan, cover with the brine solution and simmer gently for 1½–2 hours, depending on the size of the beets, or until tender.

3 Leave the beets to cool, then skin and thinly slice them. Pack the slices into jars and cover with cold spiced vinegar. If the beets were baked, add 10 ml (2 tsp) salt for each 600 ml (1 pint) vinegar. Cover and seal the jars in the usual way.

Pickled Carrots
~

1.1 kg (2½ lb) young carrots, of uniform size, trimmed and scraped

600 ml (1 pint) distilled vinegar

225 g (8 oz) sugar

25 g (1 oz) pickling spice

~

Place the carrots in a large saucepan and cover with cold water. Bring to the boil, simmer gently for 10 minutes or until only half cooked, then drain.

2 Pour the vinegar into another pan with 300 ml (½ pint) water and the sugar. Tie the pickling spice in a piece of muslin and add to the vinegar mixture.

3 Bring the vinegar mixture to the boil and boil for 5 minutes, then remove the muslin bag. Add the carrots

and boil for 10–15 minutes or until the carrots are almost tender.

4 Pack the carrots into preheated jars and cover them with the boiling vinegar. Cover and seal the jars in the usual way.

Pickled Cucumbers
~

cucumbers

salt

spiced vinegar (see page 127)

~

Split the cucumbers from end to end and cut into 5-cm (2-inch) pieces. Place in a large bowl, cover with salt and leave for 24 hours.

2 Drain the liquid from the cucumbers, rinse and drain again. Pack into jars and fill up with cold spiced vinegar. Cover and seal the jars in the usual way. Leave to mature for about 3 months before opening.

Pickled Marrow

~

700 g (1½ lb) marrow, seeded and diced (prepared weight)
25 g (1 oz) salt
300 ml (½ pint) sweet spiced vinegar (see page 126)
175 g (6 oz) sugar
4-cm (1½-inch) piece of fresh root ginger, bruised

~

*P*lace the marrow in a bowl, sprinkle with salt and leave for about 12 hours.

2 Drain and rinse the marrow well and put in a saucepan with the vinegar, sugar and ginger. Heat gently, stirring, until the sugar has dissolved, then bring to the boil and simmer gently for about 10 minutes or until the marrow is just tender but not broken up. Remove the ginger.

3 Pack the marrow into preheated jars and cover with hot vinegar. Cover and seal the jars in the usual way.

Pickled Cauliflower

~

cauliflower
salt
spiced vinegar (see page 127)

~

*C*hoose young cauliflowers with tight heads and divide them into small florets, breaking rather than cutting them.

2 Dissolve 50 g (2 oz) salt in 600 ml (1 pint) water for every 450 g (1 lb) cauliflower, pour over the florets and leave to stand overnight.

3 The next day, rinse and drain the cauliflower thoroughly. Pack into jars and cover with cold spiced vinegar. Cover and seal the jars in the usual way.

Opposite: A rich crop of fruits and vegetables can be saved from becoming the spoils of the garden, and enjoyed all year round, in a spicy array of chutneys and pickles

Pickled Onions

~

1.8 kg (4 lb) pickling onions
450 g (1 lb) salt
1.1 litres (2 pints) spiced vinegar (see page 127)

~

*P*lace the unskinned onions in a large bowl. Dissolve half the salt in 2.3 litres (4 pints) water, pour over the onions and leave for 12 hours.

2 Drain and skin the onions, then cover with fresh brine, made with the remaining salt and a further 2.3 litres (4 pints) water. Leave for 24–36 hours.

3 Drain and rinse the onions well and pack them into jars. Cover with the spiced vinegar. Cover and seal the jars in the usual way. Leave for 3 months before use.

Pickled Red Cabbage

~

about 1.4 kg (3 lb) firm, red cabbage, finely shredded
2 large onions, skinned and sliced
60 ml (4 tbsp) salt
2.3 litres (4 pints) spiced vinegar (see page 127)
15 ml (1 tbsp) dark brown soft sugar

~

*L*ayer the cabbage and onions in a large bowl, sprinkling each layer with salt, then cover and leave overnight.

2 The next day, drain the cabbage and onions thoroughly, rinse off the salt and pack into jars.

3 Pour the spiced vinegar into a saucepan and heat gently. Add the sugar and stir until dissolved. Leave to cool, then pour over the cabbage and onion. Cover and seal the jars in the usual way. Use within 2–3 weeks as the cabbage tends to lose its crispness.

Pickled Gherkins
~

450 g (1 lb) gherkins
50 g (2 oz) salt
600 ml (1 pint) light malt vinegar
5 ml (1 tsp) whole allspice
5 ml (1 tsp) black peppercorns
2 whole cloves
1 blade of mace

~

*P*ut the gherkins in a large bowl. Dissolve the salt in 600 ml (1 pint) water and pour over the gherkins. Leave to soak for 3 days.

2 Rinse, drain and dry the gherkins well, then pack them carefully in a jar. Pour the vinegar into a saucepan, add the spices and boil for 10 minutes. Pour over the gherkins, cover tightly and leave in a warm place for 24 hours.

3 Strain the vinegar out of the jars into a saucepan, boil it up and pour it over the gherkins again. Cover tightly and leave for another 24 hours. Repeat this process until the gherkins are a good green.

4 Finally, pack the gherkins in jars and cover with vinegar, adding more if required. Cover and seal the jars in the usual way.

Pickled Jerusalem Artichokes
~

Jerusalem artichokes
salt
spiced vinegar (see page 127)

~

*W*ash and scrape the artichokes. Dissolve 25 g (1 oz) salt in 600 ml (1 pint) water for every 450 g (1 lb) artichokes. Cook the artichokes in this brine until tender but not too soft. Drain and leave until cold.

2 Pack the artichokes into jars and fill up with cold spiced vinegar. Cover and seal the jars in the usual way.

Mixed Pickle
~

1.1 kg (2¹/₂ lb) mixed cauliflower, cucumber, small onions,
peppers and French beans (prepared weight – see method)
150 g (5 oz) salt
1.4 litres (2¹/₂ pints) spiced vinegar (see page 127)

~

*B*reak the cauliflower into florets, peel and dice the cucumber, skin the onions, seed and slice the peppers and top, tail and slice the beans. Layer the vegetables in a large bowl, sprinkling each layer with salt. Add 1.4 litres (2¹/₂ pints) water and leave overnight.

2 The next day, rinse the vegetables, drain well and dry on absorbent kitchen paper. Pack the vegetables into jars and cover with spiced vinegar. Cover and seal the jars in the usual way.

Bread and Butter Pickle
~

3 large ridge or smooth-skinned cucumbers
4 large onions, skinned and sliced
45 ml (3 tbsp) salt
450 ml (³/₄ pint) distilled white vinegar
150 g (5 oz) sugar
5 ml (1 tsp) celery seeds
5 ml (1 tsp) black mustard seeds
~

Thinly slice the cucumbers, then layer the cucumber and onion slices in a large bowl, sprinkling each layer with salt. Leave for 1 hour, then drain and rinse well.

2 Put the vinegar, sugar and celery and mustard seeds in a saucepan and heat gently, stirring, until the sugar has dissolved. Bring to the boil and boil for 3 minutes.

3 Pack the vegetable slices into preheated jars and add enough hot vinegar mixture to cover. Cover and seal the jars in the usual way.

4 This pickle must be stored in a dark place or the cucumber will lose its colour. Store for 2 months to mature before eating.

Summer Pickle
~

225 g (8 oz) each of celery, carrots, cucumber, red peppers and red onions
100 g (4 oz) each of green beans, baby sweetcorn and button mushrooms
600 ml (1 pint) distilled malt vinegar
6 whole allspice
6 black peppercorns
1 blade of mace
1 bay leaf
2 cloves
pinch of saffron or ground turmeric
30 ml (2 tbsp) chopped fresh dill
90 ml (6 tbsp) light brown soft sugar
100 g (4 oz) cherry tomatoes
90 ml (6 tbsp) walnut oil
salt and pepper
~

Trim and thickly slice the celery. Trim, scrape and thinly slice the carrots lengthways and cut into triangles. Halve the cucumber lengthways and thickly slice. Seed the pepper and cut into similar-sized pieces. Trim the onions, leaving the root intact, and cut into eight 'wedges' each. Top and tail the green beans and sweetcorn; trim and wipe the mushrooms.

2 Combine all the ingredients, except the cherry tomatoes and walnut oil, in a preserving pan or large saucepan. Add salt and pepper. Bring to the boil and simmer, stirring gently, for 5 minutes.

3 Stir in the cherry tomatoes and walnut oil, then transfer to a non-metallic bowl. Cool, cover with a plate and leave to marinate overnight.

4 Pack the pickle into jars, cover and seal as usual.

Mixed Vegetable Pickle

~

1 medium cauliflower (about 700 g / 1 1/2 lb)
1 green pepper
225 g (8 oz) each of courgettes, French beans and button onions
175 g (6 oz) salt
600 ml (1 pint) cider vinegar
2 blades of mace, 2 whole dried chillies, 4 allspice berries,
1 cinnamon stick and 1 bay leaf for flavouring

~

Cut the cauliflower into small florets, discarding any leaves and coarse stalk; seed the pepper and cut into chunks; wipe the courgettes and cut into wedges; top and tail the beans and cut into 2.5 cm (1 inch) lengths; skin the onions.

2 Layer the vegetables in a non-metallic bowl, sprinkling salt between the layers. Pour over 1.7 litres (3 pints) cold water and cover with a plate to keep the vegetables beneath the liquid. Leave in a cool place overnight.

3 Place the vinegar in a saucepan. Tie the mace, chillies, allspice berries (lightly crushed), cinnamon stick and bay leaf in a piece of muslin and add to the vinegar. Bring slowly to the boil and boil for 1 minute, then remove from the heat, cover and leave to infuse overnight.

4 Rinse the vegetables well to remove the salt, then pat dry on kitchen paper. Spoon them into preheated jars to within 2.5 cm (1 inch) of the tops of the jars.

5 Reheat the vinegar, then remove the muslin bag. Pour the vinegar over to cover the vegetables completely, cover and seal as usual. Store for at least 1 month.

Above (left to right in lidded jars): Mustard Pickle (page 90), Autumn Plum Chutney (page 112), Pickled Pears with Ginger (page 95), Mixed Dill Pickle (page 87), Hot Mango Chutney (page 110), Marrow and tomato Chutney (page 104)
Opposite: Summer Pickle (page 83)

Green Tomato and Onion Pickle
~

1.8 kg (4 lb) green tomatoes, sliced
700 g (1½ lb) large onions, skinned and sliced
75 ml (5 tbsp) salt
2.3 litres (4 pints) malt vinegar
150 ml (¼ pint) black treacle
15 ml (1 tbsp) mustard powder
10 ml (2 tsp) curry powder
1.25 ml (¼ tsp) cayenne
5 ml (1 tsp) ground mixed spice

~

Layer the tomato and onion slices in a bowl, sprinkling each layer liberally with salt, and leave for 24 hours.

2 Drain and rinse the tomatoes and onions well. Put the vinegar, treacle or syrup and spices into a saucepan and bring to the boil. Add the vegetables and cook very gently for 5 minutes.

3 Pour the pickle into preheated jars, cover and seal in the usual way.

Sweet Green Tomato Pickle
~

300 ml (½ pint) malt vinegar
900 g (2 lb) sugar
5 ml (1 tsp) ground cinnamon
1.4 kg (3 lb) small green tomatoes, skinned

~

Place the vinegar, sugar and cinnamon in a large saucepan with 150 ml (¼ pint) water. Heat gently, stirring, until the sugar has dissolved, then bring to the boil.

2 Add the tomatoes and continue cooking for 5 minutes. Pour into a bowl, cover and leave for 1 week.

3 Strain the vinegar into a large saucepan and boil for 10 minutes. Add the tomatoes and boil for a further 5 minutes. Pack into preheated jars, cover and seal in the usual way.

Mixed Pickled Beans
~

450 g (1 lb) mixed dried beans, soaked overnight
1 small onion, skinned
1 bouquet garni
a few sprigs of fresh marjoram
1 litre (1¾ pints) distilled vinegar
30 ml (2 tbsp) pickling spice
45 ml (3 tbsp) sugar

~

Drain the beans, place them in a large saucepan and cover with water. Add the onion and bouquet garni and bring to the boil. Cover and simmer for about 1½ hours or until tender.

2 Drain the beans, remove the onion and bouquet garni and pack the beans into clean jars. Add a few sprigs of marjoram to each jar.

3 Place the vinegar, pickling spice and sugar in a saucepan and heat gently, stirring, until the sugar has dissolved. Bring to the boil, cover and simmer for 30 minutes. Strain the vinegar and pour it over the beans in the jars. Cover and seal the jars in the usual way.

Garden Mint Pickle
~

300 ml (½ pint) distilled vinegar
225 g (8 oz) sugar
10 ml (2 tsp) mustard powder
10 ml (2 tsp) salt
1 cinnamon stick
5 ml (1 tsp) peppercorns
1 blade of mace
700 g (1½ lb) cooking apples, peeled and sliced
225 g (8 oz) onions, skinned and sliced
25 g (1 oz) mint leaves, washed and chopped

~

Pour the vinegar into a saucepan and add the sugar, mustard, salt and spices. Simmer very gently for 30 minutes, then strain.

2 Add the apple and onion slices to the spiced vinegar and continue cooking gently for 10 minutes, then remove from the heat and leave to cool.

3 When cold, pack the apples and onions into jars, sprinkling the chopped mint liberally between the layers. Cover with the spiced vinegar and cover and seal the jars in the usual way. Leave for a month before use.

Mixed Dill Pickle
~

1 cauliflower (about 550 g/1¼ lb), trimmed
175 g (6 oz) courgettes
1 green pepper (about 225 g/8 oz)
175 g (6 oz) fine green beans
100 g (4 oz) pickling or button onions
1 cucumber
225 g (8 oz) coarse salt
1.1–1.3 litres (2–2¼ pints) white wine vinegar
30 ml (2 tbsp) pickling spice
15 ml (1 tbsp) salt
100 g (4 oz) sugar
2 garlic cloves, skinned
2 good stalks of fresh dill
5 ml (1 tsp) dried dill weed
2 stalks of tarragon

~

Wash the cauliflower and divide into small florets; wash and slice the courgettes into 0.5-cm (¼-inch) diagonal pieces; wash and seed the pepper and cut into 0.5-cm (¼-inch) strips; wash, top and tail the beans and cut in half; skin the onions, leaving the roots intact; split the cucumber in half lengthways, then slice thickly.

2 Place all the prepared vegetables in a large bowl. Cover with the coarse salt. Mix, cover and leave in a cold place for 24 hours.

3 Place the remaining ingredients in a preserving pan. Heat gently to simmering point. Remove from the heat and leave to cool completely.

4 Drain the vegetables, rinse well and drain again. Bring two large pans of water to the boil. Add the vegetables and bring back to the boil. Drain the vegetables and refresh under cold water to stop the cooking process and preserve the colour. Allow to drain well.

5 Pack the vegetables into preheated jars. Leave to stand for 1 hour, then drain off the excess liquid. Pour over the cooled pickling vinegar to cover completely. Cover and seal the jars in the usual way. The pickle will darken a little on storing but it will remain clear if stored in the refrigerator.

Piccalilli
~

2.7 kg (6 lb) mixed marrow, cucumber, beans, small onions
and cauliflower (prepared weight – see method)
350 g (12 oz) salt
250 g (9 oz) sugar
15 ml (1 tbsp) mustard powder
7.5 ml (1½ tsp) ground ginger
2 garlic cloves, skinned and crushed
1.4 litres (2½ pints) distilled vinegar
50 g (2 oz) plain flour
30 ml (2 tbsp) ground turmeric

~

Seed the marrow and finely dice the marrow and cucumber. Top, tail and slice the beans, skin and halve the onions and break the cauliflower into small florets. Layer the vegetables in a large bowl, sprinkling each layer with salt. Add 3.4 litres (6 pints) water, cover and leave for 24 hours.

2 The next day, remove the vegetables and rinse and drain them well. Blend the sugar, mustard, ginger and garlic with 1.1 litres (2 pints) of the vinegar in a large pan.

3 Add the vegetables, bring to the boil and simmer for 20 minutes or until the vegetables are cooked but still crisp.

4 Blend the flour and turmeric with the remaining vinegar and stir into the cooked vegetables. Bring to the boil and cook for 2 minutes.

5 Spoon the pickle into preheated jars, cover and seal in the usual way.

Apple and Onion Pickle
~

350 g (12 oz) sour cooking apples, washed, cored and finely
chopped
350 g (12 oz) onions, skinned and finely chopped
50 g (2 oz) sultanas
9 black peppercorns
9 whole cloves
40 g (1¹/₂ oz) chillies
450 ml (³/₄ pint) distilled vinegar
7.5 ml (1¹/₂ tsp) salt
~

Pack the apples, onions and sultanas in preheated jars. Tie the spices in a piece of muslin.

2 Pour the vinegar into a saucepan, add the salt and muslin bag and leave to soak for 30 minutes. Bring to the boil and simmer gently for 10 minutes.

3 Pour the boiling vinegar over the apples and onions and cover and seal the jars in the usual way. This pickle is ready for use the next day.

*Above (left to right): Pickled Satsumas and
Kumquats (page 95), Spiced Prunes
(page 96), Pickled Jerusalem Artichokes
(page 82), Mixed Pickled Beans (page 86)
Opposite: Piccalilli*

Mustard Pickle
~

¹/₂ cucumber
450 g (1 lb) fine green beans
4 medium green peppers
4 medium red peppers
225 g (8 oz) button or pickling onions
225 g (8 oz) green tomatoes
225 g (8 oz) cauliflower
100 g (4 oz) carrots
275 g (10 oz) coarse salt
400 g (14 oz) sugar
60 ml (4 tbsp) mustard powder
10 ml (2 tsp) ground turmeric
5 ml (1 tsp) ground ginger
2.5 ml (¹/₂ tsp) black peppercorns, lightly crushed
1 litre (1³/₄ pints) white wine vinegar
75 g (3 oz) cornflour

~

*W*ash all the vegetables, peel or trim as appropriate and cut into bite-sized pieces (about 2 cm/³/₄ inch long). Place in a large bowl and mix in the coarse salt. Cover and leave in a cold place for 24 hours.

2 Rinse the vegetables thoroughly. Drain and dry well and put into a preserving pan.

3 Put the sugar, mustard, turmeric, ginger and crushed black peppercorns in a stainless steel saucepan. Add enough of the vinegar to blend the ingredients to a smooth paste. In a small bowl, blend the cornflour with 75 ml (3 fl oz) vinegar. Set aside. Add the remaining vinegar to the spice and sugar paste, stir and bring to the boil.

4 Pour the spiced vinegar over the vegetables in the preserving pan. Bring to the boil again, then reduce the heat and simmer for about 5 minutes, stirring occasionally, until the vegetables are only just tender.

5 Strain the vegetables, retaining the liquid, and pack into jars to within 1 cm (¹/₂ inch) of the rim.

6 Add the reserved cornflour paste to the liquid left in the preserving pan. Heat gently until it boils and thickens, then pour at once over the vegetables to cover completely. Cover and seal in the usual way.

Pickle Sticks
~

3 large, firm cucumbers
salt
1 large carrot, trimmed and peeled
4 celery sticks, trimmed and washed
2 red peppers, washed and seeded
100 g (4 oz) French beans, trimmed and washed
450 ml (³/₄ pint) wine vinegar
450 g (1 lb) sugar
30 ml (2 tbsp) mustard seeds
5 ml (1 tsp) ground turmeric

~

*C*ut the cucumbers into sticks about 5 cm (2 inches) long and 0.5 cm (¹/₄ inch) wide, and place in a large bowl. Stir 30 ml (2 tbsp) salt into 600 ml (1 pint) water, pour over the cucumber and leave overnight.

2 The next day, drain and rinse the cucumber well. Cut the carrot, celery and peppers into sticks the same size as the cucumber and cook with the beans in boiling salted water for 2 minutes, then drain.

3 Place all the vegetables, including the cucumber, in a large pan with the remaining ingredients and 10 ml (2 tsp) salt. Bring to the boil, stirring, then pack into pre-heated jars. Cover and seal in the usual way.

Green Chilli Pickle
~

225 g (8 oz) fresh green chillies
300 ml (½ pint) vegetable oil
15 ml (1 tbsp) paprika
5 ml (1 tsp) ground turmeric
15 ml (1 tbsp) fennel seeds
15 ml (1 tbsp) mustard seeds
30 ml (2 tbsp) salt

~

W earing rubber gloves, cut the chillies in half lengthways, remove the seeds and discard. Put the chillies in a clean, dry jar.

2 Heat the oil, add all the spices and fry over a high heat for 1–2 minutes, stirring continuously. Stir well and leave to cool. Add the salt.

3 Pour the oil over the chillies and mix well. Cover the jar with muslin and leave in a warm place for 2–3 days, stirring the contents from time to time.

4 Remove the muslin and replace with a lid. Leave the pickle to mature in a cool place for at least 1 week.

Pickled Walnuts
~

450 g (1 lb) green walnuts
100 g (4 oz) salt
sweet spiced vinegar (see page 126)

~

W ipe the walnuts, prick well and put them in a bowl, rejecting any that feel hard when pricked.

2 Dissolve half the salt in 600 ml (1 pint) water, pour this brine over the walnuts and leave to soak for 7 days.

3 Drain off and discard the brine, cover the walnuts with fresh brine, made with the remaining salt and a further 600 ml (1 pint) water, and leave to soak for another 14 days.

4 Drain, rinse and dry the walnuts well, then spread them out and leave them exposed to the air until they blacken, then pack them into jars.

5 Pour the spiced vinegar into a saucepan, bring to the boil, then pour over the walnuts. Leave to cool and, when cold, cover and seal the jars in the usual way. Store in a cool place for 5–6 weeks before use.

VARIATION
Pickled walnuts and onions

An interesting variation is obtained by pickling walnuts and onions together. Each should be prepared according to the directions given above and in the recipe for pickled onions on page 81. Place equal quantities of each in jars, arranged in alternate layers, and pour cold spiced vinegar over them.

Pickled Eggs
~

600 ml (1 pint) white wine or cider vinegar
6 garlic cloves, skinned
25 g (1 oz) pickling spice
small piece of orange rind
1 blade of mace
6 fresh, hard-boiled eggs, shelled
~

*P*ut all the ingredients, except the eggs, in a heavy-based saucepan and bring to the boil. Cover tightly and simmer gently for 10 minutes.

2 Leave the vinegar to cool, then strain some into a large wide-mouthed jar. Put in the eggs and top up the jar with more spiced vinegar.

3 Cover and seal the jar in the usual way and leave for at least 6 weeks before opening. Add more eggs as convenient.

Pickled Lemons
~

12 lemons
salt
1.7 litres (3 pints) spiced vinegar (see page 127)
~

*W*ash the lemons thoroughly and peel very thinly. Put the lemons in a large, wide-necked jar, covering each layer thoroughly with salt. Leave for about 10 days or until the lemons feel soft.

2 Wipe off most of the salt and place the lemons in a clean jar. Bring the spiced vinegar to boiling point and pour over the lemons immediately. Cover and seal the jars in the usual way. Store for 3 months before using.

Lemon Pickle
~

450 g (1 lb) ripe, juicy lemons, washed
45 ml (3 tbsp) salt
5 ml (1 tsp) ground turmeric
7.5 ml (1½ tsp) chilli powder
10 ml (2 tsp) garam masala (see Note below)
~

*C*ut the fruit (with the skin) into small pieces, remove any pips and catch any juice in a bowl. Mix the fruit pieces and juice with the salt, turmeric, chilli powder and garam masala.

2 Pack the fruit into a large sterile screw-topped jar and keep in a warm cupboard or, when possible, in the hot sun, for a week, giving it a good shake each day.

3 The pickle is ready when the skins are tender. Store well covered.

Note Garam masala is a flavouring made by mixing 5 ml (1 tsp) ground cloves, 5 ml (1 tsp) ground cinnamon, 5 ml (1 tsp) freshly ground black pepper, 5 ml (1 tsp) ground cumin seeds and 5 ml (1 tsp) ground cardamom seeds.

VARIATION
Sweet lemon pickle

Add 75 g (3 oz) demerara sugar to the ingredients above to give a sweet pickle. A few chillies may be added to make it hotter.

VARIATION
Lime pickle

Substitute limes for the lemons in the recipe above.

Sweet Pickled Limes

~

225 g (8 oz) salt
18 limes, washed
900 ml (1½ pints) distilled vinegar
600 g (1 lb 5 oz) sugar
4 cinnamon sticks
30 ml (2 tbsp) whole allspice
15 ml (1 tbsp) whole cloves

~

*D*issolve the salt in 1.4 litres (2½ pints) water to make a brine. Pour over the limes and leave overnight.

2 Drain the limes, then place in a large saucepan. Add 2.8 litres (5 pints) water and simmer gently until the limes are tender.

3 Drain the limes and prick each one with a darning needle.

4 Place the vinegar, sugar, cinnamon, allspice and cloves in a pan. Bring to the boil and boil for 5 minutes. Add the limes and simmer for 20 minutes.

5 Pack the limes into preheated jars. Strain the vinegar syrup and pour over the limes. Cover and seal the jars in the usual way.

Pickled Orange Rings

~

6 firm oranges, wiped
900 ml (1½ pints) distilled vinegar
700 g (1½ lb) sugar
20 ml (4 tsp) ground cloves
7.5 cm (3 inches) cinnamon stick
5 ml (1 tsp) whole cloves

~

*S*lice the oranges into rounds 0.5 cm (¼ inch) thick. Put the fruit into a large saucepan with just enough water to cover and simmer gently for 45 minutes or until the orange rind is really soft.

2 Remove the oranges with a slotted spoon and add the vinegar, sugar, ground cloves and cinnamon to the juice in the pan. Bring to the boil and simmer gently for 10 minutes.

3 Return the orange rings to the pan, a few at a time, and cook gently until the rind becomes transparent.

4 Using a slotted spoon, lift the orange rings from the syrup and pack them into preheated jars. Continue to boil the syrup for about 15 minutes or until it begins to thicken, then leave to cool.

5 Pour the cooled vinegar syrup over the orange rings. Add a few whole cloves to each jar, then cover and seal in the usual way.

Orange and Lemon Pickle
~

4 medium oranges
1 lemon
300 ml (½ pint) distilled vinegar
100 g (4 oz) golden syrup
100 g (4 oz) sugar
5-cm (2-inch) piece of cinnamon stick
8 cloves
10 ml (2 tsp) coriander seeds

~

Scrub the fruits. Thinly slice the oranges and halve each slice crossways, discarding any pips. Slice the lemon, discarding the pips, and chop finely.

2 Put the fruit in a large saucepan and cover with cold water. Bring to the boil, cover and simmer for about 1 hour or until the fruits and peel are tender. Drain off the liquid through a nylon sieve.

3 Put the remaining ingredients in a medium saucepan and warm gently until evenly blended. Simmer for 10 minutes.

4 Strain the vinegar and return to the pan with the fruits. Boil gently, uncovered, for 15 minutes or until reduced to a soft pulpy consistency with only a small amount of liquid.

5 Pack into jars, cover and seal in the usual way.

Spiced Pickled Peaches
~

about 30 whole cloves
900 g (2 lb) freestone peaches, skinned, stoned and halved
450 g (1 lb) sugar
300 ml (½ pint) white wine vinegar
thinly pared rind of ½ a lemon
1 small cinnamon stick

~

Push two cloves into each peach half. Place the sugar, vinegar, lemon rind and cinnamon in a saucepan and heat gently, stirring, for about 5 minutes or until the sugar has dissolved. Add the peach halves to the pan and simmer the fruit in the sweetened vinegar until soft.

2 Drain the fruit and pack into preheated jars. Continue boiling the vinegar until it is slightly reduced and beginning to thicken. Strain the vinegar syrup and pour sufficient over the fruit to cover.

3 Cover and seal the jars in the usual way. Store for 2–3 months before use.

Cérises au Vinaigre
~

450 g (1 lb) sugar
300 ml (½ pint) distilled vinegar
4 whole cloves
1 small cinnamon stick
900 g (2 lb) cherries, washed

~

Put the sugar, vinegar and spices into a saucepan and heat gently, stirring, until the sugar has dissolved. Add the cherries and simmer gently for about 5 minutes or until the fruit is cooked but not broken up.

2 Lift the cherries out of the pan with a slotted spoon and pack them into preheated jars.

3 Strain the sweetened vinegar to remove the spices, then return it to the pan and boil until it becomes syrupy. Pour over the cherries, then cover and seal the jars in the usual way.

Pickled Bananas
~

2 blades of mace
1 small cinnamon stick
6 whole cloves
300 ml (¹/₂ pint) distilled vinegar
350 g (12 oz) demerara sugar
12 under-ripe bananas
~

Tie the spices in a piece of muslin and put in a saucepan with the vinegar and sugar. Heat gently, stirring, until the sugar has dissolved, then boil for 15 minutes.

2 Meanwhile, peel the bananas and cut them into slices about 0.5 cm (¹/₄ inch) thick. Add them to the vinegar and cook gently until almost tender.

3 Carefully lift out the banana slices with a slotted spoon and pack into preheated jars. Strain the syrup and pour over the bananas. Cover and seal in the usual way.

Pickled Pears with Ginger
~

1.8 kg (4 lb) firm pears
lemon juice
1 cinnamon stick
25-g (1-oz) piece of fresh root ginger, peeled and sliced
3–4 whole cloves
600 ml (1 pint) white wine vinegar
800 g (1³/₄ lb) sugar
~

Peel, halve and core the pears (and quarter if large). Place in a saucepan of water with a little lemon juice added and simmer gently for about 1 hour or until just tender.

2 Meanwhile, place the cinnamon, ginger, cloves, vinegar and sugar in a preserving pan and heat gently, stirring, until dissolved. Bring to the boil and simmer for 5 minutes. Remove from the heat.

3 Carefully lift the pears from the water and place in the spiced vinegar syrup. Simmer for 15–20 minutes or until the pears look translucent and are very tender.

4 Lift out the pears using a slotted spoon and drain on kitchen paper. Pack into clean, preheated jars. Boil the syrup for about 5 minutes to thicken, then pour over the pears to cover completely.

5 Cover and seal in the usual way.

Pickled Satsumas and Kumquats
~

900 g (2 lb) satsumas or other 'easy-peel' citrus fruits
225 g (8 oz) kumquats
450 g (1 lb) caster sugar
600 ml (1 pint) white wine vinegar
1 cinnamon stick
5 ml (1 tsp) each whole cloves, split green cardamom pods and coriander seeds
2.5-cm (1-inch) piece of fresh root ginger, peeled and sliced
~

Carefully remove all the peel and pith from the satsumas. Prick the kumquats with a needle. Place the fruit in a large bowl.

2 Place the remaining ingredients in a large saucepan. Bring slowly to the boil, stirring, until the sugar has dissolved, then simmer for 5 minutes. Pour over the fruit, cover and leave overnight.

3 Strain the syrup into a saucepan. Pack the fruit tightly, with some of the spices and ginger, in clean jars. Boil the syrup and bubble to reduce by half. Pour over the fruit. Cover and seal in the usual way. Store for at least one month before using.

Pickled Apples
~

30 ml (2 tbsp) whole cloves
18 cm (7 inches) cinnamon stick
30 ml (2 tbsp) whole allspice
600 ml (1 pint) distilled vinegar
1 kg (2 lb) sugar
2.5 ml (½ tsp) salt
900 g (2 lb) cooking apples, peeled, cored and quartered

~

Put all the ingredients, except the apples, in a large saucepan. Heat gently, stirring, until the sugar has dissolved, then bring to the boil. Add the apples and cook gently until they are soft but not mushy.

2 Drain the apple segments, reserving the syrup, and pack them into preheated jars.

3 Boil the syrup until it is beginning to thicken, then strain. Pour over the apples, then cover and seal the jars in the usual way.

Spiced Prunes
~

450 g (1 lb) prunes, washed
cold tea
450 ml (¾ pint) distilled vinegar
225 g (8 oz) sugar
7.5 ml (1½ tsp) ground mixed spice

~

Put the prunes in a large bowl, cover with cold tea and leave to soak overnight.

2 Pour the vinegar into a saucepan and add the sugar and spice. Heat gently, stirring, until the sugar has dissolved, then bring to the boil.

3 Put the prunes in another pan with a little of the tea and simmer gently for 10–15 minutes or until soft. Drain the prunes, reserving the juice.

4 Add 300 ml (½ pint) of the prune juice to the vinegar. Pack the prunes into small jars and pour over the syrup. Cover and seal in the usual way.

Sweet and Sour Figs
~

450 ml (³/₄ pint) distilled malt vinegar
small piece of fresh root ginger, peeled and thinly sliced
3 allspice berries
6 black peppercorns
3 whole cloves
2 cinnamon sticks
pared rind of 1 lemon
30 ml (2 tbsp) honey
250 g (9 oz) sugar
700 g (1¹/₂ lb) firm, green figs
~

Put the vinegar in a large, shallow pan with the ginger, allspice, peppercorns, cloves, cinnamon, lemon rind, honey and sugar. Heat gently, stirring, until the sugar has dissolved.

2 Bring to the boil, boil for 1 minute, then remove from the heat. Wipe the figs, trim off any long stalks and discard. Thickly slice the figs into the warm vinegar. Bring to the boil, then simmer, uncovered, for 1 minute, gently pushing the fig slices under the vinegar. Carefully transfer the figs and vinegar to a large non-metallic bowl. Cover tightly with cling film and leave overnight.

3 Remove the fig slices from the vinegar with a slotted spoon. Tightly pack into clean preheated jars. Return the vinegar mixture to a clean saucepan and bring to the boil. Boil rapidly until reduced to 150 ml (¹/₄ pint).

4 Pour the hot vinegar into the jars. Cover and seal in the usual way. Store for at least 1 week before using.

Note If you want to use the distilled malt pickling vinegar now available, use the same quantity but omit the allspice and peppercorns.

Pickled Plums
~

450 g (1 lb) sugar
thinly pared rind of ¹/₂ a lemon
2 whole cloves
small piece of fresh root ginger
300 ml (¹/₂ pint) malt vinegar
900 g (2 lb) plums
~

Place all the ingredients, except the plums, in a saucepan. Heat gently, stirring, until the sugar has dissolved. Bring to the boil, then remove from the heat. Leave until cold, then strain, return to the pan and bring to the boil again.

2 Prick the plums with a needle, put them in a deep bowl, pour the spiced vinegar over, cover and leave for 5 days.

3 Strain the vinegar from the plums into a saucepan, bring to the boil and pour over the fruit again. Cover and leave for another 5 days.

4 Strain the vinegar from the plums into a saucepan and bring to the boil again. Pack the plums into jars, pour the boiling vinegar over and cover and seal the jars in the usual way.

Sweet-Sour Apricots

~

350 ml (12 fl oz) wine vinegar
250 g (9 oz) sugar
450 g (1 lb) apricots
1 small cinnamon stick

~

*P*our the vinegar into a saucepan, add the sugar and heat gently, stirring, until the sugar has dissolved. Bring to the boil.

2 Peel the apricots. (If the skins are difficult to remove, plunge the fruit into boiling water for a few seconds, then into cold water before peeling.)

3 Put the apricots in a jar, packing as tightly as possible, add the cinnamon stick and slowly pour in the hot vinegar syrup. Cover and seal the jars in the usual way. These pickled apricots are best left for a month before using.

Spiced Crab-apples

~

2.7 kg (6 lb) crab-apples, trimmed
2–3 strips lemon rind
450 g (1 lb) sugar
450 ml (³/₄ pint) red wine vinegar
1 cinnamon stick
1–2 whole cloves
3 peppercorns

~

*P*ut the crab-apples in a preserving pan with 900 ml (1¹/₂ pints) water and the strips of lemon rind. Simmer gently until just tender.

2 Remove the pan from the heat and strain the crab-apples, reserving the liquid. Put the sugar and vinegar in a pan and add 900 ml (1¹/₂ pints) of the liquid from the fruit.

3 Tie the spices in a piece of muslin and add to the liquid. Heat gently, stirring, until the sugar has dissolved, then bring to the boil and boil for 1 minute.

4 Add the crab-apples and simmer gently for 30–40 minutes or until the syrup has reduced to a coating consistency. Remove the muslin bag after 30 minutes.

5 Pack the fruit in small jars, pour over the syrup, then cover and seal the jars in the usual way.

Pickled Melon Rind

~

450 g (1 lb) melon rind, thinly pared
100 g (4 oz) salt
600 ml (1 pint) distilled vinegar
450 g (1 lb) sugar
1 small cinnamon stick
6–8 whole cloves
2–3 drops of green food colouring (optional)

~

*C*ut the melon rind into strips and put in a saucepan. Dissolve the salt in 1.1 litres (2 pints) water and pour into the saucepan with the melon rind. Bring to the boil and simmer gently for 30 minutes.

2 Drain off the salt water, rinse the melon rind, cover with fresh water, bring to the boil and cook for a further 10 minutes.

3 Change the water again and continue boiling gently until the rind is tender. Remove from the heat, cover and leave to stand overnight.

4 Pour the vinegar into a saucepan with 300 ml (¹/₂ pint) water and the sugar. Add the spices and heat gently, stirring, until the sugar has dissolved. Add the drained rind, bring to the boil and simmer gently for 1¹/₂ hours or until the syrup is thick and the rind is clear.

5 Remove the spices, add colouring if desired and spoon into jars. Cover and seal the jars in the usual way.

Pickled Dates
~

1.4 litres (2¹/₂ pints) distilled vinegar
40 g (1¹/₂ oz) pickling spice
350 g (12 oz) dark brown soft sugar
1.4 kg (3 lb) fresh dates, halved and stoned

~

*P*our the vinegar into a saucepan and add the spices and sugar. Heat gently, stirring, until the sugar has dissolved, then bring to the boil and boil for about 45 minutes or until the liquid is reduced by half.

2 Pack the dates into preheated jars, pour the hot syrup over them and leave to cool. When cold, cover and seal the jars in the usual way. Store for 3 months before using.

Sweet Pickled Fruit
~

900 g (2 lb) firm pears, peeled, cored and quartered; or firm plums, washed; or diced melon flesh
900 g (2 lb) sugar
900 ml (1¹/₂ pints) distilled vinegar
2 whole cloves

~

*P*ut the fruit in a large saucepan, cover with water, cook gently until soft, then drain well.

2 Meanwhile, put the sugar, vinegar and cloves in another pan. Heat gently, stirring, until the sugar has dissolved, then bring to the boil and boil for 30 minutes.

3 Add the fruit to the vinegar syrup and boil for 15 minutes, then pour into preheated jars. Cover and seal the jars in the usual way. Store for 6 months before using.

Pickled Nasturtium Seeds
~

225 g (8 oz) nasturtium seeds
coarse salt
30 ml (2 tbsp) mixed whole peppercorns
15 ml (1 tbsp) allspice berries
300 ml (¹/₂ pint) tarragon vinegar
a few sprigs of dill

~

*W*ash the nasturtium seeds under cold running water, picking off any brown matter. Dry thoroughly.

2 Sprinkle a layer of salt in a large non-metallic bowl. Sprinkle over the nasturtium seeds and cover with more salt. Leave to stand for 24 hours.

3 Put the peppercorns, allspice and vinegar in a saucepan, bring to the boil and simmer gently for 10 minutes. Leave to cool, then strain.

4 Rinse the seeds in cold water and pat dry. Transfer to a jar and pour over the spiced vinegar. Push a few sprigs of dill into the jar. Cover and seal in the usual way.

Chutneys and Relishes

Chutneys and relishes are made from mixtures of fruits and/or vegetables cooked with vinegar and spices which act as preservatives. The main difference between chutneys and relishes is in the finished texture. Chutneys are made from very finely chopped or sliced fruits and/or vegetables which are cooked very slowly to produce the characteristic smooth texture and mellow flavour. The finished texture of a relish is usually far more chunky since the ingredients used are cut larger and cooking time is shorter.

Preparation and Cooking

Chutneys The fruits and/or vegetables for a chutney should be finely chopped, sliced or minced. Bruised and poorly-shaped ingredients can very often be used as their appearance in the finished preserve is of no account. They are cooked to a pulp with vinegar, sugar, spices and salt. Chutneys should be simmered very slowly, uncovered, to allow evaporation. The chutney is ready when no excess liquid remains and the mixture is the consistency of a thick sauce. The cooking time will vary between 1 and 4 hours, depending mostly on the depth of the contents of the pan.

Relishes The fruits and/or vegetables for a relish should be cut into chunks and cooked for a fairly short time so that the ingredients retain their shape. Some relishes do not need cooking at all.

Equipment

The equipment used for making chutneys and relishes is exactly the same as for making pickles (see page 77).

Potting and Covering

Chutneys and relishes should be potted and covered in the same way as pickles (see pages 77 and 78). Pour the hot mixture into clean, dry, preheated jars and cover immediately with airtight, vinegar-proof tops.

Storing

Chutneys and relishes should be stored in a cool, dry, dark place and allowed to mature for 2–3 months before eating.

All-Year-Round Chutney

~

MAKES ABOUT 3 KG (6 ¹/₂ LB)

450 g (1 lb) onions, skinned
450 g (1 lb) cooking apples, cored
450 g (1 lb) sultanas
450 g (1 lb) stoned dates
450 g (1 lb) brown soft sugar
5 ml (1 tsp) ground ginger
5 ml (1 tsp) ground allspice
15 ml (1 tbsp) salt
2.5 ml (¹/₂ tsp) pepper
600 ml (1 pint) malt vinegar

~

*M*ince the onions, apples, sultanas and dates and mix together in a large bowl. Stir in the sugar, spices and seasonings and pour over the vinegar.

2 Stir the mixture well and leave for 24 hours, stirring from time to time, so that the flavours are well blended.

3 Spoon the chutney into preheated jars and cover and seal in the usual way. Store for 2–3 months before eating.

Sweet Mixed Vegetable Chutney

~

MAKES ABOUT 1.8 KG (4 LB)

900 g (2 lb) marrow, peeled, seeded and finely chopped
1 cucumber, washed and finely chopped
700 g (1¹/₂ lb) tomatoes, skinned and finely chopped
1.1 litres (2 pints) malt vinegar
450 ml (³/₄ pint) distilled vinegar
450 g (1 lb) demerara sugar
30 ml (2 tbsp) salt
30 ml (2 tbsp) ground turmeric
5 ml (1 tsp) ground cloves
7.5 ml (1¹/₂ tsp) ground ginger

~

*P*ut all the ingredients in a large saucepan. Bring to the boil, stirring, and simmer gently, uncovered, for about 3 hours, stirring occasionally, until the mixture is fairly dark and thick.

2 Spoon the chutney into preheated jars and cover and seal in the usual way. Store for 2–3 months before eating.

Note Courgettes may be used instead of marrow, and there is no need to peel them.

Hot Indian Chutney

~

MAKES ABOUT 2 KG (4¹/₂ LB)

700 g (1¹/₂ lb) cooking apples, peeled, cored and sliced
450 g (1 lb) onions, skinned and finely chopped
700 g (1¹/₂ lb) brown soft sugar
1.4 litres (2¹/₂ pints) malt vinegar
450 g (1 lb) seedless raisins, chopped
4 garlic cloves, skinned and crushed
20 ml (4 tsp) salt
30 ml (2 tbsp) ground ginger
45 ml (3 tbsp) mustard powder
30 ml (2 tbsp) paprika
15 ml (1 tbsp) ground coriander

~

*P*lace all the ingredients in a large saucepan and bring to the boil. Simmer gently, uncovered, for about 3 hours, stirring occasionally, until no excess liquid remains and the chutney is thick and pulpy.

2 Spoon into preheated jars and cover and seal in the usual way.

Aubergine and Apple Chutney
~

MAKES ABOUT 1.4 KG (3 LB)

350 g (12 oz) aubergines, roughly chopped
450 g (1 lb) tomatoes, skinned and chopped
225 g (8 oz) cooking apples, peeled, cored and sliced
175 g (6 oz) onion, skinned and chopped
1 garlic clove, skinned and crushed
100 g (4 oz) seedless raisins
175 g (6 oz) dark brown soft sugar
5 ml (1 tsp) salt
300 ml (½ pint) distilled vinegar
10 ml (2 tsp) whole pickling spice
~

Place the aubergines, tomatoes, apples, onion and garlic in a medium saucepan and add the raisins, brown sugar, salt and vinegar.

2 Tie the pickling spice in a piece of muslin and add to the pan.

3 Bring to the boil, then simmer, uncovered, stirring occasionally, for about 1 hour or until the ingredients are soft and the contents of the pan well reduced.

4 Take out the bag of spices. Spoon the chutney into preheated jars, cover and seal in the usual way.

Tomato and Red Pepper Chutney
~

MAKES ABOUT 1.4 KG (3 LB)

900 g (2 lb) ripe tomatoes, skinned and roughly chopped
225 g (8 oz) onions, skinned and roughly chopped
1 red chilli, seeded and finely chopped
1 red pepper, seeded and finely chopped
300 ml (½ pint) distilled (white) vinegar
100 g (4 oz) demerara sugar
5 ml (1 tsp) salt
5 ml (1 tsp) paprika
1.25 ml (¼ tsp) chilli powder
~

Place all the ingredients in a medium saucepan and heat gently until the sugar dissolves.

2 Bring to the boil and boil gently, uncovered, for about 1½ hours, stirring occasionally, until the vegetables are tender and the chutney of a thick pulpy consistency. Spoon the chutney into preheated jars, cover and seal in the usual way.

Tomato and Onion Chutney
~

MAKES ABOUT 2.3 KG (5 LB)

15 ml (1 tbsp) mustard seeds
900 g (2 lb) tomatoes, skinned and roughly chopped
450 g (1 lb) onions, skinned and chopped
1 garlic clove, skinned and chopped
900 g (2 lb) cooking apples, peeled, cored and sliced
225 g (8 oz) seedless raisins
350 g (12 oz) sugar
25 ml (5 tsp) curry powder
5 ml (1 tsp) cayenne
20 ml (4 tsp) salt
900 ml (1½ pints) malt vinegar
~

Tie the mustard seeds in a piece of muslin. Put all the ingredients in a large saucepan with the muslin bag. Heat gently, stirring, until the sugar has dissolved.

2 Bring to the boil, then simmer gently, uncovered, for about 3 hours, stirring occasionally, until no excess liquid remains and the chutney is thick. Remove the muslin bag.

3 Spoon the chutney into preheated jars, cover and seal in the usual way. Store in a cool, dry, dark place for 2–3 months to mature, before eating.

Green Tomato Chutney
~

MAKES ABOUT 1.4 KG (3 LB)

450 g (1 lb) cooking apples, peeled, cored and minced
225 g (8 oz) onions, skinned and minced
1.4 kg (3 lb) green tomatoes, thinly sliced
225 g (8 oz) sultanas
225 g (8 oz) demerara sugar
10 ml (2 tsp) salt
450 ml (³/₄ pint) malt vinegar
4 small pieces of dried root ginger
2.5 ml (¹/₂ tsp) cayenne pepper
5 ml (1 tsp) mustard powder

~

*P*lace all the ingredients in a large saucepan. Bring to the boil, reduce the heat and simmer gently for about 2 hours, stirring occasionally, until the ingredients are tender and reduced to a thick consistency, and no excess liquid remains. Remove the ginger.

2 Spoon the chutney into preheated jars, cover and seal in the usual way.

Marrow and Tomato Chutney
~

MAKES 1.6–1.8 KG (3¹/₂–4 LB)

10 ml (2 tsp) black peppercorns
10 ml (2 tsp) whole allspice berries
1.4 kg (3 lb) marrow, peeled, seeded and cut into 1-cm
(¹/₂-inch) chunks
450 g (1 lb) ripe tomatoes, skinned and roughly chopped
225 g (8 oz) onions, skinned and roughly chopped
2 garlic cloves, skinned and roughly chopped
30 ml (2 tbsp) salt
10 ml (2 tsp) ground ginger
700 g (1¹/₂ lb) sugar
750 ml (1¹/₄ pints) cider vinegar

~

*F*inely crush the peppercorns and allspice in a pestle and mortar, or use the end of a rolling pin in a bowl.

2 Put all the ingredients in a large saucepan. Heat gently, stirring, until the sugar has dissolved. Bring to the boil and boil steadily for about 50 minutes or until reduced by half. (This chutney will be a little more liquid than usual.) Stir occasionally to prevent sticking.

3 Cool the chutney slightly, then pot, cover and seal in the usual way.

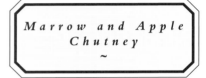

Marrow and Apple Chutney
~

MAKES ABOUT 2.7 KG (6 LB)

1.8 kg (4 lb) marrow, peeled and chopped
75 g (3 oz) salt
900 g (2 lb) cooking apples, peeled, cored and finely chopped
450 g (1 lb) shallots or onions, skinned and chopped
450 g (1 lb) dark brown soft sugar
1.1 litres (2 pints) distilled vinegar
5 ml (1 tsp) ground ginger
15 g (¹/₂ oz) pickling spice

~

*P*ut the marrow pieces in a large bowl in layers with the salt and leave for 12 hours or overnight.

2 Next day, rinse the marrow pieces, drain off the water and put them in a preserving pan. Add the apples, shallots or onions, sugar, vinegar and spice. (If using whole spice, put them in a muslin bag.)

3 Heat gently, stirring, until the sugar has dissolved, then bring to the boil and boil gently but steadily, uncovered, for about 2 hours, stirring from time to time, until the chutney becomes thick with no excess liquid. Remove the muslin bag, if used.

4 Pour the chutney into preheated jars while still warm, cover and seal in the usual way.

Beetroot Chutney
~

MAKES ABOUT 3.6 KG (8 LB)

1.4 kg (3 lb) raw beetroot, peeled and grated
900 g (2 lb) cooking apples, peeled, cored and chopped
450 g (1 lb) onions, skinned and chopped
450 g (1 lb) seedless raisins
1.4 litres (2¹/₂ pints) malt vinegar
1.1 kg (2¹/₂ lb) sugar
30 ml (2 tbsp) ground ginger
juice of 1 lemon

~

Place all the ingredients in a preserving pan and heat gently, stirring, until the sugar has dissolved. Bring to the boil and simmer gently, uncovered, stirring occasionally, for about 2¹/₂ hours or until no excess liquid remains and the mixture is thick.

2 Spoon the chutney into preheated jars, cover and seal in the usual way.

Spiced Pepper Chutney
~

MAKES ABOUT 1.6 KG (3¹/₂ LB)

3 red peppers, washed, seeded and finely chopped
3 green peppers, washed, seeded and finely chopped
450 g (1 lb) onions, skinned and sliced
450 g (1 lb) tomatoes, skinned and chopped
450 g (1 lb) cooking apples, peeled, cored and chopped
225 g (8 oz) demerara sugar
5 ml (1 tsp) ground allspice
450 ml (³/₄ pint) malt vinegar
5 ml (1 tsp) peppercorns
5 ml (1 tsp) mustard seeds

~

Place the peppers in a large saucepan with the onions, tomatoes, apples, sugar, allspice and vinegar. Tie the peppercorns and mustard seeds in a piece of muslin and add to the pan.

2 Heat gently, stirring, until the sugar has dissolved. Bring to the boil and simmer, uncovered, over a medium heat for about 1¹/₂ hours, stirring occasionally, until soft, pulpy and well reduced. Remove the muslin bag.

3 Spoon the chutney into preheated jars, cover and seal in the usual way.

Pumpkin Chutney
~

MAKES ABOUT 2.3 KG (5 LB)

900 g (2 lb) pumpkin, peeled, cored and seeded (prepared weight)
450 g (1 lb) tomatoes, skinned and roughly chopped
450 g (1 lb) onions, skinned and roughly chopped
1 garlic clove, skinned and crushed
50 g (2 oz) sultanas
700 g (1¹/₂ lb) light brown soft sugar
600 ml (1 pint) white wine vinegar
5 ml (1 tsp) ground allspice
15 ml (1 tbsp) salt
5 ml (1 tsp) freshly ground black pepper

~

Cut the pumpkin flesh into 1-cm (¹/₂-inch) cubes and put in a preserving pan with all the other ingredients.

2 Heat gently, stirring, until the sugar has dissolved, then bring to the boil and simmer gently, uncovered, for about 1 hour, stirring occasionally, especially towards the end of the cooking time, until no excess liquid remains and the mixture is thick.

3 Spoon the chutney into preheated jars, cover and seal in the usual way.

Aubergine and Pepper Chutney

~

MAKES ABOUT 1.4 KG (3 LB)

450 g (1 lb) aubergines, trimmed, washed and chopped
1 medium red pepper, washed, seeded and chopped
1 medium green pepper, washed, seeded and chopped
1 medium onion, skinned and chopped
1 garlic clove, skinned and crushed
1 large cooking apple, peeled, cored and chopped

~

Place all the ingredients in a large saucepan. Heat gently, stirring, until the sugar has dissolved, then bring to the boil and simmer gently, uncovered, for 1½ hours, stirring occasionally, until no excess liquid remains and the mixture is thick.

2 Spoon the chutney into preheated jars, cover and seal in the usual way.

Mixed Fruit Chutney

~

MAKES ABOUT 3.2 KG (7 LB)

450 g (1 lb) dried apricots, washed and chopped
450 g (1 lb) stoned dates, roughly chopped
700 g (1½ lb) cooking apples, peeled, cored and chopped
450 g (1 lb) bananas, peeled and sliced
225 g (8 oz) onions, skinned and finely chopped
450 g (1 lb) demerara sugar
grated rind and juice of 1 lemon
10 ml (2 tsp) ground mixed spice
10 ml (2 tsp) ground ginger
10 ml (2 tsp) curry powder
10 ml (2 tsp) salt
900 ml (1½ pints) distilled or cider vinegar

~

Put all the ingredients in a preserving pan. Heat gently, stirring, until the sugar has dissolved, then bring to the boil. Reduce the heat and simmer gently, uncovered, for about 1 hour, stirring occasionally, until no excess liquid remains and the mixture is thick and pulpy.

2 Spoon the chutney into preheated jars, cover and seal in the usual way.

Apple and Tomato Chutney

~

MAKES ABOUT 2.3 KG (5 LB)

900 g (2 lb) cooking apples, peeled, cored and sliced
15 ml (1 tbsp) mustard seeds
900 g (2 lb) tomatoes, sliced
350 g (12 oz) onions, skinned and chopped
1 garlic clove, skinned and chopped
225 g (8 oz) sultanas
350 g (12 oz) demerara sugar
25 ml (5 tsp) curry powder
5 ml (1 tsp) cayenne
20 ml (4 tsp) salt
900 ml (1½ pints) malt vinegar

~

Put the apples in a large saucepan with a very small quantity of water. Cook gently, stirring occasionally, until tender.

2 Tie the mustard seeds in a piece of muslin and add to the apples with the remaining ingredients.

3 Heat gently, stirring, until the sugar has dissolved, then bring to the boil. Reduce the heat and simmer gently, uncovered, for about 3 hours, stirring occasionally, until the chutney is thick and no excess liquid remains. Remove the muslin bag.

4 Spoon the chutney into preheated jars, cover and seal in the usual way.

Apple Chutney
~

MAKES ABOUT 2.7 KG (6 LB)

1.4 kg (3 lb) cooking apples, peeled, cored and diced
1.4 kg (3 lb) onions, skinned and chopped
450 g (1 lb) sultanas or seedless raisins
grated rind and juice of 2 lemons
700 g (1½ lb) demerara sugar
600 ml (1 pint) malt vinegar
~

*P*ut the apples, onions, sultanas or raisins, lemon rind and juice, sugar and vinegar in a preserving pan or large saucepan.

2 Heat gently, stirring, until the sugar has dissolved, then bring to the boil. Reduce the heat and simmer, uncovered, for about 3 hours, stirring occasionally, until the mixture is of a thick consistency, with no excess liquid remaining.

3 Spoon the chutney into preheated jars, cover and seal in the usual way.

VARIATION
Blender apple chutney

An electric blender can be used to produce a smoother texture, if preferred. In this case, cook all the ingredients, except the sultanas or raisins, until very soft. Pour into the blender goblet, a little at a time, and blend until smooth. Return to the saucepan with the sultanas or raisins and cook for a further 15 minutes or until thick.

VARIATION
Gooseberry chutney

Follow the recipe above, replacing the apples with 1.4 kg (3 lb) gooseberries, topped, tailed and washed.

Cranberry Chutney
~

MAKES ABOUT 1.4 KG (3 LB)

700 g (1½ lb) cranberries, washed
300 ml (½ pint) distilled vinegar
225 g (8 oz) sultanas
100 g (4 oz) seedless raisins
100 g (4 oz) sugar
15 g (½ oz) salt
10 ml (2 tsp) ground allspice
10 ml (2 tsp) ground cinnamon
~

*P*ut all the ingredients in a large saucepan and simmer gently for about 30 minutes or until the fruit is tender and the mixture is of a thick consistency.

2 Pour the chutney into preheated jars, cover and seal in the usual way.

Pear and Lemon Chutney

~

MAKES ABOUT 1.8 KG (4 LB)

1.8 kg (4 lb) pears, peeled, cored and chopped
450 g (1 lb) onions, skinned and chopped
350 g (12 oz) seedless raisins, chopped
50 g (2 oz) stem ginger, chopped
grated rind and juice of 2 lemons
225 g (8 oz) light brown soft sugar
30 ml (2 tbsp) salt
1.1 litres (2 pints) distilled vinegar
2 garlic cloves, skinned and crushed
6 dried chillies, crushed
4 whole cloves

~

Put the pears, onions, raisins, ginger, lemon rind and juice, sugar, salt and vinegar in a preserving pan. Tie the garlic, chillies and cloves in a piece of muslin and add to the pan.

2 Bring to the boil, then reduce the heat and simmer gently, uncovered, for about 2 hours, stirring occasionally, until the mixture is thick and no excess liquid remains. Remove the muslin bag.

3 Spoon the chutney into preheated jars, cover and seal in the usual way. Store for 2–3 months before eating.

Sweet Mango Chutney

~

MAKES ABOUT 2 KG (4¹/₂ LB)

1.8 kg (4 lb) firm mangoes, peeled, stoned and sliced
225 g (8 oz) cooking apples, peeled, cored and chopped
225 g (8 oz) onions, skinned and chopped
100 g (4 oz) seedless raisins
600 ml (1 pint) distilled vinegar
350 g (12 oz) demerara sugar
15 ml (1 tbsp) ground ginger
3 garlic cloves, skinned and crushed
5 ml (1 tsp) grated nutmeg
2.5 ml (¹/₂ tsp) salt

~

Put all the ingredients in a preserving pan. Heat gently, stirring, until the sugar has dissolved, then bring to the boil. Reduce the heat and simmer gently, uncovered, for about 1¹/₂ hours, stirring occasionally, until no excess liquid remains and the mixture is thick.

2 Spoon the chutney into preheated jars, cover and seal in the usual way. Store this chutney for 2–3 months before eating.

Opposite (left to right): Mustard Pickle (page 90),
Autumn Plum Chutney (page 112), Mixed Dill Pickle
(page 87)

Hot Mango Chutney
~

MAKES ABOUT 1.4 KG (3 LB)

1.1 kg (2½ lb) firm mangoes, just starting to ripen (about 2
large mangoes), peeled, stoned and cut into 2.5-cm (1-inch)
pieces
25 g (1 oz) piece of fresh root ginger, peeled and finely chopped
2–3 small red or green chillies, seeded and chopped
175 g (6 oz) onion, skinned and roughly chopped
1 garlic clove, skinned and roughly chopped
450 g (1 lb) cooking apples, peeled, cored and roughly chopped
15 ml (1 tbsp) salt
600 ml (1 pint) white wine vinegar
2.5 ml (½ tsp) ground cinnamon
225 g (8 oz) demerara sugar
225 g (8 oz) granulated sugar
~

Put all the ingredients, except the sugars, in a preserving pan. Bring to the boil and simmer gently
for about 10 minutes or until the fruits are beginning to
soften.

2 Add the sugars and heat gently, stirring, until the sugar
has dissolved, then bring to the boil. Reduce the heat
and simmer, uncovered, for about 45 minutes, stirring
occasionally, until thick.

3 Cool the chutney slightly, then pot, cover and seal in
the usual way.

Orange and Apple Chutney
~

MAKES ABOUT 2.3 KG (5 LB)

pared rind and juice of 2 oranges
1.8 kg (4 lb) cooking apples, peeled, cored and roughly chopped
450 g (1 lb) seedless raisins, finely chopped
750 ml (1¼ pints) malt vinegar
900 g (2 lb) sugar
~

Finely chop the orange rind. Put the apples,
raisins and orange rind in a saucepan with 600 ml
(1 pint) vinegar. Cover and cook until the apples are soft.

2 Add the sugar, remaining vinegar and orange juice and
stir to dissolve the sugar.

3 Bring to the boil and cook gently, uncovered, stirring
frequently, until the contents of the pan are reduced and
the chutney is of the desired consistency.

4 Spoon the chutney into preheated jars, cover and seal
in the usual way.

Green Fig Chutney
~

MAKES ABOUT 1.8 KG (4 LB)

1.4 kg (3 lb) fresh figs, washed and sliced
450 g (1 lb) onions, skinned and sliced
175 g (6 oz) fresh dates, stoned and chopped
100 g (4 oz) preserved ginger, chopped
1.1 litres (2 pints) malt vinegar
350 g (12 oz) demerara sugar
175 g (6 oz) seedless raisins
2.5 ml (½ tsp) cayenne pepper
5 ml (1 tsp) salt
~

Put all the ingredients in a preserving pan. Heat
gently, stirring, until the sugar has dissolved, then
bring to the boil. Reduce the heat and simmer gently,
uncovered, for about 4 hours, stirring occasionally, until
no excess liquid remains and the mixture is thick.

2 Spoon the chutney into preheated jars, cover and seal
in the usual way.

Pineapple and Date Chutney
~

MAKES ABOUT 2 KG (4 ½ LB)

450 g (1 lb) cooking apples, peeled, cored and chopped
225 g (8 oz) onions, skinned and chopped
450 ml (¾ pint) white wine vinegar
225 g (8 oz) light brown soft sugar
5 ml (1 tsp) ground cinnamon
1 medium pineapple (about 1.4 kg/3 lb), peeled, cored and diced
225 g (8 oz) fresh dates, stoned and roughly chopped

~

Put the apple and onion in a medium saucepan with the vinegar, sugar and cinnamon.

2 Heat gently, stirring, until the sugar has dissolved, then bring to the boil. Reduce the heat and simmer, uncovered, for about 20 minutes, stirring occasionally, until the apple is pulped and the onion soft.

3 Add the pineapple and dates to the pan and boil gently for a further 20–25 minutes, stirring occasionally. The fruits should be just covered in a thick syrupy liquid.

4 Spoon the chutney into preheated jars, cover and seal in the usual way.

Gooseberry Chutney
~

MAKES ABOUT 1.8 KG (4 LB)

900 g (2 lb) green gooseberries, topped, tailed and washed
175 g (6 oz) stoned dates, roughly chopped
350 g (12 oz) onions, skinned and chopped
5 ml (1 tsp) mustard seed, crushed
pinch of cayenne pepper
20 ml (4 tsp) salt
450 g (1 lb) light brown soft sugar
600 ml (1 pint) malt vinegar

~

Put all the ingredients together in a large saucepan and bring slowly to the boil, stirring, until the sugar has dissolved.

2 Boil gently, uncovered, for about 1½ hours, stirring occasionally, until the gooseberries are thoroughly pulped, adding a little more vinegar if necessary. The chutney should be thick and pulpy but not at all dry.

3 Spoon the chutney into preheated jars, cover and seal in the usual way.

Sweet Cherry Chutney
~

MAKES ABOUT 900 G (2 LB)

100 g (4 oz) onion, skinned and finely chopped
225 g (8 oz) cooking apple, peeled, cored and roughly chopped
900 g (2 lb) morello cherries, stoned
small piece of fresh root ginger, peeled
300 ml (½ pint) red wine vinegar
175 g (6 oz) demerara sugar
a little grated nutmeg
large pinch of salt

~

Put all the ingredients together in a medium saucepan.

2 Bring to the boil, cover and simmer for 5 minutes. Uncover the pan and continue to simmer, stirring occasionally, for 35–40 minutes or until the mixture is thick and pulpy and there is very little excess liquid. Remove the ginger and discard.

3 Spoon the chutney into preheated jars, cover and seal in the usual way. Store in a cool, dry place for 1 month before using.

Rhubarb and Orange Chutney

~

MAKES ABOUT 3.6 KG (8 LB)

900 g (2 lb) rhubarb, trimmed, washed and chopped
grated rind and juice of 2 oranges
450 g (1 lb) onions, skinned and chopped
900 ml (1½ pints) malt vinegar
900 g (2 lb) demerara sugar
450 g (1 lb) seedless raisins
5 ml (1 tsp) whole allspice berries
15 ml (1 tbsp) mustard seeds
15 ml (1 tbsp) peppercorns

~

Put the rhubarb, orange rind and juice, onions, vinegar, sugar and raisins in a large saucepan. Tie the spices in a piece of muslin and add to the ingredients in the pan.

2 Heat gently, stirring, until the sugar has dissolved, then bring to the boil. Reduce the heat and simmer gently, uncovered, for about 1½ hours, stirring occasionally, until the mixture is thick and pulpy and no excess liquid remains. Remove the muslin bag.

3 Spoon the chutney into preheated jars, cover and seal in the usual way. Store for 2–3 months before eating.

Autumn Plum Chutney

~

MAKES ABOUT 2.3 KG (5 LB)

900 g (2 lb) firm but ripe red plums, washed, halved and stoned
450 g (1 lb) cooking apples, peeled, cored and chopped
450 g (1 lb) onions, skinned and roughly chopped
2 garlic cloves, skinned and chopped
450 g (1 lb) sultanas
600 ml (1 pint) distilled malt vinegar
2.5 ml (½ tsp) ground mixed spice
pinch of ground mace
2.5 ml (½ tsp) ground ginger
450 g (1 lb) demerara sugar

~

Put all the fruit and vegetables in a preserving pan with the sultanas, vinegar and spices. Bring to the boil, stirring frequently, then cover and simmer gently for 30 minutes or until all the ingredients are very soft.

2 Add the sugar and heat gently, stirring, until the sugar has dissolved, then bring to the boil. Reduce the heat and simmer, uncovered, for 30–45 minutes or until thick and jam-like. Stir frequently to prevent sticking.

3 Cool the chutney slightly, then spoon into preheated jars, cover and seal in the usual way.

Pear Chutney
~

MAKES ABOUT 2.3 KG (5 LB)

1.4 kg (3 lb) pears, peeled, cored and sliced
450 g (1 lb) cooking apples, peeled, cored and chopped
225 g (8 oz) seedless raisins, chopped
225 g (8 oz) sultanas
450 g (1 lb) onions, skinned and chopped
1.1 litres (2 pints) malt vinegar
450 g (1 lb) demerara sugar
1.25 ml (¼ tsp) cayenne pepper
2.5 ml (½ tsp) grated nutmeg
10 ml (2 tsp) salt
~

Put all the fruit and vegetables in a preserving pan with the vinegar, sugar, spices and salt. Heat gently, stirring, until the sugar has dissolved.

2 Bring to the boil, then reduce the heat and simmer gently, uncovered, for about 2½ hours, stirring occasionally, until the mixture is thick and no excess liquid remains.

3 Spoon the chutney into preheated jars, cover and seal in the usual way.

Peach Chutney
~

MAKES ABOUT 1.1 KG (2½ LB)

small piece of fresh root ginger, bruised
6 ripe peaches, stoned, skinned and sliced
100 g (4 oz) sultanas
2 large onions, skinned and finely chopped
15 ml (1 tbsp) salt
350 g (12 oz) demerara sugar
300 ml (½ pint) malt vinegar
15 ml (1 tbsp) mustard seeds
grated rind and juice of 1 lemon
~

Tie the root ginger in a piece of muslin. Place all the ingredients in a large saucepan with the muslin bag.

2 Heat the mixture gently, stirring, until the sugar has dissolved, then bring to the boil and simmer, uncovered, for about 1¾ hours, stirring occasionally, until no excess liquid remains and the mixture is thick. Remove the muslin bag.

3 Spoon the chutney into preheated jars, cover and seal in the usual way. Store for 2–3 months before serving with poultry, pork or lamb.

Banana Chutney
~

MAKES ABOUT 3.2 KG (7 LB)

900 g (2 lb) cooking apples, peeled, cored and roughly chopped
225 g (8 oz) seedless raisins
225 g (8 oz) stoned dates, chopped
1.8 kg (4 lb) bananas, peeled and sliced
225 g (8 oz) onions, skinned and chopped
10 ml (2 tsp) salt
350 g (12 oz) demerara sugar
30 ml (2 tbsp) ground ginger
2.5 ml (½ tsp) cayenne pepper
600 ml (1 pint) distilled vinegar
~

Put the prepared fruit and onions in a preserving pan and sprinkle with the salt, sugar and spices. Pour in the vinegar and bring gently to the boil.

2 Simmer the mixture gently, uncovered, for about 1 hour, stirring occasionally, until no excess liquid remains and the mixture is soft and pulpy.

3 Spoon the chutney into preheated jars, cover and seal in the usual way.

Lychee and Banana Chutney
~

MAKES ABOUT 900 G (2 LB)

2 lemons
12 lychees, peeled, stoned and chopped
1 large banana, peeled and sliced
100 g (4 oz) preserved ginger, sliced
2 medium onions, skinned and grated
225 g (8 oz) seedless raisins
20 ml (4 tsp) salt
5 ml (1 tsp) ground ginger
2.5 ml (1/2 tsp) pepper
300 ml (1/2 pint) vinegar
~

Peel the lemons and cut into small chunks. Put all the ingredients in a preserving pan and simmer, uncovered, for 1 1/2 hours, stirring occasionally. Mash to a rough purée.

2 Pack the chutney into preheated jars, cover and seal in the usual way.

Damson Chutney
~

MAKES ABOUT 1.8 KG (4 LB)

1.6 kg (3 1/2 lb) damsons, washed
2 medium onions, skinned and chopped
1 garlic clove, skinned and crushed
225 g (8 oz) seedless raisins, chopped
100 g (4 oz) stoned dates, chopped
700 g (1 1/2 lb) dark brown soft sugar
1.4 litres (2 1/2 pints) malt vinegar
15 g (1/2 oz) salt
25 g (1 oz) ground ginger
1.25 ml (1/4 tsp) ground allspice
~

Mix all the ingredients together in a large saucepan. Heat gently, stirring, until the sugar has dissolved, then bring to the boil. Reduce the heat and simmer, uncovered, for 1 1/2–2 hours, stirring occasionally, until no excess liquid remains and the mixture is thick. Scoop out the damson stones with a slotted spoon.

2 Pour the chutney into preheated jars, cover and seal in the usual way.

Note   If preferred, plums can be used in the above recipe instead of damsons.

Date and Orange Chutney
~

MAKES ABOUT 1.4 KG (3 LB)

450 g (1 lb) oranges
450 g (1 lb) onions, skinned and roughly chopped
700 g (1 1/2 lb) dates, stoned
225 g (8 oz) sultanas
700 g (1 1/2 lb) sugar
100 g (4 oz) golden syrup
30 ml (2 tbsp) salt
1.25 ml (1/4 tsp) cayenne pepper
1.4 litres (2 1/2 pints) malt vinegar
~

Finely grate the rind of the oranges. Peel off and discard the pith and slice the oranges, discarding the pips.

2 Mince together the oranges, onions, dates and sultanas.

3 Put the sugar, syrup, salt, cayenne and vinegar in a large saucepan. Heat gently, stirring, until the sugar has dissolved, then bring to the boil and add the minced fruits and half the orange rind.

4 Simmer gently, uncovered, for about 1 hour, stirring occasionally, until no excess liquid remains and the mixture is thick. Stir in the remaining orange rind.

5 Spoon the chutney into preheated jars, cover and seal in the usual way.

Apricot and Apple Chutney

~

MAKES ABOUT 3.2 KG (7 LB)

450 g (1 lb) dried apricots, soaked overnight
1.8 kg (4 lb) cooking apples, peeled, cored and chopped
450 g (1 lb) onions, skinned and sliced
350 g (12 oz) seedless raisins
450 g (1 lb) demerara sugar
600 ml (1 pint) distilled vinegar
15 ml (1 tbsp) salt
15 ml (1 tbsp) ground mixed spice

~

Drain the apricots and chop roughly. Put them in a preserving pan with all the remaining ingredients and heat gently, stirring, until the sugar has dissolved, then bring to the boil. Reduce the heat and simmer gently, uncovered, for about 1 hour, stirring occasionally, until the mixture thickens and no excess liquid remains.

2 Pour the chutney into preheated jars, cover and seal in the usual way.

Spiced Apricot and Raisin Chutney

~

MAKES ABOUT 1.4 KG (3 LB)

225 g (8 oz) dried apricots, soaked overnight
350 g (12 oz) onions, skinned
finely grated rind and juice of 1 orange
1 garlic clove, skinned and crushed
50 g (2 oz) seedless raisins
225 g (8 oz) sugar
5 ml (1 tsp) prepared mustard
1.25 ml (1/4 tsp) ground cinnamon
1.25 ml (1/4 tsp) ground mixed spice
5 ml (1 tsp) salt
450 ml (3/4 pint) malt vinegar

~

Drain the apricots and chop roughly. Chop the onions finely.

2 Put the apricots and onions in a medium saucepan with the orange rind and juice. Add all the remaining ingredients and bring slowly to the boil.

3 Boil gently, uncovered, for about 1 hour, stirring occasionally, until the chutney is thick and well reduced, and no excess liquid remains.

4 Pour the chutney into preheated jars, cover and seal in the usual way. Store in a cool, dry, dark place for 2–3 months to mature before eating.

Low–Sugar Chutney

~

MAKES ABOUT 1.6 KG (3 1/2 LB)

2 garlic cloves, skinned and crushed
175 g (6 oz) onions, skinned and diced
175 g (6 oz) carrots, scrubbed and diced
175 g (6 oz) cauliflower, divided into tiny florets
175 g (6 oz) gherkins, diced
175 g (6 oz) courgettes, trimmed and diced
2 tomatoes, skinned and chopped
100 g (4 oz) dates, stoned and chopped
100 g (4 oz) seedless raisins
1 cooking apple, cored and coarsely grated
175 g (6 oz) dark brown soft sugar
2.5 ml (1/2 tsp) ground ginger
5 ml (1 tsp) dry mustard
300 ml (1/2 pint) unsweetened apple juice
300 ml (1/2 pint) malt vinegar

~

Put all the ingredients in a preserving pan or large saucepan. Bring to the boil and simmer, uncovered, for about 1 hour, stirring occasionally, until the chutney is thick and the liquid evaporated.

2 Allow to cool for 5 minutes, then stir and spoon into preheated jars. Cover and seal in the usual way. Store for 1–2 weeks before using.

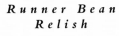

Chunky Vegetable Relish
~

MAKES ABOUT 1.4 KG (3 LB)

225 g (8 oz) carrots, peeled
225 g (8 oz) swede, peeled and diced
225 g (8 oz) onion, skinned and chopped
450 g (1 lb) cooking apples, peeled, cored and roughly chopped
225 g (8 oz) small cauliflower florets
100 g (4 oz) sultanas
30 ml (2 tbsp) molasses
45 ml (3 tbsp) tomato purée
30 ml (2 tbsp) lemon juice
1 garlic clove, skinned and crushed
175 g (6 oz) dark brown soft sugar
600 ml (1 pint) malt vinegar
salt and pepper
2.5 ml (¹/₂ tsp) ground allspice
~

Cut the carrots into 5-mm (¹/₄-inch) dice and blanch in boiling salted water for 4 minutes, then drain well. (The carrot will not tenderise sufficiently when cooking in the vinegar.)

2 Put all the ingredients in a medium saucepan and heat slowly, stirring, until the sugar has dissolved.

3 Boil gently, uncovered, for about 1¹/₄ hours, stirring occasionally, until the vegetables are just tender and the contents of the pan well reduced.

4 Spoon the relish into preheated jars, cover and seal in the usual way.

Runner Bean Relish
~

MAKES ABOUT 2.3 KG (5 LB)

700 g (1¹/₂ lb) onions, skinned and chopped
600 ml (1 pint) malt vinegar
900 g (2 lb) runner beans, trimmed and sliced (prepared weight)
45 ml (3 tbsp) cornflour
15 ml (1 tbsp) mustard powder
15 ml (1 tbsp) ground turmeric
15 ml (1 tbsp) mustard seeds
15 ml (1 tbsp) toasted sesame seeds
225 g (8 oz) light brown soft sugar
450 g (1 lb) demerara sugar
~

Put the chopped onion in a large pan with 300 ml (¹/₂ pint) of the vinegar. Simmer for 20 minutes or until tender.

2 Cook the sliced beans in boiling salted water for 5 minutes or until just tender. Drain and add to the onions.

3 Mix the cornflour, mustard, turmeric, mustard seeds and sesame seeds with a little of the remaining vinegar and add to the mixture.

4 Add the remaining vinegar and simmer for 10 minutes. Add the sugars, stirring until dissolved, then bring to the boil. Reduce the heat and simmer for a further 20–25 minutes.

5 Spoon the chutney into preheated jars, cover and seal in the usual way. Leave to mature for 1 week before eating.

Note This relish can be made equally well with frozen runner beans.

Opposite (bottom shelf, left to right): Runner Bean Relish (above), All-Year-Round Chutney (page 102), Sweetcorn Relish (page 119)

Spiced Beetroot Relish

~

MAKES ABOUT 450 G (1 LB)

350 g (12 oz) raw beetroot
50 g (2 oz) onion, skinned
25 g (1 oz) seedless raisins
150 ml (¼ pint) red wine vinegar
15 ml (1 tbsp) mustard seeds
15 ml (1 tbsp) horseradish relish
90 ml (6 tbsp) light brown soft sugar
5 ml (1 tsp) powdered gelatine

~

Wash the beetroot and wrap in foil. Bake in the oven at 180°C (350°F) mark 4 for 2–3 hours, depending on size, until the beetroot is tender.

2 Leave the beetroot to cool, then skin and finely grate in a food processor. Thinly slice the onion.

3 Put the onion, beetroot and all the remaining ingredients, except the gelatine, in a small saucepan. Bring to the boil, stirring all the time. Simmer, uncovered, for 1–2 minutes. Remove from the heat and leave to cool, then strain the vegetables, reserving the vinegar.

4 Sprinkle the gelatine over the strained, cooled vinegar mixture and leave for 3–4 minutes or until sponge-like in texture. Place over a very low heat and heat gently until the gelatine has completely dissolved. Do not stir.

5 Meanwhile, spoon the beetroot mixture into preheated jars. Pour over the vinegar. Cover and seal in the usual way.

Note If using vacuum-packed, pre-cooked beetroot, omit step 1.

Mustard Relish

~

MAKES ABOUT 1.4 KG (3 LB)

175 g (6 oz) cucumber, washed and finely chopped
175 g (6 oz) onion, skinned and finely chopped
225 g (8 oz) cauliflower, washed and broken into florets
100 g (4 oz) tomatoes, roughly chopped
1 medium green pepper, washed, seeded and finely chopped
1 medium red pepper, washed, seeded and finely chopped
225 g (8 oz) fresh gherkins, thickly sliced
25 g (1 oz) salt
15 ml (1 tbsp) mustard seeds
250 g (9 oz) sugar
25 g (1 oz) plain flour
2.5 ml (½ tsp) mustard powder
2.5 ml (½ tsp) ground turmeric
450 ml (¾ pint) malt vinegar

~

Put all the vegetables in a large bowl. Dissolve the salt in 1.1 litres (2 pints) water and pour over the vegetables. Cover and leave to stand overnight.

2 Drain and rinse the vegetables well. Blend the mustard seeds, sugar, flour, mustard powder and turmeric together in a large saucepan, then gradually stir in the vinegar. Bring to the boil, stirring.

3 Add the drained vegetables and simmer, uncovered, for 30 minutes. Stir gently from time to time to prevent sticking.

4 Spoon the relish into preheated jars, cover and seal in the usual way.

Cucumber and Celery Relish
~

MAKES ABOUT 1.6 KG (3 ½ LB)

3 cucumbers
2 large onions, skinned and chopped
4 large celery sticks, trimmed, washed and diced
1 green pepper, washed, seeded and diced
30 ml (2 tbsp) salt
100 g (4 oz) sugar
45 ml (3 tbsp) mustard powder
75 ml (5 tbsp) plain flour
5 ml (1 tsp) ground turmeric
300 ml (½ pint) cider vinegar

~

Cut the cucumbers into 0.5-cm (¼-inch) cubes and place in a bowl. Add the onion, celery, green pepper and salt and stir. Leave to stand for 30 minutes, then drain.

2 Mix the sugar, mustard, flour and turmeric with the cider vinegar. Add the chopped vegetables and cook over a medium heat for about 30 minutes, stirring.

3 Spoon the relish into preheated jars, cover and seal in the usual way. Store in a dark place.

Sweetcorn Relish
~

MAKES ABOUT 2.3 KG (5 LB)

6 corn cobs, trimmed and leaves and silk removed
½ a small white cabbage, trimmed and roughly chopped
2 medium onions, skinned and halved
1½ red peppers, washed, seeded and quartered
10 ml (2 tsp) salt
30 ml (2 tbsp) flour
2.5 ml (½ tsp) ground turmeric
175 g (6 oz) sugar
10 ml (2 tsp) mustard powder
600 ml (1 pint) distilled vinegar

~

Cook the corn cobs in boiling salted water for 3 minutes, then drain. Using a sharp knife, cut the corn from the cobs. Coarsely mince the cabbage, onions and red peppers and combine with the corn.

2 Blend the salt, flour, turmeric, sugar and mustard together in a saucepan, then gradually stir in the vinegar. Heat gently, stirring, until the sugar has dissolved, then bring to the boil. Reduce the heat, add the vegetables, and simmer for 25–30 minutes, stirring occasionally.

3 Spoon the relish into preheated jars, cover and seal in the usual way.

Tomato Relish
~

MAKES ABOUT 1.8 KG (4 LB)

1.4 kg (3 lb) tomatoes, skinned and sliced
450 g (1 lb) cucumber or marrow, peeled, seeded and roughly chopped
50 g (2 oz) salt
2 garlic cloves, skinned and finely chopped
1 large red pepper, washed, seeded and roughly chopped
450 ml (¾ pint) malt vinegar
15 ml (1 tbsp) mustard powder
2.5 ml (½ tsp) ground allspice
2.5 ml (½ tsp) mustard seeds

~

Layer the tomatoes and cucumber or marrow in a bowl, sprinkling each layer with salt. Cover and leave overnight.

2 Next day, drain and rinse well and place in a large saucepan. Add the garlic and pepper.

3 Blend the vinegar with the dry ingredients. Stir into the pan and bring slowly to the boil. Boil gently, uncovered, for about 1 hour, stirring occasionally, until the mixture is soft.

4 Spoon the relish into preheated jars, cover and seal in the usual way. Store for 3–4 months before use.

Sauces, Ketchups, Vinegars and Oils

Sauces, ketchups and vinegars are savoury, sometimes sweet, accompaniments to foods, providing a complementary piquant flavour. They all contain vinegar, which is the preservative, and herbs and/or spices. A sauce contains a mixture of fruit and vegetables and a ketchup is the extract of a single fruit or vegetable, and is a little thinner than a sauce. Flavoured oils are used for flavouring salad dressings or for stir-fries.

Sauces

Home-made bottled sauces are chutney-type mixtures of fruit, vegetables, vinegar, spices and sugar, which are sieved after cooking. They usually have one predominating flavour. Use an open pan for cooking unless otherwise stated. Since most sauces have a low acid content, they are liable to ferment and must be sterilised after bottling. Allow sauces to mature for at least 1 month before using. Some of the thinner, more pungent sauces, such as Yorkshire relish, do not need sterilising and can be used immediately.

Ketchups

Cooked with vinegar and other ingredients, a ketchup is the extract of a single fruit or vegetable. After cooking, the mixture is sieved. Like sauces, ketchups need sterilising if they have a low acid content. Home-made tomato ketchup is full of flavour and makes a delicious and unusual gift at any time of year, if bottled attractively.

Bottling and Sterilising Sauces and Ketchups

Use bottles with metal or plastic screw caps, screw stoppers or corks. Heat the bottles in the oven at 140°C (275°F) mark 1 and boil the caps or corks in

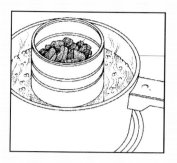

For an airtight seal, melt some pieces of paraffin wax in an old tin in a pan of simmering water.

Dip the corked bottle tops in the hot wax up to about 1 cm (½ inch) down their necks. To open, chip the wax away with a sharp knife.

water for 10 minutes immediately before using. Screw-capped bottles should be filled to just under 2.5 cm (1 inch) from the top and corked bottles to within 4 cm (1½ inches) of the top. Seal with the cap or cork immediately after filling. If using corks, they must be tied down with wire or with a strong piece of cloth and string as soon as the bottles have been filled and corked. This will prevent the corks blowing out during the sterilising process.

Wrap the bottles in cloth or newspaper and stand them upright in a deep pan with an upturned heatproof plate, a pad of newspaper or a folded cloth on the base. Fill up with warm water to reach the necks of the bottles. Heat slowly to 76°C (170°F), or simmering point if no thermometer is available. Simmer, maintaining this temperature, for 30 minutes. Remove the bottles and tighten any screw caps used. Push in the corks and, when the bottles are partly cooled, coat the corks with melted paraffin wax to make them airtight. Store the bottles in a cool, dark place.

Flavoured Vinegars and Oils

Flavoured vinegars and oils lend a subtle flavour to dressings, marinades, sauces, stews, grills and stir-fries.

To make a flavoured oil or vinegar, choose a bland oil such as sunflower, groundnut or safflower oil, or a mild olive oil, or a good quality white wine, red wine or cider vinegar.

Most culinary herbs can be used. Choose from rosemary, thyme, tarragon, marjoram, fennel, savory, sage and basil. They should all be used fresh. Lightly bruise enough herb sprigs to half-fill a glass bottle or jar. Cover them with oil or vinegar and seal with non-corrosive tops. Leave for 2 weeks in a warm place, shaking occasionally. Strain the oil or vinegar, pressing down hard on the herbs. Taste and, if the flavour is not strong enough, repeat the process. When the oil or vinegar is ready, decant into clean bottles, add a fresh herb sprig and seal.

Flower oils and vinegars are made in the same way. Remove all stalks and green parts before using the flowers. Roses, nasturtiums, violets, lavender, mint, primroses and jasmine are all suitable as well as all flowering herbs. Leave them in the oil or vinegar for about a month, on a sunny windowsill if possible, before using.

Vinegars and oils can also be flavoured with aromatics such as lemon, lime or orange, or spices such as chillies, allspice, ginger, anise, cinnamon, cloves or garlic, horseradish or summer fruits. See the recipes on pages 125–127.

Flavoured vinegars and oils do not need sterilising.

Mint Sauce
~

MAKES ABOUT 300 ML (¹/₂ PINT)

100 g (4 oz) fresh mint, washed, dried and finely chopped
225 g (8 oz) sugar
300 ml (¹/₂ pint) vinegar

~

Put the chopped mint into dry, wide-necked jars. Dissolve the sugar in the vinegar, stirring with a wooden spoon, and bring to the boil. Leave until cold. Pour over the mint and seal to make the jars airtight.
2 To serve, lift out sufficient mint with a wooden spoon, together with a little of the liquid. Put into a jug or sauceboat and add a little fresh vinegar.

Green Tomato Sauce
~

MAKES ABOUT 900 ML (1¹/₂ PINTS)

1.4 kg (3 lb) green tomatoes, washed and finely chopped
450 g (1 lb) apples, washed and finely chopped
2 small onions or shallots, skinned and finely chopped
225 g (8 oz) sugar
5 ml (1 tsp) ground pickling spice
2.5 ml (¹/₂ tsp) freshly ground pepper
2.5 ml (¹/₂ tsp) mustard powder
10 ml (2 tsp) salt
300 ml (¹/₂ pint) vinegar
gravy browning to colour

~

Put all the ingredients in a large saucepan and simmer gently for 1 hour, stirring occasionally.
2 Press through a nylon sieve and return to the pan. Bring to the boil and simmer for a few minutes.
3 Pour the hot sauce into warm bottles, seal and sterilise.

Hot Wellington Sauce
~

MAKES ABOUT 900 ML (1¹/₂ PINTS)

450 g (1 lb) red tomatoes, washed and chopped
1 onion, skinned and chopped
1 lemon, washed and chopped
900 g (2 lb) apples, peeled, cored and chopped
1.1 litres (2 pints) malt vinegar
15 g (¹/₂ oz) whole mixed spice
25 g (1 oz) salt
225 g (8 oz) dark brown soft sugar
5 ml (1 tsp) soy sauce

~

Put the tomatoes, onion and fruit in a large saucepan and cover with the vinegar and 1.1 litres (2 pints) water. Tie the spice in a piece of muslin and add to the pan with the salt and sugar.

2 Bring to the boil, then reduce the heat and simmer for about 3 hours or until well reduced. Remove the muslin bag and press the mixture through a nylon sieve.

3 Add the soy sauce and return to the pan. Simmer for 15 minutes, stirring occasionally, until the sauce thickens. Pour the hot sauce into warm bottles, seal and sterilise.

Hot Tomato and Apple Sauce
~

MAKES ABOUT 600 ML (1 PINT)

450 g (1 lb) tomatoes, washed and chopped
450 g (1 lb) cooking apples, peeled, cored and chopped
2 medium onions, skinned and chopped
150 ml (¹/₄ pint) distilled vinegar
100 g (4 oz) sugar
12 peppercorns
8 whole cloves
15 g (¹/₂ oz) fresh root ginger
2 chillies
15 g (¹/₂ oz) salt

~

Put the tomatoes, apples and onions in a saucepan, cover and cook gently until soft, then add all the remaining ingredients.

2 Simmer the mixture for about 30 minutes, uncovered, then press the mixture through a nylon sieve. Return to the pan and cook gently for about 15 minutes, stirring occasionally, until the sauce thickens.

3 Pour the hot sauce into warm bottles, seal and sterilise.

Plum Sauce
~

MAKES ABOUT 1.1 LITRES (2 PINTS)

1.8 kg (4 lb) plums, washed and stoned
225 g (8 oz) onions, skinned and sliced
100 g (4 oz) currants
600 ml (1 pint) spiced vinegar (see page 127)
225 g (8 oz) sugar
25 g (1 oz) salt

~

Put the plums, onions and currants in a saucepan with 300 ml (¹/₂ pint) of the spiced vinegar and simmer for 30 minutes.

2 Press through a nylon sieve and return to the pan with the remaining vinegar, the sugar and the salt. Simmer for about 1 hour, stirring occasionally, until the sauce is thick and creamy.

3 Pour the hot sauce into warm bottles, seal and sterilise.

Pear Sauce
~

MAKES ABOUT 300 ML (½ PINT)

8 large ripe dessert pears, peeled, cored and chopped
50 g (2 oz) caster sugar
5 ml (1 tsp) pickling spice
1 cinnamon stick
5 ml (1 tsp) whole cloves

~

*P*ut the pears in a large saucepan with 450 ml (¾ pint) water, the sugar and spices. Bring to the boil and cook for about 10 minutes or until tender and broken up. Press the mixture through a nylon sieve.

2 Return the purée to a clean pan, bring to the boil and boil for 5 minutes, stirring occasionally, until the sauce thickens.

3 Pour the hot sauce into warm bottles, seal and sterilise.

Tomato Ketchup
~

MAKES ABOUT 1.1 LITRES (2 PINTS)

2.7 kg (6 lb) ripe tomatoes, sliced
225 g (8 oz) sugar
300 ml (½ pint) spiced vinegar (see page 127)
15 ml (1 tbsp) tarragon vinegar (optional)
pinch of cayenne
5 ml (1 tsp) paprika pepper
5 ml (1 tsp) salt

~

*P*ut the tomatoes in a pan and cook over a very low heat until they pulp. Bring to the boil and boil rapidly, stirring frequently, until the pulp thickens.

2 Press through a nylon sieve and return to the pan. Add the remaining ingredients. Simmer until the mixture thickens. Pour the hot ketchup into warm bottles, seal and sterilise.

Mushroom Ketchup
~

MAKES ABOUT 900 ML (1½ PINTS)

1.4 kg (3 lb) mushrooms, washed and roughly broken
75 g (3 oz) salt
5 ml (1 tsp) peppercorns
5 ml (1 tsp) whole allspice berries
2.5 ml (½ tsp) ground mace
2.5 ml (½ tsp) ground ginger
1.25 ml (¼ tsp) ground cloves
600 ml (1 pint) distilled vinegar

~

*P*ut the mushrooms in a bowl and sprinkle with the salt. Cover and leave overnight.

2 Rinse away the excess salt, drain the mushrooms and mash with a wooden spoon. Put in a saucepan with the spices and vinegar, then cover and simmer for about 30 minutes or until the excess vinegar is absorbed.

3 Press through a nylon sieve, then pour the ketchup into warm bottles, seal and sterilise.

Yorkshire Ketchup
~

MAKES ABOUT 1.7 LITRES (3 PINTS)

25 g (1 oz) black peppercorns
7 g (¼ oz) cayenne pods or dried chilli
15 g (½ oz) whole cloves
100 g (4 oz) salt
225 g (8 oz) sugar
30 ml (2 tbsp) gravy browning
1.1 litres (2 pints) vinegar

~

*P*ut all the ingredients in a saucepan with 600 ml (1 pint) water, bring to the boil and simmer for 5–10 minutes. Leave to cool.

2 Press the ketchup mixture through a nylon sieve, then pour into warm bottles, seal and sterilise.

Fruit Vinegars
~

raspberries, blackberries or blackcurrants
red or white wine vinegar
sugar

~

*P*ut the fruit in a bowl and break it up slightly with the back of a wooden spoon. For each 450 g (1 lb) fruit, pour in 600 ml (1 pint) red or white wine vinegar. Cover with a cloth and leave to stand for 3–4 days, stirring occasionally.

2 Strain through muslin, measure the vinegar and add 450 g (1 lb) sugar for each 600 ml (1 pint). Boil for 10 minutes, then cool.

3 Strain again, pour into bottles and seal with airtight and vinegar-proof tops. Add a few whole pieces of fruit to each bottle.

Above (left to right): Herb and Garlic Oil (page 127),
Tomato Ketchup (opposite), Yorkshire Ketchup
(opposite), Mushroom Ketchup (opposite)

Herb and Garlic Vinegar
~

MAKES ABOUT 1 LITRE (1³/₄ PINTS)

1 litre (1³/₄ pints) white wine vinegar
fresh parsley or rosemary
garlic cloves
~

Pour the vinegar into a saucepan and add a few sprigs of parsley or rosemary. Bring slowly to the boil, then boil rapidly for 1 minute. Remove from the heat, cover and leave to infuse overnight.

2 The next day, carefully skin a few cloves of garlic. Place in warm sterilised jars.

3 Strain the vinegar into a jug and pour into the jars. Add a fresh sprig of parsley or rosemary to each jar. Cover with a vinegar-proof lid.

4 Store in a cool, dark place for at least 2 weeks.

Horseradish Vinegar
~

MAKES ABOUT 600 ML (1 PINT)

40 g (1¹/₂ oz) grated fresh horseradish
600 ml (1 pint) wine vinegar
~

Place the horseradish in a warmed jar. Bring the vinegar to the boil and pour it on to the horseradish.

2 Allow to cool and cover with a non-corrosive seal. Leave in a cool place for 1 week.

3 Taste the vinegar and, if the flavour is strong enough, strain the vinegar and bottle. If you prefer a stronger flavour, leave the vinegar for a few more days, then bottle and seal.

Spiced Summer Fruit Vinegar
~

MAKES ABOUT 1.1 LITRES (2 PINTS)

700 g (1¹/₂ lb) frozen mixed summer fruits
1 litre (1³/₄ pints) red wine vinegar
30 ml (2 tbsp) pickling spice
30 ml (2 tbsp) chopped fresh thyme or 10 ml (2 tsp) dried
~

Put the frozen fruit in a medium glass bowl and break down roughly with a wooden spoon. Bring the vinegar to the boil with the spice and pour over the fruit. Add the thyme.

2 Cover and leave to infuse for 2 days, stirring occasionally. Strain into a jug, then pour into preheated, sterilised jars. Add a few pieces of fruit and spices to each jar and cover with vinegar-proof lids. Store in a cool, dark place for at least 2 weeks before using.

Sweet Spiced Vinegar
~

MAKES ABOUT 1.7 LITRES (3 PINTS)

1.7 litres (3 pints) vinegar
450 g (1 lb) sugar
7.5 ml (1¹/₂ tsp) salt
5 ml (1 tsp) whole mixed spice
5 ml (1 tsp) peppercorns
2.5 ml (¹/₂ tsp) whole cloves
~

Put the vinegar, sugar, salt and spices in a saucepan, bring to the boil and pour into a bowl. Cover with a plate to preserve the flavour and leave to marinate for 2 hours.

2 Strain the vinegar through muslin, pour into bottles and seal with airtight and vinegar-proof tops.

Rosemary and Lime Vinegar

~

MAKES ABOUT 1 LITRE (1³/₄ PINTS)

1 litre (1³/₄ pints) white wine vinegar
large sprigs of fresh rosemary
2–3 garlic cloves
1 lime

~

Place the vinegar in a saucepan with a few sprigs of rosemary. Bring slowly to the boil, then boil rapidly for 1 minute. Remove from the heat, cover and leave to infuse overnight.

2 Carefully skin a few cloves of garlic. Place in warm, sterilised jars. Strain the vinegar into a jug and pour into the jars. Add a fresh sprig of rosemary and thin slices of lime to each jar. Seal with a vinegar-proof lid. Store in a cool, dry place for at least 2 weeks before using, then for up to 6 months.

Spiced Vinegar

~

MAKES ABOUT 1.1 LITRES (2 PINTS)

1.1 litres (2 pints) vinegar
30 ml (2 tbsp) blades of mace
15 ml (1 tbsp) whole allspice berries
15 ml (1 tbsp) whole cloves
18 cm (7 inches) cinnamon stick
6 peppercorns
4 dried red chillies
1 small bay leaf

~

Put the vinegar, spices and bay leaf in a saucepan, bring to the boil and pour into a bowl or bottles. Cover and leave to marinate for 2 hours.

2 Strain the vinegar through muslin, pour into sterilised bottles and seal with airtight and vinegar-proof tops.

Herb and Garlic Oil

~

MAKES ABOUT 1.1 LITRES (2 PINTS)

2 sprigs of fresh rosemary or 10 ml (2 tsp) dried
2 sprigs of fresh tarragon or mint
2 bay leaves
2 garlic cloves, skinned
6 black peppercorns
3 juniper berries
about 1 litre (1³/₄ pints) olive oil
150 ml (¹/₄ pint) walnut oil

~

Place all the ingredients in a glass jar or bottle with a tight-fitting lid. Seal and then shake well to mix.

2 Leave in a cool, dry place for 2 weeks before using. Store for up to 3 months.

VARIATION
Herb and Saffron Oil

Add 2.5 ml (¹/₂ tsp) saffron strands (ground) to the Herb and Garlic Oil.

Overleaf (left to right): Spiced Vinegar (above), Fruit Vinegars (page 125), Rosemary and Lime Vinegar (above)

Bottling and Fruits in Alcohol

Bottling is a process of preserving by sterilisation, which kills yeasts and moulds already present on the food and prevents others spreading into the bottling jars. This is done by heating the jars of fruit in the oven, in a water bath or in a pressure cooker and then sealing the jars while hot.

It is not possible to use bottling as a method of preserving meat, fish, poultry or vegetables in the home. In order to kill the bacteria which can lead to food poisoning, the food must be preserved in acid conditions – which is why most fruits can be bottled successfully – or heated to extremely high temperatures. Heat processing carried out at home, even when using a pressure cooker, is inadequate and cannot ensure that bottled vegetables are free from bacteria. Extra acid needs to be added when bottling tomatoes but almost any type of fruit can be bottled, providing the general rules for preparing and processing are followed. As with any other preserving process, the fruit must be fresh, sound, clean and properly ripe – neither too soft, nor too hard. Choose fruits of a similar shape, size and ripeness for any one bottle. Fruit should be prepared according to the chart on pages 138 and 139.

Bottling Jars

These are wide-necked jars with glass caps or metal discs, secured by screw-bands or clips. If the cap or disc has no integral rubber gasket, a thin rubber ring is inserted between it and the top of the bottle. Neither the rubber rings nor the metal discs with fitted seals should be used more than once. Jars can be obtained in different sizes ranging from 450 g (1 lb) upwards.

Before use, check all jars and fittings for any flaw and test to make sure they will be airtight. To do this, fill the jars with water, put the fittings in place, then turn them upside-down. Any leak will show in 10 minutes.

Jars must be absolutely clean, so wash them well and rinse in clean hot water. There is no need to dry them – the fruit slips into place more easily if the jar is wet.

Syrup for Bottling

Fruit may be preserved in either syrup or water, but syrup imparts a much better flavour and colour (see following recipe).

Sugar Syrup
~

225 g (8 oz) sugar

Dissolve the sugar in 300 ml (½ pint) water. Bring to the boil for 1 minute, then add a further 300 ml (½ pint) water. (This method cuts the time required for the syrup to cool.) If the syrup is to be used while still boiling, keep a lid on the pan to prevent evaporation, which would alter the strength.

2 Lemon and orange rind, liqueurs or whole spices can be added to the syrup if liked.

3 Golden syrup may be substituted for sugar. In this case, put the syrup and water into a pan, bring to the boil and simmer for 5 minutes before use. The flavour will, of course, be different.

Packing the Fruit

Put the fruit in the jars layer by layer, using a packing spoon or the handle of a wooden spoon to push down the fruit. When a jar is full, the fruit should be firmly and securely wedged in place, without bruising or squashing. The more closely the fruit is packed, the less likely it is to rise after the shrinkage which may occur during processing.

Normal pack Most fruit should be packed as above and the jars then filled up with syrup or water before or after processing.

Tight pack Fruit such as gooseberries and chopped

Use the handle of a wooden spoon to push the fruit down in the jars.

For the oven method, process jars on newspaper on a baking sheet in the centre of the oven.

For the water bath method, process jars covered with cold water in a large pan.

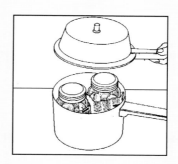

For the pressure cooker method, process jars in hot water in a pressure cooker.

rhubarb may be packed much more tightly, leaving space for only a very little syrup or water to be added. Fruit packed in this way is best used as a dessert without further cooking. If packed in the normal way, use gooseberries and rhubarb in pies or other dishes which require further cooking.

Solid pack Apple slices and tomato halves may be packed so tightly into jars that they need no syrup or water added either before or after processing.

Processing

Bottles can be sterilised in the oven, in a water bath or in the pressure cooker. The method you choose will depend on the equipment you have and the time available.

Oven method

The advantages of the oven method are that jars can be processed at one time and no special equipment is needed. It is, however, not quite as exact as the water bath method, as it is not easy to maintain a constant temperature throughout the oven and it is easier to over-cook the fruit. If you use this method, use only one shelf of the oven, placed just below the centre. Don't crowd too many jars in the oven or the heat will not penetrate evenly.

Wet pack oven method Heat the oven to 150°C (300°F) mark 2. Fill the packed jars with boiling syrup or water to within 2.5 cm (1 inch) of the top. Dispel all air bubbles by knocking each jar on the palm of your hand. Alternatively, pack the fruit and add the liquid alternately until the jar is full. Put on the rubber rings and glass caps or metal discs but not screw-bands or clips. Place the jars 5 cm (2 inches) apart on a solid baking sheet lined with newspaper to catch any liquid which may boil over. Put in the centre of the oven and process for the time stated in the table opposite. Remove jars one by one, placing them on a wooden surface, and put on clips or screw-bands, screwing the bands as tightly as possible. Hot jars should always be placed on a wooden surface after processing as a colder surface could cause them to crack. Allow to become quite cold before testing for a good seal (see page 136).

Dry pack oven method   Heat the oven to 130°C (250°F) mark ½. Pack the bottling jars with fruit but do not add any liquid. Put on the caps but not rubber rings, discs with rings, screw-bands or clips. Place the jars 5 cm (2 inches) apart on a solid baking sheet lined with newspaper. Put in the centre of the oven and process for the time stated in the table opposite. Remove jars one at a time, placing them on a wooden surface. Use the contents of one jar to top up the others if the fruit has shrunk during cooking. Fill up at once with boiling syrup.

When the jars have been filled with syrup, give each one a quick, vigorous twist to remove as many air bubbles as possible. Remember to use a cloth as the jars will be very hot. Fill the jars to the brim before putting on the fittings. Place the rubber bands (dipped first in boiling water), caps or metal discs in position and secure with clips or screw the bands on tightly. Leave to cool.

The dry pack oven method is not recommended for fruits which discolour in the air, such as apples, pears and peaches. From the chart, it will be seen that with both oven methods the time required varies not only with the type of fruit, but also with the tightness of the pack and the total load in the oven at any one time; the load is calculated accord-ing to the total capacity of the jars. Fruits such as strawberries and raspberries can be rolled in caster sugar before packing dry; the flavour will be delicious but the appearance less attractive than if the fruits were packed plain.

Water bath method

The water bath method is a more exact method of sterilisation, but needs special equipment – a large vessel about 5 cm (2 inches) deeper than the height of the bottling jars, a thermometer and bottling tongs. The vessel can be a very large saucepan, a zinc bath or a zinc bucket; it must have a false bottom such as a metal grid, strips of wood nailed together trellis-fashion, or even a folded coarse cloth. A sugar-boiling thermometer will be satisfactory. Bottling tongs are not essential, but they make it easier to remove the jars from the water bath.

Slow water bath   Pack the jars with fruit, then fill up with cold syrup. Put the rubber bands and glass caps or metal discs and screw-bands or clips in place, then turn the screw-bands back a quarter-turn. Place the jars in the large vessel and cover with cold water, immersing them completely if possible, but at least up to the necks. Heat gently on top of the cooker, checking the temperature of the water regularly. Raise the temperature to 54°C (130°F) in 1 hour, then to the processing temperature given in the chart on page 134 within a further 30 minutes. Maintain the temperature for the length of time given in the chart.

Remove the jars with the tongs (or bale out enough water to remove them with the aid of an oven cloth). Place the jars one at a time on a wooden surface, and tighten the screw-bands immediately. When cool, test for a seal (see page 136).

Quick water bath   If you have no thermometer, this is a good alternative method. Fill the packed jars with hot (not boiling) syrup, cover and place in the vessel of warm water. Bring the water to simmering point in 25–30 minutes, and keep simmering for the time stated in the table.

Times for Oven Method

These are the temperatures and processing times recommended by the AFRC Institute of Food Research.

Type of fruit	Wet pack		Dry pack	
	Preheat oven to 150°C (300°F) mark 1. Process time varies with quantity in oven, as below.		Preheat oven to 130°C (250°F) mark ½. Process time varies with quantity in oven, as below.	
	Quantity	Time	Quantity	Time
Soft fruit, normal pack: blackberries, currants, loganberries, mulberries, raspberries:	450 g–1.8 kg (1–4 lb) 2–4.5 kg (4½–10 lb)	30–40 minutes 45–60 minutes	450 g–1.8 kg (1–4 lb) 2–4.5 kg (4½–10 lb)	45–55 minutes 60–75 minutes
gooseberries and rhubarb (for made-up dishes)	As above	As above	As above	As above
apples, sliced	450 g–1.8 kg (1–4 lb) 2–4.5 kg (4½–10 lb)	30–40 minutes 45–60 minutes	Not recommended	
Soft fruit, tight pack: As above, including gooseberries and rhubarb (for stewed fruit)	450 g–1.8 kg (1–4 lb) 2–4.5 kg (4½–10 lb)	40–50 minutes 55–70 minutes	450 g–1.8 kg (1–4 lb) 2–4.5 kg (4½–10 lb)	55–70 minutes 75–90 minutes
Stone fruit, dark, whole: cherries, damsons, plums	As soft fruit (tight pack)		As soft fruit (tight pack)	
Stone fruit, light, whole: apricots, cherries, gages, plums	As above		Not recommended	
Apples, solid pack; Apricots, halved; Nectarines; Peaches; Pineapples; Plums, halved	450 g–1.8 kg (1–4 lb) 2–4.5 kg (4½–10 lb)	50–60 minutes 65–80 minutes	Not recommended	
Figs	450 g–1.8 kg (1–4 lb) 2–4.5 kg (4½–10 lb)	60–70 minutes 75–90 minutes	450 g–1.8 kg (1–4 lb) 2–4.5 kg (4½–10 lb)	80–100 minutes 105–125 minutes
Pears	As Figs		Not recommended	

Times for water bath method

These are the temperatures and processing methods recommended by the AFRC Institute of Food Research.

TYPE OF FRUIT	SLOW METHOD	QUICK METHOD
	Raise from cold in 90 minutes and maintain as below	Raise from warm 38°C (100°F) to simmering 88°C (190°F) in 25–30 minutes and maintain as below
Soft fruit, normal pack: blackberries, currants, loganberries, mulberries, raspberries; Gooseberries and rhubarb (for made-up dishes); Apples, sliced	74°C (165°F) for 10 minutes	2 minutes
Soft fruit, tight pack: As above, including gooseberries and rhubarb (for stewed fruit) Stone fruit, whole: apricots, cherries, damsons, gages, plums	82°C (180°F) for 15 minutes	10 minutes
Apples, solid pack Apricots, halved; Nectarines; Peaches; Pineapple; Plums, halved	82°C (180°F) for 15 minutes	20 minutes
Figs Pears	88°C (190°F) for 30 minutes	40 minutes

Times for pressure cooker method

Prepare the fruit as for ordinary bottling, unless otherwise stated. Bring to pressure and process as below.

FRUIT	PROCESSING TIME IN MINUTES AT LOW (5 LB) PRESSURE
Apples (quartered)	1
Apricots or plums (whole)	1
Blackberries	1
Loganberries	1
Raspberries	1
Cherries	1
Currants (red and black)	1
Damsons	1
Gooseberries	1
Pears, eating	5
Pears, cooking (very hard ones can be pressure-cooked for 3–5 minutes before packing in jars)	5
Plums or apricots (stoned and halved)	3–4
Rhubarb (in 5-cm/2-inch lengths)	1
Strawberries	Not recommended
Soft fruit, solid pack: put the fruit in a large bowl, cover with boiling syrup – 175 g (6 oz) sugar to 600 ml (1 pint) water – and leave overnight. Drain, pack in jars and cover with same syrup. Process as usual.	3
Puréed fruit, eg. apples: prepare as for stewing. Pressure cook with 150 ml (¼ pint) water at high (15 lb) pressure for 2–3 minutes, then purée and sieve. While still hot, fill jars and process.	1

Times for Sterilising Bottled Tomatoes

Oven method		
	Wet pack Preheat oven to 150°C (300°F) mark 1, process as below	*Dry pack* Preheat oven to 130°C (250°F) mark ½, process as below
Whole tomatoes (unskinned)	450 g–1.8 kg (1–4 lb) for 60–70 minutes 2–4.5 kg (4½–10 lb) for 75–90 minutes	450 g–1.8 kg (1–4 lb) for 80–100 minutes 2–4.5 kg (4½–10 lb) for 105–125 minutes
Solid pack tomatoes (halved or quartered)	450 g–1.8 kg (1–4 lb) for 70–80 minutes 2–4.5 kg (4½–10 lb) for 85–100 minutes	Not recommended

Water bath method		
	Slow method Raise from cold in 90 minutes and maintain as below	*Quick method* Raise from warm (38°C/100°F) to simmering (88°C/190°F) in 25–30 minutes and maintain as below
Whole tomatoes (skinned)	88°C (190°F) for 30 minutes	40 minutes
Solid pack tomatoes (halved or quartered)	88°C (190°F) for 40 minutes	50 minutes

Pressure cooker method	
Whole or halved tomatoes in brine (prepare as for ordinary bottling)	Process for 5 minutes at low (5 lb) pressure
Solid pack	Process for 15 minutes at low (5 lb) pressure

Puréed Fruit

Soft and stone fruits can be bottled as purée. Prepare as for stewing, then add only the minimum of water and stew until just cooked. If desired, the fruit can be puréed and sieved at this point. While still boiling, pour into hot jars and place the rubber bands and glass caps or metal discs and screw-bands in position.

Immerse the jars in a deep pan and add hot water up to the necks. Raise the temperature to boiling point and maintain for 5 minutes. Remove the jars and allow to cool.

Pressure Cooker Method

This method shortens the time and also ensures that the temperature is controlled exactly. The cooker must have a low (5 lb) pressure control. Any pressure cooker will take the 450-g (1-lb) bottling jars, but you will need a cooker with a domed lid when using larger bottling jars.

Prepare the fruit as for ordinary bottling, but look at the additional notes in the opposite chart. Pack the fruit into clean, warm jars, filling them right to the top. Cover with boiling syrup or water to within 2.5 cm (1 inch) of the top of the jars. Put on the rubber bands, glass caps or metal discs, clips or screw-bands, screwing these tight, then turning them back a quarter-turn. Next, as an extra precaution, heat the jars by standing them in a bowl of boiling water.

Put the inverted trivet into the pressure cooker and add 900 ml (1½ pints) water, plus 15 ml (1 tbsp) vinegar to prevent the pan from becoming stained. Bring the water to the boil. Pack the bottles into the cooker, making sure they do not touch by packing newspaper between. Fix the lid in place, put the pan on the heat without weight and heat until steam comes steadily from the vent. Put on the low (5 lb) pressure control and bring to pressure on a medium heat. Reduce the heat and maintain the pressure for the time given in the chart on page 134. Any change in pressure will cause liquid to be lost from the jars and under-processing may result.

Remove the pan carefully from the heat and reduce the pressure at room temperature for about 10 minutes before taking off the lid. Lift out the jars one by one, placing them on a wooden surface, and tighten the screw-bands. When cool, test for a seal (see below).

Testing for a Good Seal

After processing, allow the jars to cool, then test for correct sealing by removing the screw-band or clip and trying to lift the jar by the cap or disc. If this holds firm, it shows that a vacuum has been formed as the jar cooled and it is 'hermetically' sealed. If the cap or disc comes off, there is probably a flaw in the rim of the jar or on the cap. If, however, several bottles are unsealed, the processing procedure may have been faulty. Use the fruit from the jars at once; it can be re-processed but with loss of quality.

Storing

Store bottled fruits without clips or screw-bands as this can stretch them. If you do leave screw-bands on, smear each one with a little oil and screw on loosely. This helps to prevent rust and makes for ease of opening later. Label the bottles and store in a cool, dark place.

Bottling Tomatoes

Whole unskinned tomatoes (recommended for oven-method sterilising). The fruit must be small or medium and even in size, ripe yet firm. Remove the stalks and wash or wipe the tomatoes. Pack into jars and fill up with a brine solution made with 15 g (½ oz) salt per 1.1 litres (2 pints) water. Add 1.25 ml (¼ tsp) citric acid or 10 ml (2 tsp) lemon juice to each 450-g (1-lb) jar. Process as in the charts on page 135.

Solid pack, with no liquid added Any size of fruit may be used, but they must be firm. Skin the tomatoes. Small tomatoes may be left whole but larger ones should be cut in halves or quarters, so that they may be packed really tightly with no air spaces, making it unnecessary to add water. The flavour is improved if about 5 ml (1 tsp) salt and 2.5 ml (½ tsp) sugar are added with the fruit in each 450-g (1-lb) jar. Add 1.25 ml (¼ tsp) citric acid or 10 ml (2 tsp) lemon juice to each 450-g (1-lb) jar. Process as in the charts on page 135.

Bottling Tomato Purée

This method enables poorly shaped tomatoes to be used, though they must be sound and ripe. Wash, place in a covered pan with a little water and salt and cook until soft. Press the pulp through a nylon sieve and return it to the pan, then bring to the boil. Pour it at once into hot jars and put the rubber bands and glass caps or metal discs and screw-bands or clips in place. (It is very important that this process should be carried out quickly, as the pulp deteriorates if left exposed to the air.) Immerse the bottles in a pan of hot water (padded at the base and between the bottles with thick cloth or newspaper), bring to the boil and boil for 10 minutes. Finish and test for a seal as usual.

Opposite: Bottled fruits

Preparing Fruit for Bottling	
Fruit	**Preparation**
Apples	*Normal pack* Peel, core and cut into thick slices or rings; during preparation put into a brine solution made with 10 ml (2 tsp) salt to 1.1 litres (2 pints) water. Rinse quickly in cold water before packing into jars. *Solid pack* Prepare slices as above, remove from brine and dip in small quantities in boiling water for 1½–3 minutes, until the fruit is just tender and pliable. Pack as tightly as possible into the jars.
Apricots	*Whole* Remove stalks and wash fruit. *Halves* Make a cut round each fruit up to the stone, twist the two halves apart and remove the stone. Crack some stones to obtain the kernels and include with the fruit. Pack quickly, to prevent browning.
Blackberries	Pick over, removing damaged fruits, and wash carefully.
Blackberries with apples	Prepare apples as for solid pack (see above) before mixing with the blackberries.
Blackcurrants and Redcurrants	String, pick over and wash.
Cherries	*Whole* Remove stalks and wash fruit. *Stoned* Use a cherry stoner or small knife to remove stones. Collect any juice and include with the fruit. If liked, add 7 g (¼ oz) citric acid to each 4.5 litres (8 pints) syrup to improve the colour and flavour.
Damsons	Remove stems and wash fruit.
Figs	Remove stems and peel, if liked. Add 2.5 ml (½ tsp) citric acid to each 600 ml (1 pint) syrup. Pack with an equal amount of syrup.
Gooseberries	Small green fruit are used for pies and made-up dishes; larger, softer ones are served as stewed fruit. Top, tail and wash. To prevent shrivelling if fruit is preserved in syrup, the skins can be pricked.
Mulberries	Pick over, handling fruit carefully. Try to avoid washing it.
Peaches	Immerse the fruit in a saucepan of boiling water for 30 seconds, then rinse in cold water and peel off the skin. Peaches can be bottled whole but are more usually cut in half (as for Apricots). Bottle quickly before fruit discolours.
Pears (dessert)	Peel, halve and remove cores with a teaspoon. During preparation, keep in a solution of 15 g (½ oz) salt and 7 g (¼ oz) citric acid per 1.1 litres (2 pints) water. Rinse quickly in cold water before packing. Add 1.25 ml (¼ tsp) citric acid or 10 ml (2 tsp) lemon juice to each 450-g (1-lb) jar.

Pears (cooking)	As these are very hard, prepare as for dessert pears, but, before packing, stew gently in a sugar syrup – 100–175 g (4–6 oz) sugar to 600 ml (1 pint) water – until just soft. Add 1.25 ml ($\frac{1}{4}$ tsp) citric acid or 10 ml (2 tsp) lemon juice to each 450-g (1-lb) jar.
Pineapple	Peel, trim off leaves, and remove central core and as many 'eyes' as possible. Cut into rings or chunks.
Plums and Greengages	*Whole* Remove stalks and wash fruit. *Halves* Make a cut round the middle of each fruit to the stone, twist the halves and remove the stone. Crack some stones to obtain the kernels and include with the fruit.
Quinces	Prepare as for pears. Always pack into small jars, as they are usually used in small quantities only, eg. as flavouring in apple dishes.
Raspberries/Loganberries	Remove the hulls and pick over the fruit. Avoid washing if possible.
Rhubarb	The thicker sticks are generally used for made-up dishes; the more delicate, forced rhubarb is used as stewed fruit. Cut rhubarb into 5-cm (2-inch) lengths. To make it pack more economically and taste sweeter when bottled, it may be soaked first; pour hot syrup over and leave overnight. Pack rhubarb in jars and use the syrup to top up the jars.
Strawberries	These do not bottle well.

Bottling Tomato Juice

Simmer tomatoes until soft and press through a nylon sieve. To each 1.1 litres (2 pints) pulp, add 300 ml ($\frac{1}{2}$ pint) water, 5 ml (1 tsp) salt, 30 ml (2 tbsp) sugar, 30 ml (2 tbsp) lemon juice and a pinch of pepper. Process as for tomato purée.

Bottling Problems

When the seal fails   Check jars and sealing discs for chips, cracks or other flaws. (You must use a new sealing disc every time.) The instructions for each method of sterilising must be followed exactly.

When fruit rises in the jar   This does not affect the keeping qualities, but it does spoil the appearance. It is due to over-processing, too high a temperature during processing, loose packing or over-ripe fruit.

When mould appears or fermentation takes place   These are caused by poor-quality fruit, insufficient sterilising or badly sealed bottles.

When fruit darkens   This is due to fruit not being fully covered by liquid or to under-processing. If the contents are darkened throughout, this is probably due to using produce in poor condition, to over-processing or failure to store in a cool, dark place.

Fruits in Alcohol

This is a method of preserving fruit with the minimum of cooking. Although fruits in alcohol do not have the keeping qualities of jams and jellies made by the traditional method, they retain a flavour much closer to the original taste of the fruit.

Brandied Cherries
~

MAKES ABOUT 450 G (1 LB)

450 g (1 lb) fresh cherries, washed
225 g (8 oz) sugar
1 cinnamon stick
about 150 ml ('/4 pint) brandy

~

Prick the cherries all over with a darning needle. Make a light syrup by dissolving 100 g (4 oz) of the sugar in 300 ml ('/2 pint) water. Add the cherries and cinnamon stick and poach gently for 4–5 minutes.

2 Remove the pan from the heat and drain the cherries, reserving the syrup but removing the cinnamon stick. Cool, then arrange the fruit in small jars.

3 Add the remaining sugar to the reserved syrup and dissolve it slowly. Bring to the boil and boil to 110°C (230°F), then allow to cool.

4 Measure the syrup and add an equal quantity of brandy. Pour over the cherries. Cover as for pickles (see page 78).

Brandied Peaches
~

MAKES ABOUT 450 G (1 LB)

450 g (1 lb) fresh peaches or one 822-g (1 lb 13-oz) can peach halves
225 g (8 oz) sugar (if using fresh peaches)
about 150 ml (¼ pint) brandy or orange flavoured liqueur
~

*I*f using fresh peaches, skin the peaches by plunging them into boiling water, then gently peeling off the skins. Halve the peaches and remove the stones.

2 Make a light syrup by dissolving 100 g (4 oz) of the sugar in 300 ml (½ pint) water. Add the peaches and poach gently for 4–5 minutes.

3 Remove the pan from the heat, drain the peaches, reserving the syrup, and leave to cool. Arrange the fruit in small jars.

4 Add the remaining sugar to the reserved syrup and dissolve it slowly. Bring to the boil and boil to 110°C (230°F), then allow to cool.

5 Measure the syrup and add an equal quantity of brandy or liqueur. Pour over the peaches. Cover as for pickles (see page 78). Leave for 2–3 months before eating.

6 If using canned peaches, drain the syrup from the peaches and put in a saucepan (this size of can yields about 450 ml/¾ pint syrup). Reduce the syrup to half the quantity by boiling gently, remove from the heat and leave to cool.

7 Prick the peaches with a fine skewer or darning needle and place in small jars. Add brandy or liqueur to the syrup and pour over the fruit. Cover as for pickles (see page 78).

Brandied Pineapple
~

MAKES ABOUT 450 G (1 LB)

1 small fresh pineapple or one 822-g (1 lb 13-oz) can pineapple pieces
225 g (8 oz) sugar (if using fresh pineapple)
3 whole cloves
5-cm (2-inch) cinnamon stick
150 ml (¼ pint) brandy or kirsch
~

*I*f using fresh pineapple, peel and trim off the leaves. Remove the central core and as many 'eyes' as possible and cut the fruit into chunks.

2 Make a light syrup by dissolving 100 g (4 oz) of the sugar in 300 ml (½ pint) water. Add the cloves, cinnamon and pineapple and poach gently for 10 minutes.

3 Remove the pan from the heat and drain the pineapple, reserving the syrup but removing the cinnamon and cloves. Leave to cool, then arrange the fruit in a wide-necked bottle.

4 Add the remaining sugar to the reserved syrup and dissolve it slowly. Bring to the boil and boil to 110°C (230°F), then allow to cool.

5 Measure the syrup and add an equal quantity of brandy or kirsch. Pour over the fruit. Cover as for pickles (see page 78).

6 If using canned pineapple, drain the juice from the pineapple and put it in a saucepan. Add the cloves and cinnamon and simmer gently until of a syrupy consistency. Add the pineapple pieces and simmer for a further 10 minutes.

7 Remove the pan from the heat and add the brandy or kirsch. Cool, then bottle the fruit. Pour over the syrup and cover as for pickles (see page 78).

Peaches in Strawberry Caramel
~

MAKES ABOUT 900 G (2 LB)

450 g (1 lb) sugar
275 g (10 oz) ripe strawberries, hulled and roughly chopped
100 ml (4 fl oz) brandy
1.4 kg (3 lb) ripe but firm peaches
~

Put the sugar in a wide, heavy-based saucepan with 150 ml (¼ pint) water. Heat gently until all the sugar has dissolved, then bring to the boil and bubble until it has turned pale caramel. Do not stir.

2 Remove the pan from the heat and carefully add 450 ml (¾ pint) warm water (the mixture will splutter at this stage). Bring to the boil and boil for 2–3 minutes, stirring, until the caramel has completely dissolved. Add the strawberries and simmer for a further 3 minutes. Leave to cool for 3–4 minutes.

3 Purée the strawberry and caramel mixture in a blender or food processor, then press through a fine sieve or leave to drain through muslin. The caramel should be a clear and pinky-brown colour. Stir in the brandy and leave to cool completely.

4 Meanwhile, carefully peel the peaches, then, with a large, heavy chopping knife, carefully split the peaches in half right through the kernels. Place in jars, packing the fruit tightly to within 1 cm (½ inch) of the top.

5 Pour in the strawberry caramel to cover the fruit completely. Cover and seal the jars with airtight lids and store in a cold place, preferably the refrigerator. Store for 2–3 days before opening, then use within 2 weeks.

Apricots and Prunes in Brandy
~

MAKES ABOUT 700 G (1½ LB)

225 g (8 oz) dried apricots
225 g (8 oz) stoned prunes
225 g (8 oz) sugar
10 cloves
50 ml (2 fl oz) brandy
~

Place the apricots and prunes in separate bowls, cover with plenty of cold water, then leave to soak overnight.

2 Drain the apricots, reserving 300 ml (½ pint) soaking water. Drain the prunes and discard the water.

3 Place the reserved water in a saucepan with the sugar and cloves. Heat gently, stirring occasionally, until the sugar dissolves, then bring to the boil and boil rapidly until the syrup has reduced to about 300 ml (½ pint). Pour in the brandy.

4 Meanwhile, layer the apricots and prunes in jars. Pour over the syrup and seal the jars well. Store for about 3 weeks before opening.

Orange Slices in Cointreau
~

MAKES ABOUT 900 G (2 LB)

350 g (12 oz) sugar
6 firm oranges
1 small cinnamon stick
5 ml (1 tsp) cloves
150 ml (¼ pint) Cointreau

~

*P*ut the sugar and 450 ml (¾ pint) water in a saucepan. Heat gently, stirring, until the sugar has dissolved, then bring to the boil. Boil for 1 minute, then add a further 450 ml (¾ pint) water.

2 Scrub the orange skins clean. Cut the oranges into 0.5 cm (¼ inch) thick slices.

3 Add the oranges and spices to the sugar syrup and poach gently for about 45 minutes or until tender. Remove from the heat and drain, reserving the syrup but removing the cinnamon stick. Leave to cool for about 30 minutes.

4 Pack the fruit in jars, adding a few of the cloves. Add the liqueur to the reserved syrup and pour over the orange slices. Cover at once with airtight tops, label and leave to mature for at least 1 month before opening.

Rumtopf
~

MAKES ABOUT 450 G (1 LB)

450 g (1 lb) prepared fruit (see Note)
225 g (8 oz) caster sugar
rum, brandy or kirsch

~

*T*horoughly clean a large, deep, glazed stone or pottery jar with a wide neck and tightly fitting lid (not metal) and a saucer that will fit inside it.

2 Carefully wash the fruit and dry on absorbent kitchen paper. Berry fruits should be hulled; currants, goose-berries and grapes stalked. Skin large-stoned fruits, if preferred, then halve them and remove the stones. Remove the tough flesh and outer skin of fruits like pineapples; dip banana slices in lemon juice; peel, core and slice pears; scrub the skin of oranges and slice into rings.

3 Spread a layer of any fruit on a plate; sprinkle with the sugar and turn gently so that every part of the fruit is covered. Leave for about 1 hour.

4 Transfer the fruit and sugar to the jar and spread evenly. Completely cover with alcohol.

5 Place the saucer on top to keep the fruit submerged, then cover the jar tightly with cling film and cover with the lid. Store this batch in a cool, dry place until ready to add the next layer, but for no longer than 1 year. Check for fermentation or mould growth before adding next batch.

6 When the time comes to add more fruit repeat the process, replacing a clean saucer each time and resealing the jar as before. Stir the contents or, alternatively, leave in the original layers.

7 When the last batch of fruit has been added, top up with more alcohol, cover and label. Store for at least 1 month. Check the level of the liquid occasionally and add more if necessary.

Note A *Rumtopf* is a delicious way of preserving fresh fruit with sugar and alcohol, by layering two or more different types over a period of time, as they come into season. Rum is used in the original German recipe, but brandy or a liqueur such as kirsch are equally suitable. Choose ripe, unblemished fruit for best results. Most fruits are suitable, except rhubarb, which tends to give a bitter taste, and apples, which may ferment. Soft fruits such as raspberries, loganberries and currants are delicious, but they will disintegrate with time. Very watery fruits like melons should be kept to a minimum as they dilute the alcohol, which may result in mould growth or fermentation.

Soft Fruits in Wine
~

MAKES ABOUT 900 G (2 LB)

900 g (2 lb) mixed soft red fruits, eg. strawberries, redcurrants,
raspberries
225 g (8 oz) caster sugar
1/2 bottle red wine
6 whole green cardamom pods, crushed

~

Hull the strawberries, then halve and slice any large ones. Remove the redcurrants from their stalks. Wash and dry the fruit.

2 Place the sugar, wine and cardamom pods in a small saucepan. Heat gently, stirring occasionally, until the sugar has dissolved. Strain.

3 Layer the fruit in a large, wide-necked jar. When the fruit reaches the neck of the jar, fill it up with the red wine mixture. Cover tightly with cling film or a screw-top lid. Store in the refrigerator for 2–3 days before using. Use within 2 weeks.

Above: Soft Fruits in Wine Opposite:
Chestnuts in Syrup (page 146)

Chestnuts in Syrup
~

MAKES ABOUT 350 G (12 OZ)

225 g (8 oz) sugar
225 g (8 oz) glucose or dextrose
350 g (12 oz) whole chestnuts, peeled and skinned (prepared weight) or 350 g (12 oz) canned chestnuts, drained
vanilla pod

~

Put the sugar and glucose or dextrose in a saucepan large enough to hold the chestnuts. Add 180 ml (¼ pint plus 2 tbsp) water and heat gently until the sugars have dissolved, then bring to the boil. Remove from the heat, add the chestnuts and bring to the boil again. Remove from the heat, cover and leave overnight, preferably in a warm place.

2 The next day, re-boil the chestnuts and syrup in the pan, without the lid. Remove from the heat, cover and again leave standing overnight.

3 On the third day, add the vanilla pod and repeat the boiling process. Warm some 450-g (1-lb) bottling jars in the oven, fill with the chestnuts and cover with syrup. Cover with airtight lids and test for a seal.

Note This recipe gives a delicious result, but the chestnuts are not exactly like commercially prepared Marrons Glacés, which cannot be reproduced under home conditions.

Plum and Almond Hooch
~

small, firm but ripe plums
vanilla sugar
blanched almonds
dark or light rum

~

Wash the plums and dry thoroughly. Place them in an earthenware container, sprinkling generously with sugar and a few almonds as you push them in tightly. Cover the top with a layer of sugar.

2 Pour over enough rum to cover. Cover the jar with a tightly fitting lid and store in a cool dark place for at least 6 months, preferably a year, before eating.

Spiced Peaches with Plums and Greengages
~

MAKES ABOUT 900 G (2 LB)

450 g (1 lb) sugar
300 ml (½ pint) white wine vinegar
5 ml (1 tsp) whole allspice berries
1 small cinnamon stick
1 small piece of fresh root ginger, peeled and sliced
450 g (1 lb) peaches, halved and stoned
225 g (8 oz) plums, halved and stoned
225 g (8 oz) greengages, halved and stoned

~

Put the sugar, vinegar, allspice, cinnamon and ginger in a large pan. Heat gently, stirring, until all the sugar has dissolved.

2 Poach the peaches, plums and greengages gently in the liquid until just tender.

3 Lift the fruits out of the liquid and pack in a jar. Reduce the poaching liquid a little by boiling, then pour over the fruits to cover completely. Seal and label the jar.

4 Store for a few months before using.

Summer Fruits in Vodka
~

MAKES ABOUT 450 G (1 LB)

450 g (1 lb) prepared summer fruits (such as raspberries, redcurrants and loganberries)
175 g (6 oz) caster sugar
vodka

~

Thoroughly clean a large, deep, glazed stone or pottery jar with a wide neck and tightly fitting lid, and a saucer that will fit inside it.

2 Toss the fruit in the sugar until thoroughly coated, then leave for 2 hours.

3 Layer the fruit in the jar, then pour in enough vodka to cover completely.

4 Place the saucer on top of the fruit to keep the fruit submerged, then cover the jar tightly with cling film, then with the lid. Store in a cool, dry place.

5 Repeat the process, adding more fruit and alcohol as required. Every week or so, the mixture should be stirred to ensure that the fruits absorb the sugar and alcohol.

6 When the last batch of fruit has been added, top up with more alcohol, cover and label. Store for at least 1 month. Check the level of the liquid occasionally and add more if necessary.

Aniseed Grapes in Vodka
~

MAKES ABOUT 1 LITRE (1³/₄ PINTS)

450 g (1 lb) seedless black and green grapes
25 g (1 oz) caster sugar
2.5 ml (¹/₂ tsp) aniseed
1–2 star anise
450 ml (³/₄ pint) vodka

~

Strip the grapes from their stalks, wash and dry. Prick the grapes with a needle and pack into sterilised, wide-necked jars.

2 Put the sugar in a saucepan with 150 ml (¹/₄ pint) water and heat gently, stirring, until the sugar has dissolved. Bring to the boil and bubble for 2–3 minutes.

3 Pour over the grapes with the aniseed, star anise and vodka. Cover and seal. Refrigerate for at least a week before using. Keeps for about 3 months.

Overleaf: Aniseed Grapes in Vodka (above)

Salting, Storing, Drying, Curing and Smoking

Salting, storing, drying, curing and smoking are the original methods of preservation. Except storing, they are all types of dry preserving – for without moisture, micro-organisms cannot grow and eventually spoil foods. Storing vegetables and fruits carefully under certain conditions enables them to be kept fresh for longer periods. Salting, storing and drying processes are economical and simple to carry out at home.

Curing

Curing is the name give to a method of preserving fish or meat by salting and smoking. We do not recommend that this method of preserving be carried out at home as commercially cured foods are more convenient and safer to eat.

Smoking

Smoking is a method of preserving meat and fish by drying them in the smoke of a wood fire. The flavour of the food depends on the type of wood used, for example oak, beech and juniper, each of which gives its own special flavour. Some old houses had chimneys specially constructed for smoking and in others a special outhouse was used. Since few homes now have these chimneys, and a wide variety of good quality commercially smoked foods is now available, lengthy home smoking is no longer necessary.

A type of home smoker is now on the market for use domestically. It is particularly suitable for fish, poultry and meat. Food smoked in this way is for immediate consumption and not for preservation.

Salting

This method of preserving fish and meat dates back to Roman times. It was widely used until the advent of refrigeration. For best results at home, salting is limited to certain fish, vegetables and nuts. Choose rock, kitchen or block, or sea salt; kitchen or block salt is cheaper and perfectly adequate. Do not use free-running table salt.

Storing

There are various methods and techniques of storing some root vegetables, hard fruits and nuts to keep them in good condition. (Green vegetables and soft fruits do not store well.) Select produce in prime condition for storing. Although storage life is fairly limited, it is well worth the effort if you have a suitable space. The ideal storage area should be cool, moist and dark. A cellar, shed or outbuilding with an earth, brick or concrete floor is ideal. It must be well ventilated and protected from frost and mice. It may be necessary to dampen the floor to keep the atmosphere moist.

Storing Root Vegetables

There are many different methods and techniques of storing, ranging from racks and shelves, boxes, wire trays, sacks, sand, peat and nets to old-fashioned clamps and 'pies'. The method used depends on what is being stored.

Never store anything which is not in perfect condition, as rot or disease will spread quickly. Watch out for the following conditions which indicate that produce should not be stored.

Onions Softness, especially round the neck, or black areas on the bulbs.

Carrots Scored by fly maggots.

Parsnips Soft, dark areas of canker.

Any root vegetables Skin damaged on lifting: the skin is the insulation.

Making a clamp or 'pie'

This cheap and simple method gives complete protection to root vegetables through the winter, although the clamp cannot be opened during a frost without risk to the stored roots. Use a well protected, well drained part of the garden. Put down a

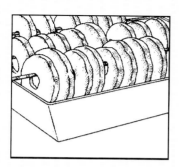

For drying, thread apple rings on sticks and leave in a warm place (see page 156).

For salting, pack fish between layers of salt in a wide-necked jar (see page 160).

Use a bottle filled with water to press down the fish and salt in the jar.

layer of dry straw or clinker about 1.5 metres (5 feet) wide. Build the roots into a broad-based, tapering heap on the straw base. Cover the heap with a 15-cm (6-inch) thickness of straw and leave the root vegetables to sweat for a few days.

After a few days, cover the straw and the whole heap with a layer of packed soils of the same depth, made smooth and firm by patting with the back of a spade. The heap must be entirely soil-crusted apart from a tuft of straw at the peak to act as a chimney and ventilator. To cover the clamp, use soil dug from around the base, so forming a drainage trench. This will prevent the bottom of the clamp becoming waterlogged in wet weather.

Note: This system is best used where a large quantity of root vegetables have to be stored, and when a good number can be taken out at a time. A clamp should not be opened too regularly. To remove moderate quantities, plunge your hand down the 'chimney'. For large quantities, break the 'pie crust' and then replace after removing the vegetables.

Storing Apples and Pears

Usually the early varieties do not keep well and should be used quickly, but the later varieties can be stored for several months. Pick them only when they are fully matured and then only store perfectly sound fruit. Apples or pears with bruises, scars, bird pecks, missing stalks or other blemishes should be preserved by a different method. Handle the fruit very carefully. Pears need particularly careful handling as they are usually only at their best for a few days.

After picking, the fruit should be allowed to stand in a cool, airy place overnight. Store different varieties separately. Each fruit must then be individually wrapped. Use oiled paper preferably, or tissue paper or newspaper. Lay the fruit in single layers, not touching each other, in trays, racks or

boxes or on the floor. Boxes can be stacked on top of each other as long as air can circulate underneath and between them. Store in a dark place. Covering with straw or paper will help if the store cannot be darkened. Examine and turn occasionally.

Storing Nuts

You can store most nuts for several months, providing they are quite dry and in good condition when gathered. Discard any that appear diseased. Do not remove the shells.

Walnuts   Gather the nuts when they are mature and fall to the ground. Remove the husk and then any fibrous material as this is where mould begins to grow. If necessary, quickly scrub the nuts in cold water using a soft brush, for only a few seconds as scrubbing may crack them. Then spread the nuts out to dry at room temperature, in a current of air if possible, turning them occasionally. When dry, store the nuts in a large jar or earthenware crock with alternate layers of a mixture of equal quantities of cooking salt and coconut-fibre refuse, or sawdust, bulb fibre or well dried hardwood shavings. Store in a cool, dry place for up to 6 months.

Chestnuts   Remove the husks, wipe and store the nuts in sacks or boxes in a cool, dry place.

Sweet almonds   Store as for walnuts.

Hazelnuts, filberts and cobnuts   Gather when the husks begin to dry and lay the nuts out thinly on wire trays in an airy room. Turn occasionally to prevent mildew.

Above: Storing vegetables (page 150)
Opposite: Drying fruit and herbs (page 156)

Storing Vegetables

VEGETABLE	CONDITION AND/OR PREPARATION	STORING
BEETROOT	After lifting, remove any excess earth. Twist off the tops, leaving about 5 cm (2 inches) of leaf stalk. This reduces 'bleeding' which occurs if the leaves are cut from the root.	Line a deep box with 2.5 cm (1 inch) of slightly damp sand or peat, put in a single layer of the prepared beetroots, followed by a layer of sand, and so on. Keep the boxes in a cool, dry, frostproof place, and watch out for mice. The sand, peat or other strong material should not be over-wet; just sufficient to stop shrivelling but not enough to cause rotting or encourage fresh growth. Beetroot can also be stored in a clamp or 'pie' (see page 150).
CARROTS	As for beetroot, except tops are cut off close to the head.	As for beetroot, with the roots laid head to tail.
CELERIAC	Lift before the frost arrives. Remove excess earth.	Store in sand in an airy shed. In warmer parts, they can be left in the ground covered with bracken or straw and dug up during winter as needed.
CUCUMBER	Select firm cucumbers.	Store in a cool place. Stack on racks, or on a stone floor.
KOHLRABI	As for beetroot.	Store for a short time as for beetroot. Late-sown ones can be left in the ground and used as wanted.
MARROW pumpkin squash	The skins must be hard for storing purposes.	Store marrows, etc., hung up in netting, string bags or anything which will let the air circulate around them. Small ones can be stored on a shelf in a well-ventilated, frostproof place. Turn to prevent bruising or mould.
ONIONS	Lift when the leaves are yellow and drooping. Leave on the surface of the soil to dry off. In wet weather, spread the onions in a single layer and dry under cover. They must be thoroughly dry before storing.	Store so the air can move freely between them. They can be placed on slatted, wooden trays, wire-based boxes, or strung up in ropes. Hang up stout lengths of thin rope or strong twine on a pole or beam in a shed or garage. Pull the roots off the onions and tie the necks round the cord. If necks are too short, use string or raffia. Stop before an onion 'rope' is too heavy to carry about. Keep one rope handy, in or near the kitchen, and the rest in a dry, ventilated, frostproof place. Alternatively, use old nylon stockings or tights. Put the onions down the legs, tying a knot between each one. Cut them off as you want them, below a knot.
PARSNIPS leeks celery Jerusalem artichokes	Remove any excess earth.	These are best left in the ground and lifted as required. If parsnips cannot be left in the ground, lift them and leave in a heap where the frost can touch and sweeten them, and the rain can wash them clean.

Storing Vegetables, cont.

VEGETABLE	CONDITION AND/OR PREPARATION	STORING
POTATOES	Remove any excess earth.	Large quantities can be stored in clamps (see page 150). Put small quantities in orange boxes lined with straw and topped with more straw or newspapers, or keep in slatted trays topped with straw. Sacks of hessian, paper or polythene are other alternatives. The roots must be allowed to 'sweat' for a few days before being bagged, and must be inspected regularly for mice and rotting. Make small holes in polythene and paper sacks so the potatoes can breathe.
SALSIFY	Remove any excess earth.	If they cannot be left in the ground until needed, store in layers of sand or peat.
SHALLOTS	Leave to dry as for onions. Separate bulbs, take off the dried outer skin, leaves, etc.	Store as for onions on wire or wooden trays and racks. They are rather fiddly to 'rope'.
SWEDES	As for beetroot, carrots and potatoes.	As for beetroot, carrots and potatoes.
TOMATOES	Choose firm tomatoes with no skin blemishes or cuts.	Hang whole green trusses in a frostfree place which need not be dark. Alternatively, keep green tomatoes on trays under a bed, in a cupboard or in drawers lined with newspapers. Much depends on their condition when harvested. If you want them for Christmas, keep them cool but frostfree and bring a few at a time into the warmth. Place them in a wide fruit bowl in the living room; the ripe tomatoes will help to ripen the green ones among them.
TURNIPS	As for beetroot, carrots and potatoes.	As for beetroot, carrots and potatoes.

Drying

Some foods, such as apples, pears, plums, mushrooms, herbs and onions, are more suitable than others for drying and can be dried at home using basic kitchen equipment.

Select good quality fruit that is just ripe. Avoid any with blemishes or bruises, or cut out the blemishes.

In the home, any source of heat can be utilised for drying, providing it is applied with ventilation.

Unfortunately the average oven does not have a low enough temperature setting to dry foods slowly and instead tends to bake and shrivel the food. However, the heat left in the oven after cooking can be used to dry food. This method of using residual heat means the food has to be dried over a longer period. A warm airing cupboard or the area over a central heating boiler is ideal because there is a continuous supply of gentle heat and the air can circulate freely. The prepared food should be placed on an open rack – a wire rack is ideal.

If this method of preservation appeals to you, you may want to invest in an electrical 'food dehydrator' that dries larger quantities of foods at once.

Drying Fruit

Apples and pears Prepare by peeling and coring. Slice apples into rings about 0.5 cm (¼ inch) thick, and cut pears in half or into quarters using a stainless steel knife. Put the prepared fruit in a solution of 50 g (2 oz) salt to 4.5 litres (8 pints) water, to prevent discoloration. Leave in the solution for 5 minutes, then drain and dry on a cloth.

Spread the fruit on baking sheets or trays, or thread rings of fruit on thin sticks and place across a roasting tin. Dry in a cooling oven, in an airing cupboard or over a central heating boiler until leathery in texture. This will take 6–8 hours. When dried, remove the fruit from the heat and allow to cool. Pack into jars, tins, or paper-lined boxes – they needn't be airtight containers – and store in a cool, dry, well-ventilated place.

Plums and apricots For best results, cut the fruit in half and remove the stones, although smaller fruit can be dried whole. Wash the fruit, dry carefully and arrange, cut sides up, on trays or baking sheets. Dry as for apples and pears.

To cook dried fruit Soak in cold water overnight or for several hours before use. Drain well before using for stewed fruit or in puddings and pies.

Drying Vegetables

Mushrooms Wipe with a damp cloth; do not wash. Leave whole or cut into slices or quarters. Dry as for apples, etc. Add dried mushrooms to soups, stews and casseroles. Soak dried mushrooms in water for 30 minutes before frying or grilling.

Onions Remove the skins and cut into 0.5-cm (¼-inch) slices. Separate into rings and dip each ring into boiling water for 30 seconds. Drain, dry and spread on trays or thread on to thin sticks. Dry as for apples, etc. Soak dried onions in hot water for 30 minutes. Drain and dry on absorbent kitchen paper before frying or grilling.

Drying Tomatoes

Imported sun-dried tomatoes are richly flavoured and make a wonderful addition to casseroles, soups, stews and sauces. If you are unable to buy them, and have a plentiful supply of tomatoes, it is possible to dry your own in the oven. Choose small, even-sized tomatoes and cut them in half. Lay the tomatoes, cut sides up, on baking sheets and put them in the oven at 100°C (200°F) mark low for 2–3 hours or until thoroughly dried and shrivelled. Pack in jars with herbs, garlic or spices for added flavour, cover with olive oil and store in the refrigerator.

Drying Herbs

Herbs should be picked on a dry day, when the dew has lifted, before the sun dispels the volatile oils. The best time is shortly before they flower – usually June or July – when they contain the maximum amount of oil. Pick off any damaged leaves and rinse dusty stems and leaves quickly in cold water.

Herbs can be dried in the sun over a period of 4–5 days. However, this method tends to result in loss of the colour and aromatic properties of some herbs. It is much quicker and better to dry them in an airing cupboard or the oven on the lowest possible setting, both with the door left slightly ajar to allow air to circulate. The oven temperature should not exceed 32°C (90°F). Place the herbs on wire racks covered with muslin or cheesecloth which lets the air through. Herbs will dry in an airing cupboard in 3–5 days and in 2–3 hours in the oven. From time to time, turn the herbs gently to ensure quicker, more even drying.

Herbs can also be dried very successfully in a microwave cooker. Place herbs on a paper towel, in a single layer, and cook on HIGH, the time depending on the quantity. When cool, crumble between your fingers and store (see below).

Parsley and mint will keep green if dipped in boiling water for 1 minute and then dried fairly quickly.

Herbs are dry when the stem and leaves become brittle but remain green and will crumble easily when rubbed between the fingers. If you are not quite sure about this, check by putting the dried herbs into a glass jar, cover it and watch for a few days to see if moisture appears. If it does, turn them out and continue the drying process. If the leaves turn brown you know that they have been over-dried and are of no further use.

It is also possible to dry herbs by hanging bunches in a dry place. Pick the stems as long as possible, tie them loosely in small bunches and suspend them out of direct sunlight. If this is difficult, place them in brown paper bags and hang them up. Check at regular intervals after 3 days until they are dry.

Once dried, you can strip the leaves from the stems and crumble them for storage. Don't rub so hard that they turn to dust as some of the flavouring properties will be lost. The exception are bay leaves which should be left whole as they contain large amounts of oil and, if crushed, they will release it before it is required. Store dried herbs in small screw-topped jars.

When using dried herbs, remember that they have a more concentrated flavour than fresh. Use half the quantity if substituting dried herbs for fresh in a recipe. You can make your own bouquet garni by placing a bay leaf, a sprig of parsley and a sprig of thyme on a square of muslin cloth and tying into a small bag with string. Dry and add to soups, stews and casseroles.

Drying Flowers

Marigolds, nasturtiums, rose petals and violets are all worth drying for flavouring cakes, creams, ice creams, sorbets, syrups, sauces and drinks.

Pick the flowers on a warm, dry day after the morning dew has evaporated. Choose open but not fully-blown buds and remove any green parts before drying. Dry them in a cool airy place away from direct sunlight. Leave for a few days until completely dry, then store in an airtight container or sealed polythene bag.

Spiced Black Pepper
~

15 g (½ oz) freshly ground black pepper
15 g (½ oz) dried marjoram
15 g (½ oz) dried thyme
15 g (½ oz) dried rosemary
15 g (½ oz) dried winter savory
15 g (½ oz) ground mace

~

Mix all the ingredients together well, sift them and store in a labelled jar.

Herb Spice
~

25 g (1 oz) ground dried bay leaves
25 g (1 oz) dried thyme
25 g (1 oz) dried marjoram
25 g (1 oz) dried basil
22 ml (1½ tbsp) ground mace
7.5 ml (1½ tsp) grated nutmeg
7.5 ml (1½ tsp) freshly ground pepper
7.5 ml (½ tsp) ground cloves

~

Mix and sift the herbs and spices together. Put into clean, dry, glass jars and label. This herb spice may be used for flavouring meat or sausage dishes, stuffings, etc.

Mixed Dried Herbs
~

50 g (2 oz) parsley
25 g (1 oz) winter savory
25 g (1 oz) lemon-scented thyme
25 g (1 oz) sweet marjoram

~

Weigh the herbs before drying. When dry, crumble, mix well and sift. Store in a labelled screw-topped jar.

Salted Almonds or Hazelnuts
~

350 g (12 oz) shelled almonds or hazelnuts
25 g (1 oz) butter or margarine
10 ml (2 tsp) salt

~

If the almonds are not blanched, put them in a bowl, cover with boiling water and leave for 3–4 minutes. Plunge into cold water for 1 minute, then slide off the skins between your fingers.

2 To skin hazelnuts, put them in a grill pan and grill for 2–3 minutes, shaking the pan occasionally. Rub off the skins between your fingers or in a clean cloth.

3 Melt the butter or margarine in a roasting tin and add the almonds or hazelnuts, tossing them until they are evenly coated. Roast in the oven at 150°C (300°F) mark 2 for 30 minutes, stirring occasionally.

4 Add the salt and toss well. When cold, store in an airtight container.

Salted Beans

~

350 g (12 oz) salt for each 900 g (2 lb) French or runner beans

~

Choose small, young, fresh and tender French or runner beans: it isn't worth preserving old, stringy ones. Cut off the stalks, wash and string if necessary. French beans can be left whole, but runner beans should be sliced.

2 Place a layer of salt in a glass or stoneware jar, then a layer of beans. Fill the jar with alternate layers, pressing the beans down well and finishing with a layer of salt.

3 Cover with a moisture-proof covering – cork or plastic material – and tie tightly. Leave for a few days to allow a strong brine solution to form.

4 The beans will shrink considerably as the salt draws out the moisture from them, and so the jars can be filled up with more layers of beans and salt – always finishing with salt. Store in a cool, dry, dark place. Use within 6 months.

5 To cook, remove some beans from the jar. (Put a layer of salt on top of the remaining beans and re-cover the jar.) Wash thoroughly several times in cold water, then soak for 2 hours in warm water.

6 Cook as for fresh beans, but in boiling unsalted water, until tender. Drain and serve in the usual way.

Sauerkraut

~

15 g (¹/₂ oz) sea salt for each 450 g (1 lb) cabbage, trimmed and washed

~

Choose firm, white cabbages and finely shred them. Put layers of shredded cabbage in a large stoneware jar (or crock) or wooden tub and sprinkle each layer with salt.

2 Toss the cabbage with your hands, then pack the cabbage down after each layer. When the container is filled, cover the cabbage with a large piece of cling film (not foil) and place an inverted plate or lid on top. Press down with a heavy, non-metal weight, such as a jar filled with water. Make sure it is airtight. In a few days the lid should be under the surface of the brine.

3 Leave at room temperature for about 3 weeks, for fermentation to take place, removing any scum every few days, as necessary. If the level of brine falls, top it up with a solution of 25 g (1 oz) salt in 1.1 litres (2 pints) water.

4 After about 3 weeks, when the salted cabbage has stopped frothing and fermentation is complete, the cabbage is ready to use.

5 For storage, the sauerkraut must be bottled. Drain the brine into a large saucepan and bring to the boil. Add the cabbage and bring back to the boil, stirring occasionally. If liked, add caraway seeds or juniper berries to flavour.

6 Put the cabbage at once into hot, clean jars, packing the sauerkraut down to remove any air pockets. Leave a headspace of 2.5 cm (1 inch) at the top of the jars. Cover and process for 25 minutes (see page 131). Test the seal, cover and store.

7 Sauerkraut is generally cooked in its own liquid and served with bacon, smoked sausages or pork.

Salted Fish
~

1.4 kg (3 lb) very fresh anchovies or sprats
900 g − 1.1 kg (2−2¹/₂ lb) sea salt

~

Remove the heads and gut the fish. Wash under cold running water, then dry thoroughly on absorbent kitchen paper. Place the fish in a dish between two layers of salt and leave for at least 12 hours or overnight. Drain the fish on absorbent kitchen paper.

2 Put a 1-cm (¹/₂-inch) layer of salt in the bottom of a wide-necked jar. Pack a layer of fish tightly together on top of the salt, head to tail.

3 Add another layer of salt and then a layer of fish, crossways to the first layer. Repeat layering until the jar is full, finishing with a layer of salt. Leave about 1 cm (¹/₂ inch) between the salt and the rim of the jar.

4 Continue until all the fish have been packed into jars. Place a non-metal weight inside each jar on top of the final layer of salt. A bottle filled with water is ideal.

5 Leave in a cool place for 5–6 days, until an oily substance rises to the surface. Remove the oil with a spoon. Cover the jars and store in a cool place.

6 Fish preserved in this way will keep for up to 6 months. Before using the fish, soak them in cold water for about 15 minutes to remove excess salt.

Drinks and Liqueurs

Fruit drinks, such as fruit syrups, squashes, cordials and liqueurs are most rewarding to make at home. Almost any fruit can be used. Autumn is an excellent time to prepare them as many of the fruits are ripe then and some can simply be gathered from the garden or the hedgerows. Home-made squashes and cordials are usually diluted before drinking. They will keep for about 6 weeks unopened. Making liqueurs during autumn is especially well timed as the liqueur has three months to mature before the Christmas season. Syrups, squashes and cordials need sterilising, liqueurs do not.

Note When using rosehip syrup, squash and cordial recipes, refer to the fruit syrup method for detailed bottling and sterilising instructions (see right).

Liqueurs

Liqueurs are made by infusing fruits in spirits for several weeks or months and require no fermentation. After infusion and before bottling, the fruits can be eaten separately as a dessert. Liqueurs are surprisingly simple to prepare and keep well. Serve with coffee after dinner.

Fruit Syrups

These are made with soft berry fruits, such as blackberries, blackcurrants, raspberries, bilberries, loganberries and strawberries. The fruit must be fresh and ripe; choose fruit that is too ripe for bottling or jam making. Use fruit syrups as a sauce with ice creams, steamed or baked puddings and desserts; or serve as a drink diluted with water or soda water.

No water is necessary when extracting the juice from the fruit, except when using blackcurrants – 300 ml (½ pint) per 450 g (1 lb), and blackberries – 300 ml (½ pint) per 2.7 kg (6 lb). There are three methods of extracting the juice:

Method 1 Wash the fruit and drain thoroughly. Place in a bowl over a saucepan of boiling water. Break up the fruit with a wooden spoon or stainless steel masher, and leave for about 1 hour for 2.7 kg (6 lb) fruit until the juice flows freely, keeping the pan replenished with boiling water as it evaporates. This method ensures that the fruit is not overcooked, which spoils the colour and flavour.

Method 2 Wash the fruit and drain thoroughly. Place in a saucepan with the water (if used) and bring quickly to the boil, stirring continuously. Boil for 1 minute, crushing any whole fruit with a wooden spoon or stainless steel masher.

Method 3 There are various types of electric juice extractor on the market which can be used.

Remove the fruit from the heat, if necessary, and strain overnight through a scalded jelly bag or cloth. Transfer the pulp to a clean linen cloth and fold over the ends. Twist them in opposite directions to squeeze out as much juice as possible. Measure the extracted juice, adding 350 g (12 oz) sugar for every 600 ml (1 pint) juice. Stir to dissolve.

Pour into small sterilised bottles to within 4 cm (1½ inches) of the top for corks, or under 2.5 cm (1 inch) for screw type caps, to leave room for expansion on heating. Before use, bottles must be sterilised and corks, caps, stoppers, etc, must be submerged in boiling water for 15 minutes. Seal the bottles with a cork, which must be cut off level with the top of the bottle and covered by a metal or plastic screw cap, a screw stopper or a cork alone which must be tied with wire or string to prevent being blown off during the sterilisation process.

To sterilise, place the bottles of fruit drink in a deep pan padded on the base and between the bottles with thick cloth or newspaper. Fill to the base of the corks, caps or stoppers with warm water, then raise to simmering point and maintain this temperature for 20 minutes. (If you have a thermometer, maintain at 77°C/170°F for 30 minutes.) Remove the bottles. If using corks only, seal by dipping into melted sealing wax as soon as the bottles are cold and corks dry (see page 121).

Store in a cool dry place; the bottles may be wrapped to preserve the colour of the syrup.

Apricot Brandy
~

MAKES ABOUT 750 ML (1¼ PINTS)

12 apricots
600 ml (1 pint) brandy
225 g (8 oz) caster sugar
~

Cut the fruit into small pieces, reserving the stones. Crack open the stones to obtain the kernels, crush the kernels and place in a jar with the fruit.

2 Add the brandy and sugar, seal the jar and shake to dissolve the sugar. Leave in a dark place for 1 month, shaking the jar several times a week.

3 Strain off the fruit and eat separately. Bottle the liqueur and store until required.

VARIATION
Peach brandy

Follow the recipe above using peaches instead of apricots.

Cherry Brandy
~

MAKES ABOUT 750 ML (1¼ PINTS)

450 g (1 lb) Morello cherries, washed
75 g (3 oz) caster sugar
600 ml (1 pint) brandy
~

Either remove the stalks from the cherries or cut them within 0.5 cm (¼ inch) of the fruit. Dry the cherries and prick all over with a darning needle.

2 Put the fruit and sugar in alternate layers into a wide-necked jar. Cover with the brandy, then seal the jar. Leave in a dark place for at least 3 months, shaking the jar two or three times a week until the brandy is a rich cherry colour.

3 Strain off the fruit and eat separately. Bottle the liqueur and store until required

Sloe Gin
~

MAKES ABOUT 900 ML (1½ PINTS)

450 g (1 lb) sloes, stalks removed and washed
75–100 g (3–4 oz) sugar
a few drops of almond essence
75-cl (26.4-fl oz) bottle of gin
~

Prick the sloes all over with a darning needle and put them in a screw-topped jar. Add the sugar and almond essence. Cover with gin, then screw down tightly. Leave in a dark place for 3 months, shaking occasionally.

2 Strain the gin through muslin until clear. Bottle the gin and store until required.

For cherry brandy, layer the fruit and sugar
in a jar and cover with brandy

Redcurrant Gin
~

MAKES ABOUT 750 ML (1¼ PINTS)

450 g (1 lb) redcurrants, stalks removed and washed
225 g (8 oz) caster sugar
600 ml (1 pint) gin
~

*P*ut the redcurrants in a bowl with the sugar and stir well, crushing the fruit.

2 Transfer the redcurrant mixture to a clean wide-necked bottle or jar. Pour in the gin. Seal tightly and shake gently to blend the mixture.

3 Store in a cool, dry, dark place for 3 months, shaking occasionally. Strain, reserving the redcurrants. Pour the liquid into a clean bottle and seal with a non-metallic covering. Label and store in a cool, dry place.

Raspberry Gin
~

MAKES ABOUT 1.3 LITRES (2¼ PINTS)

450 g (1 lb) raspberries
350 g (12 oz) sugar
one 75-cl (26.4-fl oz) bottle of gin
~

*P*ut all the ingredients in a jar and seal securely. Leave in a dark place for 3 months, shaking the jar every day for the first month, then occasionally.

2 Strain the liqueur through muslin, then bottle and store until required.

Orange Gin
~

MAKES ABOUT 1.1 LITRES (2 PINTS)

peel of 10 medium oranges
one 75-cl (26.4-fl oz) bottle of gin
225 g (8 oz) sugar
~

*C*ut the peel of each orange into eight sections and place on a baking sheet. Heat in the oven at the lowest setting for several hours until hard and brittle.

2 Place the peel in a wide-necked glass jar and pour in the gin to cover. If necessary, remove some of the peel or add more gin to ensure that the gin covers the peel. Seal the jar and leave in a dark place for 6 weeks, shaking the jar several times a week.

3 Put the sugar and 300 ml (½ pint) water in a pan and heat gently, stirring, until the sugar has dissolved, then bring to the boil and boil for 3 minutes. Remove from the heat and leave until cold.

4 Strain the peel and gin through a nylon sieve, pressing the peel lightly with the back of a wooden spoon. Add the syrup to the orange gin, then strain through muslin.

5 Pour into small bottles and seal. Store in a cool place for 2 months before serving as a liqueur.

Opposite: Redcurrant Gin (above)

Orange Whisky
~

MAKES ABOUT 750 ML (1¼ PINTS)

2 oranges
100 g (4 oz) sugar
1 cinnamon stick
600 ml (1 pint) whisky
~

Thinly pare the rind from the oranges. Cut the rind into thin strips and put in a jar.

2 Squeeze out the juice from the fruit and add to the rind with the sugar and cinnamon stick. Pour in the whisky, then seal the jar. Shake to dissolve the sugar. Leave in a cool, dark place for 1 month, shaking the jar occasionally.

3 Strain off the fruit and bottle the whisky. Store until required.

Blackberry Liqueur
~

MAKES ABOUT 2 LITRES (3½ PINTS)

1.8 kg (4 lb) blackberries, washed
15 ml (1 tbsp) whole cloves
15 ml (1 tbsp) grated nutmeg
about 450 g (1 lb) sugar
300 ml (½ pint) brandy
~

Place the blackberries, cloves and nutmeg in a saucepan and add 600 ml (1 pint) water. Bring to the boil, then simmer gently for about 15 minutes or until the blackberries are soft. Leave until cold.

2 Strain the blackberries through a piece of muslin. Measure the juice and add 225 g (8 oz) sugar for every 600 ml (1 pint) juice. Pour into a saucepan and heat gently, stirring, until the sugar has dissolved.

3 Remove the pan from the heat and stir in the brandy. Pour into bottles and store until required.

Prune Liqueur
~

MAKES ABOUT 750 ML (1¼ PINTS)

450 g (1 lb) prunes
one 70-cl bottle of red wine
150 g (5 oz) sugar
150 ml (¼ pint) rum
~

Pierce the prunes right through using a skewer, but do not remove the stones. Put the prunes in a large glass jar.

2 Pour the wine into a large saucepan, add the sugar and heat gently until just beginning to boil. Remove from the heat and stir in the rum.

3 Pour the wine and rum mixture over the prunes to cover. Leave until cold, then seal the jar. Leave in a dark place for at least 1 month before drinking.

4 To serve, place a prune on a cocktail stick in a small glass and pour in enough liqueur to cover the fruit

Orange Liqueur
~

MAKES ABOUT 600 ML (1 PINT)

peel of 6 thin-skinned oranges
600 ml (1 pint) white wine
150 g (5 oz) caster sugar
150 ml (1/4 pint) white rum

~

Cut the orange peel into quarters, then cut into strips as fine as possible.

2 Leave the wine in the wine bottle and add as many strips of peel as possible by pushing them down the neck of the bottle with a wooden spoon. Cork the bottle and leave in a dark place for at least 2 months, shaking the bottle several times a week.

3 Strain the peel and wine through a nylon sieve, pressing the peel lightly with the back of a wooden spoon.

4 Add the sugar to the wine and stir until dissolved. Add the rum and mix well together, then strain through muslin. Bottle and leave for 1 month before serving.

Pineapple Liqueur
~

1 fresh pineapple
sugar
brandy

~

Remove the skin and 'eyes' from the pineapple and slice very thinly. Put in a large bowl, sprinkle with a little sugar, cover and leave for 24 hours.

2 Strain off the juice, measure it and add an equal amount of brandy. With each 300 ml (1/2 pint) brandy, add 50 g (2 oz) sugar.

3 Pour into a screw-topped jar with a few slices of the fresh pineapple, then screw down tightly. Leave in a dark place for 3 weeks.

4 Strain off the fruit and eat separately. Bottle the liqueur.

Cassis
~

MAKES ABOUT 1.1 LITRES (2 PINTS)

450 g (1 lb) blackcurrants, stalks removed and washed
600 ml (1 pint) gin or brandy
sugar

~

Crush the blackcurrants. Place with the gin or brandy in screw-topped jars, then screw down tightly. Leave in a dark place for about 2 months.

2 Strain the spirit, then add 175 g (6 oz) sugar to each 600 ml (1 pint) liquid. Pour into a jug, cover and leave for 2 days, stirring at intervals to dissolve the sugar. Strain through muslin. Bottle the liqueur and store for 6 months to mature before using.

Apricot Liqueur
~

MAKES ABOUT 1.4 LITRES (2¹/₂ PINTS)

450 g (1 lb) apricots, washed and halved
450 g (1 lb) sugar
one 70-cl bottle of dry white wine
300 ml (¹/₂ pint) gin

~

Crack the apricot stones and remove the kernels, then blanch in boiling water for 1 minute.

2 Place the apricots, sugar and wine in a saucepan and heat gently, stirring, until the sugar has dissolved. Bring to the boil, then remove from the heat.

3 Stir in the gin and apricot kernels. Pour into a large bowl or jug, cover tightly and leave for 5–6 days.

4 Strain, then bottle and store for 1 month.

Above: Apricot Liqueur
Opposite: (on chair) Blackcurrant and Rosemary Syrup
(page 171) with white wine to dilute; (on grass) Sweet
and Sour Figs (page 97), Redcurrant Gin (page 165)

Hot Chilli Vodka
~

MAKES ABOUT 300 ML (¹/₂ PINT)

1 red and 1 green chilli
300 ml (¹/₂ pint) vodka
~

*S*plit the chillies lengthways. Mix with the vodka in a bottle with a tight-fitting lid.
2 Shake and leave in a cool place for at least 2 weeks before using. Store for up to 3 months.

VARIATION
Citrus vodka

This produces a pale lemon-coloured spirit. Try adding a little to sautés of beef or chicken, or stir a couple of spoonfuls into fruit salads or over slices of fresh pineapple. Omit the chillies from the above recipe and add the pared rind of 3 lemons.

VARIATION
Pepper vodka

Omit the chillies from the above recipe and add 30 ml (2 tbsp) lightly crushed green peppercorns. This variation is also delicious served in a Bloody Mary.

Redcurrant Wine
~

MAKES ABOUT 750 ML (1³/₄ PINTS)

700 g (1¹/₂ lb) frozen redcurrants, thawed
1 bottle of red wine
450 g (1 lb) caster sugar
45–60 ml (3–4 tbsp) brandy
~

*P*lace the redcurrants and wine in a large bowl. Mash the fruit with the back of a wooden spoon. Cover tightly with cling film and leave in a cool place to infuse for 3 days.
2 Strain the fruit and wine liquid carefully into a large saucepan and stir in the caster sugar. Heat gently, stirring occasionally, until the sugar has dissolved completely. Bring to the boil, then simmer gently for 10 minutes.
3 Add the brandy to the redcurrant syrup and pour into sterilised bottles. Seal.
4 Store the wine in a cool, dark place for at least 1 week before using. The wine can be stored for up to 3 months. Shake well before serving.

Orange Wine
~

MAKES ABOUT 600 ML (1 PINT)

600 ml (1 pint) dry white wine
pared rind of 2 oranges
pared rind of 1 lemon
1 cinnamon stick
1 vanilla pod
~

*M*ix all the ingredients in a bottle with a tight-fitting top. Shake well and leave in a cool, dark place for up to 2 weeks.
2 Strain the wine, re-bottle and store for up to 3 months.

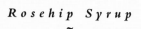

Blackcurrant and Rosemary Syrup
~

MAKES ABOUT 600 ML (1 PINT)

900 g (2 lb) blackcurrants, stalks removed and washed
2 sprigs of fresh rosemary
caster sugar
juice of 1 lemon

~

*D*ry the blackcurrants thoroughly. Place in a medium saucepan with the rosemary and 300 ml (½ pint) water. Bring slowly to the boil and simmer for 5 minutes or until the fruit is very soft and pulpy.

2 Press the mixture through a nylon sieve, extracting all the liquid. Measure the liquid into a small saucepan. Add 150 g (5 oz) caster sugar and the juice of 1 lemon to each 600 ml (1 pint).

3 Heat the mixture gently, stirring, until the sugar has dissolved, then bring to the boil and boil for 10 minutes or until syrupy.

4 Pour the syrup into clean, warmed bottles and seal with corks or snap-on plastic lids. Cool, label and store in a cool, dark place for up to 1 month.

Rosehip Syrup
~

MAKES ABOUT 600 ML (1 PINT)

900 g (2 lb) ripe rosehips
450 g (1 lb) sugar
~

*H*ave ready 1.7 litres (3 pints) boiling water, preferably in an aluminium or unchipped enamel saucepan.

2 Press the rosehips through the coarse blade of a mincer and place immediately in the boiling water. Bring to the boil again. As soon as the mixture boils, remove the pan from the heat and leave for 15 minutes.

3 Pour the rosehips into a scalded jelly bag and allow the bulk of the juice to drip through.

4 Return the pulp in the jelly bag to the saucepan, add 900 ml (1½ pints) boiling water, re-boil, then allow to stand without further heating for another 10 minutes.

5 Pour the juice into a clean saucepan and simmer to reduce to about 900 ml (1½ pints), then add 450 g (1 lb) sugar. Stir until dissolved, then boil for a further 5 minutes.

6 Pour the hot syrup into hot bottles and seal at once (see page 162). Sterilise for 5 minutes. If using corks only, seal with melted paraffin or sealing wax (see page 121).

Note It is advisable to use small bottles, as the syrup will not keep for more than a week or two once it is opened.

Overleaf (left to right): Raspberry Butterscotch Sauce (page 206), Sparkling Strawberry Water (page 174), Harvest Preserve with Port (page 32), Soft Fruits in Wine (page 144), Redcurrant and Cinnamon Jelly (page 45), Blueberry Bay Jam (page 16), Redcurrant Gin (page 165), Blackcurrant and Rosemary Syrup (above), Sweet Cherry Chutney (page 111)

Sparkling Strawberry Water
~

MAKES ABOUT 600 ML (1 PINT)

450 g (1 lb) strawberries, hulled, washed and dried
30 ml (2 tbsp) icing sugar
grated rind and juice of 1 large orange
soda or sparkling mineral water, to serve
fresh mint, to garnish
~

Thickly slice the strawberries into a bowl and sprinkle with the sugar, adding the grated orange rind and juice. Cover and leave in a cool place to marinate for 2–3 hours.

2 Put the mixture in a medium saucepan with 300 ml (½ pint) water. Bring to the boil, cover and simmer for 5–10 minutes. Purée in a blender or food processor until smooth.

3 Press the mixture through a muslin-lined nylon sieve, then leave to cool. Store, covered, in the refrigerator for up to 1 week.

4 When ready to serve, divide the mixture between four chilled glasses and top up with soda or sparkling mineral water. Garnish with fresh mint.

Lemon Squash
~

MAKES ABOUT 900 ML (1½ PINTS)

about 4 lemons, washed
700 g (1½ lb) sugar
1.25 ml (¼ tsp) citric acid (optional)
~

Grate the rind of two lemons and squeeze out the juice from all the fruit to make 300 ml (½ pint) juice. Place the lemon rind, sugar and 450 ml (¾ pint) water in a saucepan and heat slowly until boiling, stirring until the sugar has dissolved.

2 Strain the syrup into a jug, add the lemon juice and

citric acid, if used, and stir well. Pour into bottles, seal and sterilise (see page 162).

3 To serve, dilute the squash with water or soda water – allow 1 part squash to 23 parts water, according to taste. Do not store for longer than 1–2 months, as the colour and flavour deteriorate.

Orange Squash
~

MAKES ABOUT 900 ML (1½ PINTS)

about 3 oranges, washed
700 g (1½ lb) sugar
15 g (½ oz) citric acid
~

Grate the rind of the oranges, squeeze out the juice and measure 300 ml (½ pint) juice.

2 Place the orange rind, sugar and 450 ml (¾ pint) water in a saucepan and heat slowly until boiling, stirring until the sugar has dissolved.

3 Strain the syrup into a jug, add the orange juice and citric acid, and stir well. Pour into bottles, seal and sterilise (see page 162).

4 To serve, dilute with water or soda water – allow 1 part squash to 2–3 parts water, according to taste. Do not store for longer than 1–2 months, as the colour and flavour deteriorate.

Ginger Cordial
~

MAKES ABOUT 4.5 LITRES (8 PINTS)

25 g (1 oz) fresh root ginger, bruised
450–700 g (1–1½ lb) sugar
7.5 ml (1½ tsp) tartaric acid
½ a lemon, washed and sliced
~

Put the ginger (use the larger amount if you like sweet ginger cordial), tartaric acid and lemon in a large bowl. Cover with 4.5 litres (8 pints) boiling water, stir until the sugar has dissolved, then leave for 3–4 days.
2 Strain the cordial through muslin, then pour into bottles, seal and sterilise (see page 162). This cordial is ready to drink, undiluted, after a few days.

Elderflower Cordial
~

MAKES ABOUT 2 LITRES (3½ PINTS)

10 large elderflower heads
900 g (2 lb) sugar
2 lemons, washed and sliced
25 g (1 oz) tartaric acid
2.3 litres (4 pints) boiling water
~

Place all the ingredients in a bowl. Cover and leave for 24 hours, stirring occasionally.
2 Strain the cordial through muslin, pour into bottles, seal and sterilise (see page 162). To serve, dilute to taste with sparkling mineral water.

Elderberry Cordial
~

MAKES ABOUT 2.8 LITRES (5 PINTS)

700 g (1½ lb) elderberries
about 225 g (8 oz) caster sugar
~

Strip the berries from their stalks, then wash and drain. Place in a saucepan with 2.3 litres (4 pints) water and bring gently to the boil. Simmer for about 15 minutes or until the fruit is pulpy. Cool slightly.
2 Strain the elderberry liquid through a nylon sieve lined with muslin.
3 Return the liquid to a saucepan, adding sugar to taste. Heat gently to dissolve the sugar, then leave to cool. Decant into clean bottles, cover and store in the refrigerator for up to 2 weeks.

Rose Water Cordial
~

MAKES ABOUT 600 ML (1 PINT)

450 g (1 lb) sugar
juice of ½ lemon, strained
45 ml (3 tbsp) triple distilled rose water
red food colouring
~

Put the sugar in a saucepan and add 300 ml (½ pint) cold water. Stir well and bring slowly to the boil. Boil for 1 minute.
2 Remove the pan from the heat and stir in the lemon juice, rose water and enough red food colouring to give the syrup a dark jewel-like colour. Cool for 5 minutes, then pour into clean, dry bottles and seal.
3 To serve, dilute to taste with iced water or soda water. This cordial can be stored in the refrigerator for 10 days.

Overleaf: Rose Water Cordial (above)

Candying and Crystallising

Candying and crystallising are methods of preservation that use sugar as a preserving agent. Candied fruits may be preserved as a dessert or eaten as sweets. The peel of such citrus fruits as oranges, lemons and citrons can also be candied and is widely used in making cakes, cookies, puddings, mincemeats, etc. Crystallised flowers, petals or leaves are used as cake or dessert decorations.

Candying

Candying essentially consists of soaking the fruit in a syrup, the sugar content of which is increased daily over a stated period of time until the fruits are completely impregnated with sugar. Candied fruits can be left plain or given a crystallised or glacé finish.

Candied fruits are expensive to buy because of the labour involved and the amount of sugar used. The process is possible to do at home provided certain basic rules are followed. The most suitable fruits to treat are those with a really distinctive flavour − pineapples, peaches, plums, apricots, oranges, cherries, crab-apples and pears. Both fresh and canned fruits may be used, but different types should not be candied in the same sugar syrup.

Fruit and Syrup for Candying

Fresh fruit The fruits must be ripe, but firm and free from blemishes. Prepare them according to kind. Small whole crab-apples, apricots and plums should be pricked all over with a stainless steel fork; cherries must be stoned and peaches and pears peeled and halved or cut into quarters. Fruits which are peeled and cut up need not be pricked.

Place the prepared fruits in sufficient boiling water to cover them and cook gently until just tender. Tough fruits such as apricots may take 10–15 minutes; soft ones need only 2–4 minutes. Overcooking spoils the shape and texture, while under-cooking results in slow penetration of the syrup and causes dark colour and toughness.

Canned fruits Use good quality fruit. Pineapple chunks or small rings, plums, sliced and halved peaches and halved apricots are all suitable for candying.

The syrup Granulated sugar is generally recommended for the preparation of the syrup. Part of the sugar may be replaced by glucose − see the charts on pages 179–180 which gives full details of the proportion of sugar to liquid at the different stages.

Notes on Candying Fruit

Amount of syrup If the syrup is not sufficient to cover the fruit, make up more of the same strength, but remember that the amount of sugar to add later must be increased accordingly. For example, if you increase the amount used for fresh fruit on Day 1 to 450 ml (¾ pint) liquid and 250 g (9 oz) sugar, on Day 2 you must add 75 g (3 oz) sugar and on Day 8 add a further 125 g (4½ oz) sugar.

Soaking time It is important that the fruit should soak for a full 24 hours (or as specified) before the next amount of sugar is added.

Days 5, 7, 8, 10 When the added sugar is increased to 75 g (3 oz), first dissolve the sugar in the strained syrup, then add the fruit and boil it in the syrup for 2–3 minutes.

Day 11 or 14 Once the syrup has reached the consistency of honey, the fruit may be left to soak for as little as 3 days or up to 2–3 weeks, depending on how sweet you like the candied fruit to be.

Finishing the Candied Fruit

When the fruits are thoroughly dried, pack them as described opposite, or give them one of the following finishes before packing.

Crystallised finish Take the pieces of candied fruit and dip each quickly into boiling water. Drain off excess moisture, then roll in caster sugar.

Glacé finish Prepare a fresh syrup, using 450 g (1 lb) sugar and 150 ml (¼ pint) water, bring to the boil and boil for 1 minute. Pour a little of the syrup into a cup. Dip the candied fruit into boiling water for 20 seconds, then dip them one at a time in the syrup, using a skewer. Place the fruit on a wire rack to dry. Cover the rest of the syrup in the pan with a damp cloth and keep it warm (a double pan is useful for this purpose). As the syrup in the cup becomes cloudy, replace it with fresh. Dry the fruit as before, turning it occasionally.

Using the Surplus Syrup

After the fruit has been removed, the surplus syrup can be used in several different ways. It has a delicious fruity flavour and is the consistency of honey. Add a little to fruit salads and sauces or use to sweeten puddings or stewed fruit.

Packing the Candied Fruit

Pack the fruits in cardboard or wooden boxes, keeping each piece separate between layers of waxed paper. If preferred, they may be stored in jars with a piece of paper or cloth over the top. Containers must not be sealed or airtight as the fruit may become mouldy under these conditions.

Crystallising

Flowers, petals and leaves crystallised at home usually look more attractive than the commercially prepared ones and are quite easy to make. The flowers or leaves are simply painted with lightly beaten egg white and then sprinkled with caster sugar (see page 184).

Most flowers are suitable to use, except those grown from bulbs as they are poisonous. The best results are obtained from flattish flowers with a small number of petals, eg. violets, primroses, rose petals, fruit blossoms – apple, pear or cherry. Choose whole flowers that are fresh and free from damage, bruises or brown marks. Pick them in the morning once the dew has lifted and the petals are completely dry. The most popular leaves to crystallise are mint because of their pleasant taste. Be just as selective when picking leaves, making sure they are blemish-free.

Processing Charts for Candied Fruit

Using 450 g (1 lb) prepared fruit (see Notes on page 178).

CANNED FRUIT		
Day	Syrup	Soaking time
1	Drain off canning syrup and make up to 300 ml (½ pint); add 225 g (8 oz) sugar (or 100 g/4 oz sugar and 100 g/4 oz glucose). Dissolve, bring to the boil and pour over fruit.	24 hours
2	Drain off syrup, add 50 g (2 oz) sugar, dissolve, bring to the boil and pour over fruit.	24 hours
3	Repeat Day 2	24 hours
4	Repeat Day 2	24 hours
5	Repeat Day 2, using 75 g (3 oz) sugar.	48 hours
6	–	–
7	Repeat Day 2, using 75 g (3 oz) sugar.	4 days
8	–	–
9	–	–
10	–	–
11	Dry in the oven at lowest setting or cover lightly and leave in a warm place until quite dry (this may take from a few hours to 2–3 days), turn them 2–3 times.	–

FRESH FRUIT		
Day	Syrup	Soaking time
1	Drain 300 ml (½ pint) cooking liquid from fruit, add 175 g (6 oz) sugar (or 50 g/2 oz sugar and 100 g/4 oz glucose). Dissolve, bring to the boil and pour over fruit.	24 hours
2	Drain off syrup, add 50 g (2 oz) sugar, dissolve, bring to the boil and pour over fruit.	24 hours
3	Repeat Day 2	24 hours
4	Repeat Day 2	24 hours
5	Repeat Day 2	24 hours
6	Repeat Day 2	24 hours
7	Repeat Day 2	24 hours
8	Repeat Day 2, using a further 75 g (3 oz) sugar	48 hours
9	–	–
10	Repeat Day 8	4 days
11	–	–
12	–	–
13	–	–
14	Dry as for canned fruit (page 179).	–

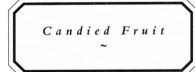

Candied Fruit
~

*fresh fruit, such as oranges, apricots, pineapple,
kiwi, pears, apples*
sugar
30 ml (2 tbsp) orange flower water
~

Choose firm, ripe fruits, free from blemishes. Small fruits can be left whole but if they have tough skins – such as plums or apricots – prick them all over.

2 Remove the stones from cherries with a cherry stoner. Remove the peel from citrus fruits and divide oranges into segments, removing all pith and membrane. Peel pears, apples and peaches and halve them or cut into thick slices. Remove all the skin, core and 'eyes' and cut the pineapple into chunks or rings.

3 Weigh the fruit after preparation but before cooking. Always candy different types of fruit separately.

4 Put the prepared fruit in a saucepan, just cover with boiling water and simmer gently until just tender. Take care not to over-cook the fruit, as soft fruits will have less taste and will lose their shape. On the other hand, if you under-cook the fruit, the finished product will be tough.

5 For every 450 g (1 lb) prepared fruit, use 175 g (6 oz) sugar and 300 ml (½ pint) of the water the fruit was cooked in.

6 Lift out the fruit carefully from the cooking liquid with a slotted spoon and place it in a large bowl.

7 Dissolve the sugar very slowly in the water, stirring continuously with a metal spoon. Bring to the boil and pour the syrup over the fruit. The fruit must be completely covered with syrup. Leave for 24 hours.

8 Drain off the syrup into a saucepan and add another 50 g (2 oz) sugar. Dissolve it slowly over gentle heat, stirring continuously. Bring to the boil and pour the syrup back over the fruit. Soak for another 24 hours.

9 Repeat step 8 every day for the next five days, so that the syrup gradually gets stronger and stronger.

10 At the beginning of the second week, drain off the syrup and add 75 g (3 oz) sugar (instead of the 50 g/2 oz you have been adding up to now). Dissolve it and then add the fruit to the syrup in the pan. Simmer gently for 3–4 minutes. Carefully return the fruit and syrup to the bowl. Leave to soak for a full 48 hours.

11 Repeat the same procedure with 75 g (3 oz) sugar. Then add 30 ml (2 tbsp) orange flower water and leave to soak for 4 full days. This is the last soaking and you can leave it longer if you wish, up to about 2 weeks. The fruit becomes sweeter, the longer it is left.

12 Finally, drain off the syrup and spread the pieces of fruit out on a wire rack. Place the rack on a tray and cover the fruit without touching it (use an inverted roasting tin, a loose tent of foil, or a plastic box) just to protect it from dust, flies, etc. Leave the fruit in a warm place for 2–3 days or until thoroughly dry. Turn each piece two or three times while drying.

13 When dry, carefully pack the fruits in boxes with waxed paper or parchment between each layer.

*Opposite: Candied fruits with crystallised finish
(above and page 178), Crystallised violets (page 184)*

Candied Peel
~

6 oranges, lemons, limes or grapefruit, or a mixture
350 g (12 oz) granulated sugar
~

*W*ash or scrub the fruit thoroughly, halve or quarter them and remove the peel. Large pieces of peel retain their moisture better, so do not cut them up.

2 Simmer the peel in a little water for 1–2 hours, stirring occasionally, until tender. (Change the water 2–3 times when cooking grapefruit peel.)

3 Drain the liquid into a measuring jug and make up to 300 ml (1/2 pint) with water.

4 Pour the liquid into a clean pan, add 225 g (8 oz) sugar and heat gently, stirring, until the sugar has dissolved. Bring to the boil, then add the peel, remove from the heat and leave in a cool place for 2 days.

5 Drain off the syrup again into a clean pan. Add the remaining sugar. Add the peel and simmer until semi-transparent. The peel can be left in this thick syrup for 2–3 weeks.

6 Drain off the syrup and place the peel on a wire rack to dry. Put the rack in a warm place such as an airing cupboard. (The temperature should not exceed 50°C/120°F or the peel may brown and the flavour spoil.)

7 The drying will take several hours and is completed when the peel is no longer sticky. When thoroughly dried, pack as described on page 179. If liked, finish the peel with a glacé or crystallised finish (see page 178).

VARIATION
Spiced candied peel

Add six cloves and a cinnamon stick to the syrup in step 4. Remove and discard the spices in step 5.

Caramelled Fruits
~

about 450 g (1 lb) mixed fruits, prepared (see method)
225 g (8 oz) preserving sugar
5 ml (1 tsp) powdered glucose
a large pinch of cream of tartar
~

*S*uitable fruits are orange or mandarin segments, small pieces of pineapple, black or white grapes, cherries or strawberries. Select only perfect fruit without bruises or defects.

2 Wash and dry the fruit carefully and drain any canned fruit used thoroughly. Skewer each piece of fruit on a fork or cocktail stick.

3 Make a syrup of the sugar and 60 ml (4 tbsp) water in a small, deep, heavy-based saucepan. When the sugar has dissolved, add the glucose and cream of tartar. Boil gently until it is golden brown and has reached a temperature of 143°C (290°F).

4 Dip the prepared fruit, one piece at a time, into the syrup. Drain well by tapping the fork or stick gently on the edge of the saucepan.

5 Place each piece of fruit on an oiled marble slab or an oiled plate. Leave, without touching, until quite dry, then place in paper cases. Serve as petits fours.

Candied Angelica
~

angelica

salt

sugar

~

*D*rop the angelica shoots (which can be picked in April or May) immediately into brine – 7 g (¼ oz) salt to 2.3 litres (4 pints) water – and leave to soak for 10 minutes, to preserve the green colour. Rinse in cold water.

2 Cook the angelica in boiling water for about 5 minutes or until quite tender. Drain, retaining the liquid, and scrape the angelica to remove the outer skin.

3 Using the angelica cooking liquid, make a syrup using 175 g (6 oz) sugar to 300 ml (½ pint) liquid. Place the angelica in a bowl, add the syrup, cover and leave for 24 hours.

4 Drain off and measure the syrup, add 50 g (2 oz) sugar for every 300 ml (½ pint) and bring to the boil. Pour back into the bowl over the angelica, cover and leave for 24 hours.

5 Repeat this process a further five times until the syrup is of the consistency of runny honey. Boil the angelica for 2–3 minutes at the last addition of the sugar, then leave for 2 days.

6 Dry off on a wire rack in a warm place or in the oven at 110°C (225°F) mark ¼. Store in screw-topped jars.

VARIATION
Quick method

Choose tender shoots and cut into 7.5–10-cm (3–4-inch) pieces. Place in a pan with 450 g (1 lb) sugar to each 450 g (1 lb) shoots, cover and leave to stand for 2 days. Bring slowly to the boil and boil until the angelica is clear and green, then drain in a colander. Toss the shoots in caster sugar and dry them off in the oven at 110°C (225°F) mark ¼ before storing.

Fruit Sweetmeats
~

*U*nusual and attractive sweets can be made from sweetened fruit pulp.

2 Choose fully ripe fruit, chop roughly and put in a saucepan with a very little water. Simmer until soft, then sieve to remove pips and skin.

3 Add sugar to taste (except in the case of ripe dessert pears). Simmer the sweetened pulp gently, stirring constantly until it is very thick.

4 Spread it out on a baking sheet or on muslin stretched over a wire cooling tray and dry slowly at a low temperature as for candied fruit (see page 179). This may take from a few hours to 2–3 days.

5 When firm enough to handle, cut the fruit into small bars, squares or rounds and roll the pieces in caster sugar.

To vary the sweets, add suitable spices or flavourings, or a little food colouring.

Glacé Fruit
~

candied fruit (see page 180)
450 g (1 lb) sugar
~

The candied fruit must be thoroughly dry. Put the sugar in a saucepan with 150 ml (¼ pint) water and dissolve the sugar slowly over a gentle heat, stirring. Bring to the boil and boil for about 1 minute.

2 Pour a little of the syrup into a small bowl and keep the rest warm over hot water. Put a little boiling water in another bowl.

3 Using a dipping fork or skewer, dip the candied fruit, one piece at a time, into the boiling water for about 20 seconds, then into the syrup. Place on a wire rack to dry. Replace the boiling water as it cools, and the syrup as it becomes cloudy.

4 Dry the fruit again for 2–3 days, turning occasionally.

Crystallised Flowers, Petals or Leaves
~

1 egg white
flowers, petals or leaves (see page 179)
caster sugar
~

Lightly whisk the egg white. Divide the flowers, petals or leaves, leaving a short piece of stalk on each one, if possible.

2 Paint both sides of each flower, petal or leaf with the lightly whisked egg white.

3 Sprinkle both sides with caster sugar, shaking off the excess. Leave to dry.

4 If necessary, sprinkle a second time with sugar to ensure they are evenly coated. Leave to dry completely before storing in an airtight container or jar.

To crystallise leaves, paint both sides with lightly whisked egg white.

Dip wet leaves in caster sugar, shake off surplus and leave to dry.

Mincemeats

Mincemeat was originally a way of preserving meat without using the smoking or salting methods. Today, mincemeat is a mixture of fruits, mostly dried, preserved in alcohol and sugar. The only reminder of the past is the addition of suet.

Pot and cover mincemeat in the same way as jam (see page 12).

Vegetarian Mincemeat

Vegetarian 'suet' is now available from supermarkets and can be substituted for beef suet in any of the following recipes.

Mincemeat-Making Problems

Fermentation   This is usually marked by oozing out of the jars, and is generally caused by lack of care in preparation, eg. mixing on a floury board, insufficient sugar, not enough lemon juice, unsuitable apples, or poor storage conditions. Possibly the most frequent cause is using insufficient sugar, or the inclusion in the mixture of too large a proportion of soft sweet or semi-sweet apples instead of a measured quantity of hard sour apples. It is important not to introduce excess flour, but small amounts of flour, such as are contained in packaged suet, do not seem to cause trouble. If fermentation has occurred, boil the mincemeat in a saucepan, and re-pot in sterilised jars. This will spoil the natural appearance, but will not affect the taste of the finished product.

Fermentation should not, however, be confused with the juiciness which develops once the sugar has begun to form a syrup. This syrupy condition is a sign that the mincemeat is maturing well.

Drying after storage   If mincemeat becomes dry with keeping, stir in a little of the type of alcohol used in the original mixture.

Mixed Fruit and Nut Mincemeat
~

MAKES ABOUT 2.5 KG (5 ¹/₂ LB)

1.6 kg (3¹/₂ lb) dried mixed fruit
225 g (8 oz) cooking apples, peeled, cored and grated
100 g (4 oz) blanched almonds, chopped
450 g (1 lb) dark brown soft sugar
175 g (6 oz) shredded suet
5 ml (1 tsp) grated nutmeg
5 ml (1 tsp) ground cinnamon
grated rind and juice of 1 lemon
grated rind and juice of 1 orange
300 ml (¹/₂ pint) brandy or sherry
~

Put the dried fruits, apples and almonds in a large bowl. Add the sugar, suet, spices, lemon and orange rinds and juice and brandy or sherry, then mix all the ingredients together thoroughly.

2 Cover the mincemeat and leave to stand for 2 days. Stir well, put into jars and cover as for jam (see page 12). Allow at least 2 weeks to mature before using.

Note   For mincemeat that will keep well, use a firm, hard type of apple, such as Wellington; a juicy apple, such as Bramley's, may make the mixture too moist.

Cherry and Nut Mincemeat
~

MAKES ABOUT 1.5 KG (3 LB)

175 g (6 oz) currants
175 g (6 oz) seedless raisins
175 g (6 oz) sultanas
225 g (8 oz) glacé cherries
225 g (8 oz) cooking apples, peeled, cored and grated
100 g (4 oz) walnuts, chopped
100 g (4 oz) shredded suet
350 g (12 oz) demerara sugar
5 ml (1 tsp) ground mixed spice
300 ml (½ pint) brandy or rum
~

Place all the ingredients in a large bowl. Mix well together, cover and leave for 2 days.

2 Stir well, put into jars and cover as for jam (see page 12). Allow at least 2 weeks to mature before using.

Eliza Acton's Mincemeat
~

MAKES ABOUT 3 KG (6 LB)

4 lemons
350 g (12 oz) currants
350 g (12 oz) seedless raisins
350 g (12 oz) chopped mixed peel
350 g (12 oz) apples, peeled and cored (prepared weight)
350 g (12 oz) shredded suet
450 g (1 lb) sugar
5 ml (1 tsp) ground mace
5 ml (1 tsp) ground cloves
5 ml (1 tsp) ground ginger
5 ml (1 tsp) salt
about 300 ml (½ pint) rum or brandy
~

Put the lemons in a saucepan of water, bring to the boil and simmer until tender.

2 Meanwhile, mince the fruit and suet and mix well together.

3 When the lemons are soft, cut them open, remove the pips and mince the rind and pulp. Add to the rest of the fruit with the sugar, spices, salt and rum or brandy (using more if liked).

4 Mix well, put into jars and cover as for jam (see page 12). Allow at least 2 weeks to mature before using.

Note This mincemeat improves with storing and keeps for 1 year. If necessary, add a little more rum or brandy to moisten.

Apricot and Orange Mincemeat
~

MAKES ABOUT 2 KG (4 LB)

225 g (8 oz) dried apricots, soaked overnight
grated rind and juice of 2 large oranges
225 g (8 oz) seedless raisins
225 g (8 oz) currants
225 g (8 oz) sultanas
100 g (4 oz) chopped mixed peel
450 g (1 lb) demerara sugar
100 g (4 oz) blanched almonds, chopped
225 g (8 oz) shredded suet
30 ml (2 tbsp) marmalade
10 ml (2 tsp) ground mixed spice
2.5 ml (½ tsp) salt
60 ml (4 tbsp) sherry
100 ml (4 fl oz) rum
~

Drain the apricots, pat dry with absorbent kitchen paper and chop.

2 Mix the grated orange rind and juice, the dried fruit (including the apricots), mixed peel, sugar, almonds, suet, marmalade, spice and salt thoroughly together. Cover and leave for 24 hours.

3 Add the sherry and rum and stir well to mix, then pot and cover as for jam (see page 12).

Almond Whisky Mincemeat
~

MAKES ABOUT 1.1 KG (2¹/₂ LB)

100 g (4 oz) blanched almonds, finely chopped
100 g (4 oz) no-soak dried apricots, finely chopped
50 g (2 oz) dried figs, finely chopped
50 g (2 oz) stoned dried dates, finely chopped
350 g (12 oz) cooking apples, peeled, cored and finely chopped
225 g (8 oz) sultanas
150 g (5 oz) seedless raisins
175 g (6 oz) shredded suet
5 ml (1 tsp) ground cinnamon
5 ml (1 tsp) grated nutmeg
pinch of ground allspice
100 g (4 oz) dark brown soft sugar
300 ml (¹/₂ pint) whisky
finely grated rind and juice of 2 oranges
finely grated rind and juice of 1 small lemon
~

*P*ut the almonds, apricots, figs, dates and apples in a non-metallic bowl with the next eight ingredients.

2 Stir in the grated rind and strained juice of the oranges and lemon. Cover and leave to stand overnight.

3 Stir well, pack tightly into jars and cover as for jam (see page 12). Store in a cool, dry place for about 6 weeks before using. (Will store for a further 3 months.)

Citrus Mincemeat
~

MAKES ABOUT 1.1 KG (2¹/₂ LB)

100 g (4 oz) each dried apricots, raisins and flaked almonds
350 g (12 oz) sultanas
225 g (8 oz) carrots, peeled and grated
175 g (6 oz) shredded suet
100 g (4 oz) dark brown soft sugar
7.5 ml (1¹/₂ tsp) ground cinnamon
2.5 ml (¹/₂ tsp) grated nutmeg
6 whole green cardamoms
finely grated rind and juice of 1 orange
finely grated rind and juice of 1 lemon
finely grated rind and juice of 1 lime
45 ml (3 tbsp) Grand Marnier
150 ml (¹/₄ pint) medium sherry
~

*S*nip the apricots into small pieces and place in a bowl with the roughly chopped raisins, almonds and sultanas. Stir in the carrot with the suet, sugar and ground spices.

2 Split the cardamoms and remove the seeds. Crush the seeds, using a pestle and mortar or in a strong bowl with the end of a rolling pin. Add to the fruit with the orange, lemon and lime rinds and 90 ml (6 tbsp) strained mixed juices.

3 Pour in the Grand Marnier and sherry and stir well to mix. Leave to stand for about 1 hour, then pack tightly into jars and cover as for jam (see page 12). Store in a cool place for at least 2 weeks before using.

Opposite: Almond Whisky Mincemeat (above)

Apricot, Walnut and Cointreau Mincemeat
~

MAKES ABOUT 1.8 KG (4 LB)

350 g (12 oz) no-soak dried apricots, chopped
225 g (8 oz) sultanas
100 g (4 oz) chopped mixed peel
175 g (6 oz) walnut halves, chopped
225 g (8 oz) stoned dried dates, chopped
15 ml (1 tbsp) ground mixed spice
10 ml (2 tsp) ground cinnamon
100 g (4 oz) dark brown soft sugar
finely grated rind of 1 lemon
300 ml (½ pint) Cointreau
175 g (6 oz) shredded suet

~

Mix all the ingredients in a large bowl. Cover and leave in a cool place for 2 days, stirring occasionally.

2 Stir again, then pot and cover as for jam (see page 12). Allow at least 2 weeks to mature before using.

Quick Mincemeat
~

MAKES ABOUT 900 G (2 LB)

225 g (8 oz) cooking apples, peeled, cored and roughly chopped
450 g (1 lb) seedless raisins and currants, mixed, or
450 g (1 lb) sultanas
100 g (4 oz) chopped mixed peel
100 g (4 oz) demerara sugar
225 g (8 oz) seedless green grapes, skinned and chopped
grated rind of 1 orange and 1 lemon
15 ml (1 tbsp) lemon juice
5 ml (1 tsp) ground cinnamon or mixed spice
a pinch of salt

~

This is a quick, fruity mincemeat, not suitable for long keeping, but popular with those who do not like suet.

2 Mix the apples, dried fruit and peel in a large bowl. Add the sugar and mix well together.

3 Add the remaining ingredients, mix well, pot and cover as for jam (see page 12). Store in a cool place for no more than a week.

Spicy Carrot Mincemeat
~

MAKES ABOUT 1.2 KG (2³/₄ LB)

225 g (8 oz) cooking apples, peeled and cored
100 g (4 oz) carrots, peeled
450 g (1 lb) sultanas
225 g (8 oz) currants
grated rind and juice of 1 orange
100 g (4 oz) shredded suet
pinch of salt
100 g (4 oz) demerara sugar
60 ml (4 tbsp) sherry
5 ml (1 tsp) grated nutmeg
5 ml (1 tsp) ground cloves
5 ml (1 tsp) ground cinnamon
5 ml (1 tsp) ground allspice

~

Finely grate the apples and carrots. Place in a large bowl and add all the remaining ingredients. Mix well together. Put into jars and cover as for jam (see page 12). Allow 2 weeks to mature before using.

Mixed Fruit Mincemeat
~

MAKES ABOUT 2 KG (4¹/₂ LB)

100 g (4 oz) dried apricots
100 g (4 oz) dried figs
100 g (4 oz) chopped mixed peel
225 g (8 oz) currants
225 g (8 oz) seedless raisins
225 g (8 oz) sultanas
225 g (8 oz) shredded suet
175 g (6 oz) chopped mixed nuts
450 g (1 lb) demerara sugar
30 ml (2 tbsp) orange marmalade
finely grated rind and juice of 1 medium orange
finely grated rind and juice of 1 lemon
45 ml (3 tbsp) rum
45 ml (3 tbsp) sherry

~

Snip the apricots and figs in small pieces into a large bowl. Add the remaining dry ingredients and mix together.

2 Stir in the marmalade with the finely grated orange and lemon rinds. Add the orange and lemon juices with the rum and sherry. (If the mincemeat is to be stored for more than 6 weeks, add an extra 45 ml/3 tbsp each of rum and sherry.) Mix well.

3 Pack into warmed jars and cover as for jam (see page 12). Store for at least 1 week before use.

Short-term and other Preserves

Although salting and curing are no longer recommended as practical methods of preserving meat and fish in the home, it is possible to preserve some meat and fish for a limited length of time by other methods. Many of these short-term preserves make worthwhile and delicious additions to the busy cook's storecupboard. This chapter contains a mixture of short-term preserves which take their inspiration from all corners of the world, ranging from the traditional *rillettes* (see right) through more modern and flavoursome spreads, sauces and butters to melt in the mouth cheeses or mushrooms in oil.

Methods of short-term preserving allow foods to be stored for anything from a few days to 3 months.

Meat can be prepared in the form of *rillettes* and stored in the refrigerator for up to 2 months before serving. This method of preserving best suits meats that are naturally fatty, such as pork or duck. It is important to remove all moisture from the meat, so it is first salted and then cooked for a long time until it is very tender. After cooking, the fat is strained off the meat and reserved. The meat is then separated into strands with a fork and piled into small pots or a large dish before being covered with the reserved fat.

Potted beef or shrimps make useful starters for a dinner party as they can be made a few days in advance and sealed under clarified butter until required.

Sealing with Fat or Clarified Butter

Cooked meat or fish will keep for a longer period if stored under a seal of fat or clarified butter. The seal excludes air and moisture which encourage the growth of bacteria. Once the seal has been broken, the meat or fish should be eaten within a week.

Preserving in Vinegar

Vinegar acts as a preservative and some fish can be stored in much the same way as fruit and vegetables are pickled (see pages 76–78). Fish prepared in this way will keep for about a month in the refrigerator (see the recipe for Rollmop Herrings on page 203).

Tapenade
~

SERVES 3−4

50 g (2 oz) can anchovy fillets
milk
75 g (3 oz) stoned black olives (about 36)
60 ml (4 tbsp) capers
100 g (4 oz) can tuna fish in oil, drained
50 ml (2 fl oz) olive oil
15 ml (1 tbsp) lemon juice
about 15 ml (1 tbsp) brandy
black pepper

~

*S*oak the anchovies overnight in a little milk. Drain well.

2 Place the anchovies, olives, capers and tuna fish in a blender or food processor and blend to a thick paste.

3 Gradually add the olive oil and juice drop by drop, as if making mayonnaise, to form a smooth paste. Add the brandy and black pepper to taste.

4 Pack into small attractive pots or jars, cover with a layer of olive oil and seal tightly. The mixture will keep in the refrigerator for several weeks.

5 To serve, stir in the top layer of oil and serve with hot bread or toast, or warm steamed crudités of your choice.

Harissa (Fiery Sauce)
~

MAKES ABOUT 30 ML (2 TBSP)

25 g (1 oz) dried red chillies
1 garlic clove, skinned and chopped
5 ml (1 tsp) caraway seeds
5 ml (1 tsp) cumin seeds
5 ml (1 tsp) coriander seeds
pinch of salt
olive oil

~

*S*oak the chillies in hot water for 1 hour. Drain well, then put in a pestle and mortar or electric mill with the garlic clove and spices, and grind to a paste.

2 Put into a small jar, cover with olive oil and seal. *Harissa* will keep in the refrigerator for up to 2 months. The oil can be used in salad dressings.

Pesto
~

MAKES ENOUGH TO DRESS 4 SERVINGS OF PASTA

50 g (2 oz) fresh basil leaves
2 garlic cloves, skinned
30 ml (2 tbsp) pine nuts
salt and freshly ground pepper
100 ml (4 fl oz) olive oil
50 g (2 oz) Parmesan cheese

~

*P*lace the basil, garlic, pine nuts, salt and pepper and olive oil in an electric blender or food processor and blend until very creamy.

2 Transfer the mixture to a bowl, grate in the cheese and mix together thoroughly. Transfer to a screw-topped jar. Pesto will keep for up to 2 weeks in the refrigerator. Taste and adjust the seasoning before serving.

Hazelnut and Coriander Pesto
~

**MAKES ABOUT 300 ML (¹/₂ PINT)
(ENOUGH FOR 4–6 SERVINGS OF PASTA)**

75 g (3 oz) hazelnuts
1 large bunch of coriander, weighing about 100 g (4 oz)
2–3 garlic cloves, skinned and crushed
finely grated rind and juice of ¹/₂ lemon
about 150 ml (¹/₄ pint) olive, sunflower or corn oil
salt and freshly ground black pepper

~

Spread the hazelnuts on a baking sheet and cook under a hot grill until lightly toasted. Tip into a blender or food processor.

2 Trim the stalks from the coriander and discard. Put the leaves into the blender with the garlic and the lemon rind and juice. Process until finely chopped, then, with the machine still running, gradually add the oil in a thin, steady stream until you have a fairly thick, sauce-like consistency.

3 Season with black pepper and a little salt. Turn into a bowl or a jar and cover tightly. Store in the refrigerator for up to 2 weeks.

Anchovy Caper Spread
~

MAKES ABOUT 60 ML (4 TBSP)

2 tins anchovy fillets
15 ml (1 tbsp) capers
25 g (1 oz) stoned black olives
15 ml (1 tbsp) coarse-grained mustard
pinch of dried basil and thyme
freshly ground pepper
30–45 ml (2–3 tbsp) olive oil (optional)

~

Drain the anchovies, reserving the oil. Put the anchovies in a food processor with the capers, olives, mustard, basil, thyme and pepper.

2 Blend until smooth, then add the oil from the anchovies, or the olive oil if preferred, and process again until reduced to a soft paste.

3 Pack the spread into small attractive pots or jars, cover with a layer of oil and seal tightly. Store in the refrigerator for several weeks.

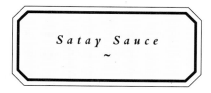

Satay Sauce
~

MAKES ABOUT 300 ML (¹/₂ PINT)

15 ml (1 tbsp) vegetable oil
1 small onion, skinned and finely chopped
5 ml (1 tsp) chilli powder
5 ml (1 tsp) chopped fresh lemon grass or finely
grated lemon rind
1 garlic clove, skinned and crushed
50 g (2 oz) creamed coconut
60 ml (4 tbsp) crunchy peanut butter
30 ml (2 tbsp) soy sauce

~

Heat the oil in a heavy-based saucepan and fry the onion for about 10 minutes or until brown and crisp. Add the remaining ingredients and 150 ml (¹/₄ pint) boiling water.

2 Bring to the boil, stirring all the time, then simmer for 3–4 minutes. Leave to cool.

3 Pour the sauce into a screw-topped jar and store in the refrigerator for up to 2 weeks.

4 Serve the sauce warm or cold with grilled chicken, prawns, beef or vegetables.

Salsa Verde
~

MAKES ABOUT 200 ML (7 FL OZ)

100 ml (4 fl oz) olive oil
15 ml (1 tbsp) white wine vinegar or lemon juice
45 ml (3 tbsp) chopped fresh parsley
30 ml (2 tbsp) capers, chopped
1 garlic clove, skinned and finely chopped
3 anchovy fillets, drained and finely chopped
2.5 ml (¹/₂ tsp) prepared mustard
freshly ground pepper

~

Put all the ingredients in a bowl or screw-topped jar and whisk or shake together.

2 Transfer to a screw-topped jar, if necessary, cover tightly and store in the refrigerator for 2–3 weeks. Serve with pasta, baked potatoes, fish, grilled meat or salads.

Salsa di Noci
(Walnut Dressing)
~

MAKES ABOUT 225 ML (8 FL OZ)

1 small slice of wholemeal bread
40 g (1¹/₂ oz) shelled walnuts
10 ml (2 tsp) lemon juice
1 garlic clove, skinned
salt and freshly ground pepper
200 ml (7 fl oz) olive oil

~

Remove the crusts from the slice of bread and soak it in cold water for a few minutes.

2 Squeeze out the excess moisture and put the bread in a food processor.

3 Add the walnuts, lemon juice, garlic, salt and pepper, and blend until the mixture is very finely ground.

4 Gradually add the oil through the funnel, while the machine is still running, until it is all incorporated.

Transfer the dressing to a screw-topped jar and store in the refrigerator for up to 1 week.

5 Check the seasoning and stir well before serving the sauce with salads, baked potatoes, pasta or steamed vegetables.

Preserved Wild Mushrooms
~

MAKES ABOUT 2 LITRES (3¹/₂ PINTS)

1 small onion, skinned and chopped
1 carrot, chopped
olive oil
2 garlic cloves, skinned
salt and freshly ground pepper
450 ml (³/₄ pint) white wine vinegar
sprigs of rosemary, thyme and parsley
3 fresh bay leaves
6 coriander seeds, crushed
12 whole white peppercorns, crushed
900 g (2 lb) wild mushrooms, eg. chanterelles, ceps, etc.

~

Sauté the onion and carrot in a little oil with the garlic for about 5 minutes or until beginning to soften. Add the salt, pepper, vinegar, herbs, coriander and peppercorns and 450 ml (³/₄ pint) water. Bring to the boil, then boil, uncovered, for 10 minutes.

2 Put the mushrooms in a large, non-metallic bowl and pour over the vinegar mixture. Cover and leave to soak overnight.

3 Strain the mushrooms from the liquid and pack into a jar. Add the bay leaves, herbs and seasoning. Cover with olive oil and seal with a lid. Store for 3–4 weeks before using. Serve with thick slices of warm bread to absorb the mushroom juices.

Opposite: Preserved Wild Mushrooms (above)

Sweet and Sour Cranberry Sauce
~

MAKES ABOUT 900 G (2 LB)

2 cinnamon sticks
6 whole allspice berries
6 cloves
225 g (8 oz) cooking apples, peeled, cored and chopped
1-cm (1/2-inch) piece of fresh root ginger, peeled and finely chopped, or 5 ml (1 tsp) ground ginger
450 g (1 lb) cranberries
300 ml (1/2 pint) cider vinegar
350 g (12 oz) demerara sugar

~

*T*ie the cinnamon, allspice and cloves in a piece of muslin and put in a saucepan with the apples, ginger, cranberries and vinegar. Bring to the boil, cover and simmer for 10 minutes or until the fruits are soft but still retain their shape.

2 Remove the pan from the heat and stir in the sugar. Return to the heat and simmer gently, uncovered, stirring continuously, for a further 20 minutes. Remove the spices.

3 Transfer the sauce to sterilised jars and cover with vinegar-proof lids. Store in a cool, dry place for up to 3 months.

Elderberry Sauce
~

MAKES ABOUT 900 ML (1 1/2 PINTS)

900 g (2 lb) elderberries
175 g (6 oz) onion, skinned and chopped
10 ml (2 tsp) salt
300 ml (1/2 pint) spiced vinegar (see page 127)
700 g (1 1/2 lb) sugar

~

*S*trip the berries from their stalks, wash and drain. Place all the ingredients in a saucepan and simmer gently until the fruit is well broken down and the onions are tender.

2 Press the mixture through a nylon sieve, then return to the pan. Simmer until the sauce has thickened and no excess vinegar remains.

3 Cool, then transfer to sterilised bottles and cover tightly with vinegar-proof lids. Store in the refrigerator for up to 2 weeks.

Zahter Seasoning
~

MAKES ABOUT 60 ML (4 TBSP)

15 ml (1 tbsp) sesame seeds
15 ml (1 tbsp) ground dried marjoram
15 ml (1 tbsp) ground dried thyme
15 ml (1 tbsp) grated lemon rind
5 ml (1 tsp) salt

~

*M*ix all the ingredients together and store in a screw-topped jar for up to 2 weeks. Use to flavour salads, stews and breads or beat into softened butter and spread on to a French loaf cut in 2.5-cm (1-inch) slices. Wrap in foil and bake in the oven until hot.

Wholegrain Mustard with Honey

~

MAKES ABOUT 800 G (1 LB 12 OZ)

225 g (8 oz) white mustard seeds
about 300 ml (½ pint) garlic wine vinegar
15 ml (1 tbsp) ground cinnamon
pinch of ground ginger
75 ml (5 tbsp) clear honey

~

Place the mustard seeds, vinegar and spices in a medium bowl. Cover and leave to soak overnight.

2 Pound the mixture to a coarse paste with the honey, using a pestle and mortar, or in a strong bowl with the end of a rolling pin. Add a little more vinegar, if necessary, to mix to a stiff paste.

3 Transfer to sterilised jars, cover tightly with vinegar-proof lids and store in the refrigerator for up to a month.

Goats' Cheeses in Herb and Saffron Oil

~

MAKES ABOUT 1.6 LITRES (2½ PINTS)

8 fresh goats' cheeses (about 50 g/2 oz each) such as Crottin
1.1 litres (2 pints) Herb and Saffron Oil (see page 127)

~

Place the cheeses in a large, wide-necked jar. Gently pour over the Herb and Saffron Oil to cover completely.

2 Cover tightly and store in the refrigerator for at least 1 week before using. Store for up to 1 month. To serve, spread on warm bread with a little of the flavoured oil and brown under a hot grill. The oil can also be used for drizzling over crusty bread or mixed salad leaves, or for basting grilled meats and fish.

Yogurt Cheeses in Oil

~

MAKES ABOUT 16 CHEESES

600 ml (1 pint) Greek yogurt
olive oil
sprigs of fresh herbs, such as bay leaves, coriander, thyme and rosemary
chillies (optional)
garlic cloves, skinned (optional)

~

Spoon the yogurt in a mound on to a large piece of muslin. Gather the ends of the muslin up around the yogurt and tie in a bundle with string. Hang up the yogurt over a bowl to catch the drips and leave in a cool place to drain for 24 hours.

2 Pour the olive oil into a sterile jar until it is about 2.5 cm (1 inch) deep. Unwrap the yogurt cheese and roll into small balls. Drop the cheeses, one by one, into the oil, adding more oil each time you add a cheese so they do not stick together.

3 Pour in enough oil to cover the cheeses completely. Add the herbs and chillies and garlic, if using. Cover and leave for at least 3 days. Store in a cool place for up to 2 weeks. Serve the cheeses with salads, warm breads or baked potatoes. The oil can be used to flavour salads or for sautéing vegetables.

Fresh Mango Chutney

~

MAKES ABOUT 225 G (8 OZ)

1 large ripe mango
1 fresh green chilli, seeded
juice of 1 lime
1.25 ml (1/4 tsp) cayenne
2.5 ml (1/2 tsp) salt

~

Slice the mango in half lengthways through to the stone. Cut all the way round, then, keeping the flat side of the knife against the stone, saw the mango flesh free from the stone. Repeat with the other side.

2 Using the point of a knife, make 5 or 6 diagonal cuts through the flesh, but not through the skin. Then make another 5 or 6 cuts at right angles to the first set, so that you have a diamond pattern in the flesh.

3 Turn the skin inside out so that the cubes of flesh stand up, then cut these off with the knife and place in a bowl.

4 Cut the chilli into fine rings and mix with the mango cubes, lime juice, cayenne and salt. Chill for 1 hour before serving. This chutney will keep for up to 2 days in the refrigerator.

Fresh Coriander Chutney

~

MAKES ABOUT 300 ML (1/2 PINT)

100 g (4 oz) fresh coriander, washed and dried
1 medium onion, skinned and roughly chopped
2 fresh green chillies, seeded
2.5-cm (1-inch) piece of fresh root ginger, peeled
5 ml (1 tsp) salt
30 ml (2 tbsp) lemon or lime juice
15 ml (1 tbsp) desiccated coconut

~

Put all the ingredients in a blender or food processor and blend until smooth.

2 Transfer to a glass or plastic bowl, cover and chill in the refrigerator for up to 1 week.

Fresh Carrot Chutney

~

MAKES ABOUT 450 G (1 LB)

450 g (1 lb) carrots, peeled
1 small onion, skinned
45 ml (3 tbsp) chopped fresh mint
2.5-cm (1-inch) piece of fresh root ginger, peeled and finely chopped
7.5 ml (1 1/2 tsp) salt
60 ml (4 tbsp) lemon or lime juice

~

Grate the carrots and onion finely and mix together with the mint, ginger and salt.

2 Add enough lemon or lime juice to moisten. Transfer to a screw-topped jar, cover and refrigerate until required. This chutney will keep in the refrigerator for 2–3 days.

Opposite: Yogurt Cheeses in Oil (page 199)

Fresh Mint Chutney
~

MAKES ABOUT 350 G (12 OZ)

50 g (2 oz) fresh mint leaves
60 ml (4 tbsp) fresh coriander leaves
1 medium onion, skinned and roughly chopped
juice of ¹/₂–1 lemon
2.5 ml (¹/₂ tsp) sugar
2.5 ml (¹/₂ tsp) salt
~

Wash the mint and coriander leaves and dry thoroughly with absorbent kitchen paper.

2 Put the onion in a blender or food processor with a little lemon juice and blend until minced.

3 Add the mint and coriander, sugar, salt and remaining lemon juice and blend to form a smooth paste.

4 Turn into a bowl or screw-topped jar, cover tightly and store in the refrigerator for up to 3 days.

Fresh Onion Relish
~

SERVES 4

1 medium onion, skinned
juice of 1 lemon
2.5 ml (¹/₂ tsp) paprika
salt and freshly ground pepper
~

Cut the onion crossways into very, very thin rings. Put in a bowl and add the remaining ingredients, with salt and pepper to taste.

2 Toss together, then cover tightly and leave to marinate for about 1 hour. Store for up to 3 days in the refrigerator.

Potted Beef
~

MAKES ABOUT 350 G (12 OZ)

450 g (1 lb) stewing steak, cut into 1 cm (¹/₂ inch) cubes
150 ml (¹/₄ pint) beef stock
1 clove
1 blade of mace
salt and freshly ground pepper
50 g (2 oz) butter, melted
fresh bay leaves, to garnish (optional)
~

Put the meat in a casserole with the stock, clove, mace and salt and pepper to taste. Cover and cook in the oven at 180°C (350°F) mark 4 for 2¹/₂–3 hours, or until tender.

2 Remove the clove and mace and drain off the stock, setting it aside.

3 Mince the meat twice or place it in a blender or food processor and blend for several minutes or until smooth. Add half the melted butter and enough of the reserved stock to moisten.

4 Press the mixture into small pots and cover with the remaining melted butter. Store in the refrigerator and use within a few days. Serve garnished with fresh bay leaves, if possible.

Potted Chicken with Tarragon

~

SERVES 6–8

1.4 kg (3 lb) oven-ready chicken
45 ml (3 tbsp) dry sherry
15 ml (1 tbsp) chopped fresh tarragon or 5 ml (1 tsp) dried
50 g (2 oz) butter
1 onion, skinned and chopped
1 carrot, peeled and chopped
salt and freshly ground pepper
melted butter

~

Place the chicken in a flameproof casserole with the sherry, tarragon, butter, vegetables and salt and pepper to taste. Cover tightly and cook in the oven at 180°C (350°F) mark 4 for about 1½ hours.

2 Lift the chicken out of the casserole and cut off all the flesh, reserving the skin and bones. Coarsely mince the chicken meat in a food processor or mincer.

3 Return the skin and broken up bones to the casserole. Boil the contents rapidly until the liquid has reduced to 225 ml (8 fl oz). Strain, reserving the juices.

4 Mix the minced chicken and juices together, then check the seasoning. Pack into small dishes, cover with melted butter and store in the refrigerator for up to 2 days. Serve as a starter with Melba toast.

Rollmop Herrings

~

MAKES 12

6 small herrings, cleaned and filleted
12 small pickled gherkins
2 medium onions, skinned and thinly sliced
2 bay leaves
2.5 ml (½ tsp) mustard seeds
3 whole cloves
6 peppercorns
450 ml (¾ pint) distilled vinegar
60 ml (4 tbsp) olive oil
5 ml (1 tsp) salt

~

Roll each herring fillet, skin-side out, firmly around a gherkin and secure with wooden cocktail sticks. Place in a wide-necked jar in layers, alternating with layers of onion, bay leaves, mustard seeds, cloves and peppercorns.

2 Heat the vinegar, oil and salt together and bring just to boiling point, then allow to cool slightly. Pour over the herrings.

3 Cover the jars and leave in the refrigerator to marinate for 2–3 days before serving. The rollmops will keep, under refrigeration, for 3 weeks after they are ready. Serve as an appetiser or with salad.

Rillettes de Porc
~

SERVES 4–6

900 g (2 lb) belly or neck of pork, rinded and boned
salt
450 g (1 lb) back port fat
1 garlic clove, skinned and bruised
bouquet garni
freshly ground black pepper

~

ub the meat well with salt and leave it to stand for 4–6 hours.

2 Cut the meat into thin strips along the grooves left after the bones were removed. Cut the pork fat into thin strips and put the meat and fat together in an ovenproof dish. Bury the garlic clove and bouquet garni in the centre, season with pepper and add 75 ml (5 tbsp) water.

3 Cover and cook in the oven at 150°C (300°F) mark 2 for about 4 hours. Discard the bouquet garni and garlic and season well.

4 Strain the fat from the meat and, when well drained, pound it slightly with the back of a wooden spoon. Remove the meat from the dish and pull it into fine shreds with two forks. Pile lightly into a glazed earthenware or china jar and pour the fat over the top.

5 Cover the jar with foil and keep in the refrigerator.

6 *Rillettes* should be soft-textured, so allow to come to room temperature before serving with toast or French bread. Store for 1–2 months but use within a week.

Potted Shrimps
~

SERVES 4

225 g (8 oz) butter
150 g (5 oz) peeled shrimps
pinch of ground mace
pinch of cayenne pepper
pinch of grated nutmeg

~

*M*elt half the butter in a saucepan. Add the shrimps and heat very gently without boiling. Add the seasonings.

2 Pour the shrimps into ramekin dishes or small pots and leave them to cool.

3 Gently heat the remaining butter in a pan until it melts, then continue to heat slowly, without browning. Remove from the heat and leave to stand for a few minutes for the salt and sediment to settle, then carefully pour a little clarified butter over the shrimps to cover. Leave until set. Store in the refrigerator and use within 2–3 days. Once the seal has been broken eat within 1–2 days.

4 To serve, unless the pots are really attractive, turn the shrimps out on to individual plates lined with a few lettuce leaves, but try to retain the shape of the pot. Before serving, remove from the refrigerator and leave at room temperature for about 30 minutes. Serve with lemon wedges and brown bread or Melba toast.

Whisky Butter
~

MAKES ABOUT 250 G (9 OZ)

100 g (4 oz) unsalted butter, softened
100 g (4 oz) light brown soft sugar
grated rind of 1 small orange
1.25 ml (¼ tsp) ground mixed spice
pinch of ground green cardamom
45 ml (3 tbsp) whisky
lemon juice

~

Cream the butter and sugar together until pale and soft. Add the orange rind and spices.

2 Gradually beat in the whisky and 5 ml (1 tsp) lemon juice. Spoon into small, wide-necked pots, cover and store in the refrigerator for up to a week.

Drambuie Butter
~

MAKES ABOUT 225 G (8 OZ)

100 g (4 oz) butter, softened
100 g (4 oz) light brown soft sugar
grated rind of ½ orange
1.25 ml (¼ tsp) ground mixed spice
pinch of ground green cardamom
45–60 ml (3–4 tbsp) Drambuie
lemon juice

~

Put the butter and sugar in a food processor and blend until soft and pale. Add the grated orange rind, the mixed spice and cardamom. Process until soft and well creamed, then gradually drip in the Drambuie and a good squeeze of lemon juice. Pack the butter into pots, cover and store in the refrigerator for up to a week.

Raspberry Butterscotch Sauce
~

MAKES ABOUT 750 ML (1¼ PINTS)

450 g (1 lb) raspberries, washed and dried
100 g (4 oz) unsalted butter
100 g (4 oz) light brown soft sugar
60 ml (4 tbsp) golden syrup
juice of 1 lemon

~

Put the raspberries in a saucepan with 150 ml (1/4 pint) water. Bring to the boil, cover and simmer for 5–10 minutes or until the fruit is very pulpy. Purée in a blender or food processor until smooth, then pass through a nylon sieve. Leave to cool.

2 Put the remaining ingredients in a medium saucepan and heat gently, stirring, until the sugar has dissolved and the ingredients are well blended. Bring to the boil and boil for 1 minute. Stir in the cooled raspberry purée and continue stirring over a gentle heat until well blended.

3 Pour into a clean, warmed jar and leave to cool, then cover and store in the refrigerator for up to 1 month. Reheat gently to serve.

Plum and Apple Spread

MAKES ABOUT 900 G (2 LB)

900 g (2 lb) ripe plums, such as Victoria, halved and stoned
900 g (2 lb) eating apples, quartered and cored
600 ml (1 pint) unsweetened red grape juice
2.5 ml (¹/₂ tsp) ground cinnamon

~

Put the plums and apples in a preserving pan or a large heavy-based saucepan with the grape juice and 300 ml (¹/₂ pint) cold water.

2 Bring slowly to the boil, then simmer over a low heat for about 50 minutes or until the fruit is reduced to a very thick purée. Stir frequently, pressing the fruit into the liquid with a wooden spoon so that it breaks up and becomes pulpy. Towards the end of cooking, add the cinnamon and stir continuously to ensure that the purée does not stick to the bottom of the pan.

3 Remove the pan from the heat and leave for about 5 minutes or until the mixture has settled. Spoon the hot spread into clean, warm, dry jars and leave until completely cold. Cover and seal the jars. Store in the refrigerator for up to 3 weeks.

Dried Fruit Spread

MAKES ABOUT 900 G (2 LB)

75 g (3 oz) no-soak dried apricots, chopped
175 g (6 oz) stoned dried dates, rinsed and chopped
175 g (6 oz) ready-to-eat dried apples, rinsed and finely chopped
grated rind of ¹/₂ lemon
5 ml (1 tsp) grated orange rind
1.25 ml (¹/₄ tsp) ground cinnamon
450 ml (³/₄ pint) unsweetened orange juice

~

Put all the ingredients in a saucepan. Bring to the boil, cover, lower the heat and simmer very gently for 30 minutes or until the mixture is thick and the orange juice has evaporated. If the mixture shows signs of sticking, add a little extra fruit juice.

2 Mash the fruit with a fork or process in a food processor until smooth. Put into washed and sterilised glass jars and cover as for jam (see page 12). Store in the refrigerator for up to 1 month.

Apricot and Cardamom Spread

MAKES ABOUT 700 G (1¹/₂ LB)

15 ml (1 tbsp) green cardamom pods
juice of 1 lemon
5 ml (1 tsp) ground cardamom
500 g (1 lb 2 oz) no-soak dried apricots, chopped

~

Crush the cardamom pods in a pestle and mortar or in a strong bowl with the end of a rolling pin until the pods break open. (No need to crush them finely.)

2 Make up the lemon juice to 300 ml (¹/₂ pint) with cold water. Put the liquid, crushed cardamoms and ground cardamom in a heavy-based saucepan and cook until just boiling. Remove from the heat and leave for 30 minutes to infuse.

3 Strain the liquid and return to the pan with the apricots. Bring to the boil, cover, lower the heat and simmer very gently for 20–25 minutes or until thick, stirring occasionally to prevent sticking. Add a little more water if necessary.

4 Mash the fruit with a fork or process in a food processor until smooth, then pot and cover as for jam (see page 12). Store in the refrigerator for up to 1 month.

Microwave
Preserves

Microwave cookers are particularly useful for preparing small quantities of preserves. Large quantities are best made by the conventional method. Making preserves in the microwave has its advantages: it is relatively quick; ordinary heatproof bowls can be used instead of preserving pans or saucepans and they are easy to clean afterwards.

Always use a large bowl to avoid boiling over (a capacity of about 3–4 litres/6 pints is ideal). Heatproof glass is most suitable. The bowl should never be more than one-third full. Always use oven gloves to remove the bowl from the oven; the bowl will get very hot because of the transference of heat from the boiling preserve.

Sterilising Jars in the Microwave

Quarter-fill up to four jars with water, arrange in a circle in the cooker, then bring to the boil on HIGH. Using oven gloves, remove each jar as it is ready and pour out the water. Invert the jars on a clean tea towel or kitchen paper. Fill with preserve while still warm. Cover in the same way as for conventional preserves.

Raspberry Jam
~

MAKES ABOUT 700 G (1¹/₂ LB)

450 g (1 lb) frozen raspberries
30 ml (2 tbsp) lemon juice
450 g (1 lb) sugar
~

Put the frozen fruit in a large heatproof bowl and microwave on HIGH for 4 minutes to thaw. Stir several times with a wooden spoon to ensure even thawing.

2 Add the lemon juice and sugar. Mix well and microwave on HIGH for 5 minutes or until the sugar has dissolved, stirring several times.

3 Microwave on HIGH for 13 minutes or until setting point is reached, stirring occasionally.

4 Pot and cover the jam in the usual way (see page 12).

Blackberry Jam
~

MAKES ABOUT 900 G (2 LB)

700 g (1¹/₂ lb) blackberries, washed
45 ml (3 tbsp) lemon juice
700 g (1¹/₂ lb) sugar
a knob of butter
~

Put the blackberries and lemon juice in a large heatproof bowl. Cover and microwave on HIGH for 5 minutes or until the blackberries are soft, stirring occasionally.

2 Stir in the sugar and microwave on HIGH for 2 minutes or until the sugar has dissolved, stirring frequently.

3 Microwave on HIGH for 15 minutes or until setting point is reached. Stir in the butter.

4 Pot and cover the jam in the usual way (see page 12).

Gooseberry Jam
~

MAKES ABOUT 900 G (2 LB)

700 g (1½ lb) gooseberries, topped, tailed and washed
700 g (1½ lb) sugar
a knob of butter

~

Put the gooseberries in a large heatproof bowl with 150 ml (¼ pint) water. Cover and microwave on HIGH for 8–10 minutes or until the gooseberries are soft.

2 Stir in the sugar and microwave on HIGH for 2 minutes or until the sugar has dissolved, stirring frequently. Microwave on HIGH for 20 minutes or until setting point is reached. Stir in the butter.

3 Pot and cover the jam in the usual way (see page 12).

Rhubarb and Ginger Jam
~

MAKES ABOUT 450 G (1 LB)

450 g (1 lb) rhubarb, trimmed (prepared weight)
450 g (1 lb) sugar
juice of 1 lemon
2.5-cm (1-inch) piece of dried root ginger, bruised
50 g (2 oz) crystallised ginger, chopped

~

Chop the rhubarb into short even-sized lengths and arrange in a large heatproof bowl in layers with the sugar. Pour over the lemon juice. Cover and leave in a cool place overnight.

2 Uncover the rhubarb and add the root ginger. Microwave on HIGH for 5 minutes or until the sugar has dissolved, stirring twice.

3 Remove the root ginger, add the crystallised ginger and microwave on HIGH for 14 minutes or until setting point is reached.

4 Pot and cover the jam in the usual way (see page 12).

Dried Apricot Jam
~

MAKES ABOUT 900 G (2 LB)

225 g (8 oz) no-soak dried apricots, roughly chopped
45 ml (3 tbsp) lemon juice
450 g (1 lb) sugar
25 g (1 oz) blanched almonds, split

~

Put the apricots, lemon juice and 600 ml (1 pint) boiling water in a large heatproof bowl. Cover and microwave on HIGH for 15 minutes, stirring occasionally.

2 Stir in the sugar. Microwave on HIGH for 2 minutes or until the sugar has dissolved. Microwave on HIGH for 12 minutes or until setting point is reached, stirring several times. Stir in the almonds.

3 Pot and cover the jam in the usual way (see page 12).

Lime Curd
~

MAKES ABOUT 450 G (1 LB)

finely grated rind and juice of 4 limes
3 eggs, beaten
250 g (9 oz) caster sugar
75 g (3 oz) unsalted butter, diced

~

Put the lime rind and juice in a large heatproof bowl. Gradually whisk in the eggs, sugar and butter, using a balloon whisk.

2 Microwave on HIGH for 4–6 minutes or until the curd is thick, whisking well every minute.

3 Remove the bowl from the cooker and continue whisking for 3–4 minutes or until the mixture is cool and thickens further.

4 Pot and cover the curd in the usual way (see page 65). Store in the refrigerator for up to 3 weeks.

Lemon and Grapefruit Curd
~

MAKES ABOUT 900 G (2 LB)

finely grated rind and juice of 2 lemons
finely grated rind and juice of 1 large grapefruit
4 eggs
225 g (8 oz) caster sugar
100 g (4 oz) unsalted butter, diced
~

Put the fruit rind and juice in a large heatproof bowl. Using a wooden spoon, beat in the eggs and sugar. Add the butter and stir well.

2 Microwave on HIGH for 7 minutes or until thickened, whisking occasionally to ensure even thickening.

3 Remove the bowl from the cooker and whisk for about 5 minutes or until the curd cools and thickens.

4 Pot and cover the curd in the usual way (see page 65).

Orange Marmalade
~

MAKES ABOUT 1.1 KG (2½ LB)

900 g (2 lb) Seville oranges
juice of 2 lemons
900 g (2 lb) sugar
a knob of butter
~

Pare the rind from the oranges, avoiding the white pith. Shred or chop the rind and set aside. Put the fruit pith, flesh and pips in a food processor and chop until the pips are broken.

2 Put the chopped mixture and lemon juice in a large heatproof bowl and add 900 ml (1½ pints) boiling water. Microwave on HIGH for 15 minutes.

3 Strain the mixture through a sieve into another large bowl and press the cooked pulp until all the juice is squeezed out. Discard the pulp. Stir the shredded rind into the hot juice and microwave on HIGH for 15 minutes or until the rind is tender, stirring occasionally. Stir in the sugar until dissolved.

4 Microwave on HIGH for about 10 minutes, stirring once during cooking, until setting point is reached. Stir in the butter, then remove any scum with a slotted spoon. Leave to cool for 15 minutes, then pot and cover the jam in the usual way (see page 51).

Crushed Strawberry Jam
~

MAKES ABOUT 700 G (1½ LB)

450 g (1 lb) strawberries, hulled
45 ml (3 tbsp) lemon juice
450 g (1 lb) sugar
a knob of butter
~

Put the strawberries in a large heatproof bowl with the lemon juice. Cover and microwave on HIGH for 5 minutes or until the strawberries are soft, stirring frequently.

2 Lightly crush the strawberries with a potato masher. Add the sugar and stir well. Microwave on LOW for 15 minutes or until the sugar has dissolved, stirring frequently.

3 Microwave on HIGH for 20–25 minutes or until setting point is reached. Stir in the butter.

4 Allow the jam to cool slightly, then pot and cover in the usual way (see page 12).

Lemon Curd
~

MAKES ABOUT 900 G (2 LB)

finely grated rind and juice of 4 large lemons
4 eggs, beaten
225 g (8 oz) caster sugar
100 g (4 oz) butter, diced

~

*P*ut the lemon rind in a large heatproof bowl. Mix the juice with the eggs and strain into the bowl. Stir in the sugar, then add the butter.

2 Microwave on HIGH for 5–6 minutes or until the curd is thick, whisking well every minute.

3 Continue whisking until the mixture is cool. (Lemon curd thickens on cooling.) Pot and cover the curd in the usual way (see page 65). Store in the refrigerator for up to 3 weeks.

Above: Lemon Curd
Opposite: Crushed Strawberry Jam (page 211)

Three Fruit Marmalade
~

MAKES ABOUT 1.4–1.8 KG (3–4 LB)

1 thin-skinned grapefruit
1 thin-skinned orange
1 thin-skinned lemon
1 kg (2.2 lb) Sugar with Pectin
~

*H*alve the fruit and squeeze out the juice, then thinly shred the peel. Put in a 2.8-litre (5-pint) heatproof bowl.

2 Add 900 ml (1½ pints) boiling water, cover and microwave on HIGH for 25 minutes or until the peel is tender.

3 Add the sugar and stir thoroughly to dissolve. Microwave on HIGH, uncovered, for 10 minutes, stirring once during cooking.

4 Remove any scum with a slotted spoon, then microwave on HIGH for a further 5 minutes, stirring once during cooking or until setting point is reached.

5 Pot and cover the marmalade in the usual way (see page 51).

Banana and Apple Spread
~

MAKES ABOUT 225 G (8 OZ)

75 g (3 oz) dried bananas
2 large eating apples, peeled, cored and finely chopped
large pinch of ground mixed spice
large pinch of ground cinnamon
100 ml (4 fl oz) unsweetened apple juice
~

*C*ut the bananas into small pieces and put in a medium heatproof bowl with the apples.

2 Stir in the mixed spice, cinnamon and apple juice and stir well to mix. Cover and microwave on HIGH for 10 minutes or until the apples are tender, stirring once.

3 Purée in a blender or food processor until smooth, then leave until cold. Cover, and store in the refrigerator for up to 1 week. Use as a spread for toast or bread.

Blackcurrant Jam
~

MAKES ABOUT 700 G (1½ LB)

450 g (1 lb) blackcurrants, strings removed and washed
700 g (1½ lb) sugar
a knob of butter
~

*P*ut the fruit in a heatproof bowl with 30 ml (2 tbsp) water. Cover and microwave on HIGH for 5–6 minutes or until the fruit is very soft, stirring from time to time. (As the skins of currants tend to be rather tough, it is important to cook the fruit really well before adding the sugar.)

2 Stir in the sugar and microwave on HIGH for 2 minutes or until the sugar has dissolved, stirring frequently.

3 Microwave on HIGH for 12 minutes or until setting point is reached. Stir in the butter.

4 Pot and cover the jam in the usual way (see page 12).

Apple Chutney
~

MAKES ABOUT 900 G (2 LB)

450 g (1 lb) cooking apples, peeled, cored and finely diced
450 g (1 lb) onions, skinned and finely chopped
100 g (4 oz) sultanas
100 g (4 oz) seedless raisins
150 g (5 oz) demerara sugar
200 ml (7 fl oz) malt vinegar
5 ml (1 tsp) ground ginger
5 ml (1 tsp) ground cloves
5 ml (1 tsp) ground allspice
grated rind and juice of ¹/₂ lemon

~

Put all the ingredients in a large heatproof bowl and microwave on HIGH for 5 minutes, stirring occasionally, or until the sugar has dissolved.

2 Microwave on HIGH for about 2 minutes or until the mixture is thick and has no excess liquid. Stir every 5 minutes during cooking to prevent the surface drying out.

3 Pot and cover the chutney in the usual way (see page 101). Store for 3 months before eating.

Mango Chutney
~

MAKES ABOUT 450 G (1 LB)

3 mangoes
2.5-cm (1-inch) piece of fresh root ginger, peeled
1 small green chilli, seeded
100 g (4 oz) light brown soft sugar
200 ml (7 fl oz) distilled or cider vinegar
2.5 ml (¹/₂ tsp) ground ginger
1 garlic clove, skinned and crushed

~

Peel the mangoes and cut the flesh away from the stone. Chop into small pieces. Finely chop the ginger and chilli.

2 Put all the ingredients in a large heatproof bowl and microwave on HIGH for 5 minutes or until the sugar has dissolved, stirring occasionally.

3 Microwave on HIGH for 15 minutes or until thick and well reduced. Stir two or three times during the first 10 minutes of cooking and after every minute for the last 5 minutes to prevent the surface of the chutney from drying out.

4 Pot and cover in the usual way (see page 101).

Carrot and Raisin Chutney
~

MAKES ABOUT 450 G (1 LB)

450 g (1 lb) carrots, peeled and coarsely grated
100 g (4 oz) seedless raisins
15 ml (1 tbsp) black poppy seeds
2 bay leaves
2.5 ml (¹/₂ tsp) ground mixed spice
2.5 ml (¹/₂ tsp) ground ginger
4 black peppercorns
50 g (2 oz) light brown soft sugar
300 ml (¹/₂ pint) white wine vinegar

~

Put all the ingredients in a large heatproof bowl and microwave on HIGH for 12–15 minutes or until the carrots are tender and the liquid has evaporated.

2 Pot and cover in the usual way (see page 101).

Indonesian Vegetable Pickle
~

MAKES ABOUT 700 G (1 1/2 LB)

1-cm (1/2-inch) piece of fresh root ginger, peeled and grated
2 large garlic cloves, skinned and crushed
10 ml (2 tsp) ground turmeric
45 ml (3 tbsp) vegetable oil
150 ml (1/4 pint) spiced pickling vinegar
1/2 cucumber
2 large carrots
175 g (6 oz) cauliflower florets
1–2 green chillies, seeded and sliced
60 ml (4 tbsp) sesame seeds
100 g (4 oz) dark brown soft sugar
100 g (4 oz) salted peanuts, roughly chopped
~

*P*ut the ginger, garlic, turmeric and oil in a large heatproof bowl and microwave on HIGH for 2 minutes, stirring occasionally. Add the vinegar and microwave on HIGH for 3–5 minutes or until boiling.

2 Meanwhile, cut the cucumber and carrots into 5 mm (1/4 inch) slices, and break the cauliflower into tiny florets.

3 Add the vegetables to the boiling vinegar, cover and microwave on HIGH for 2 minutes or until the liquid just returns to the boil. When boiling, microwave for a further 2 minutes. Stir in the remaining ingredients and mix thoroughly together.

4 Pot and cover as for pickles (see page 78). Store.

*Above (left to right): Indonesian Vegetable Pickle
(above), Mango Chutney (page 215)
Opposite: Blackcurrant Jam (page 214)*

Tomato Chutney

~

MAKES ABOUT 900 G (2 LB)

700 g (1½ lb) firm tomatoes
225 g (8 oz) cooking apples, peeled, cored and chopped
1 medium onion, skinned and chopped
100 g (4 oz) dark brown soft sugar
100 g (4 oz) sultanas
5 ml (1 tsp) salt
200 ml (7 fl oz) malt vinegar
15 g (½ oz) ground ginger
1.25 ml (¼ tsp) cayenne pepper
2.5 ml (½ tsp) mustard powder

~

*P*ut the tomatoes in a large heatproof bowl and just cover with boiling water. Microwave on HIGH for 4 minutes, then lift the tomatoes out one by one, using a slotted spoon, and remove their skins.

2 Put the apple and onion in a blender or food processor and blend to form a thick paste. Coarsely chop the tomatoes.

3 Mix all the ingredients together in a large heatproof bowl. Microwave on HIGH for 35–40 minutes or until the mixture is thick and has no excess liquid. Stir every 5 minutes during cooking and take particular care, stirring more frequently, during the last 5 minutes.

4 Pot and cover the chutney in the usual way (see page 101). Store for at least 2 months before eating.

Hot and Spicy Tomato Chutney

~

MAKES ABOUT 225 G (8 OZ)

45 ml (3 tbsp) vegetable oil
3 garlic cloves, skinned and crushed
2.5-cm (1-inch) piece of fresh root ginger, peeled
and finely grated
5 ml (1 tsp) black mustard seeds
5 ml (1 tsp) cumin seeds
5 ml (1 tsp) coriander seeds
2.5 ml (½ tsp) fenugreek seeds
5 ml (1 tsp) ground turmeric
1 red chilli, seeded and finely chopped
450 g (1 lb) ripe tomatoes, skinned and finely chopped
salt and freshly ground pepper

~

*P*ut the oil, garlic and ginger in a large heatproof bowl and microwave on HIGH for 1–2 minutes, stirring once.

2 Meanwhile, grind the mustard seeds, cumin seeds, coriander seeds and fenugreek seeds in a pestle and mortar.

3 Stir all the spices into the oil and microwave on HIGH for 1–2 minutes or until the spices are sizzling, stirring once.

4 Add the chilli and the tomatoes and mix thoroughly together. Microwave on HIGH for 10–12 minutes or until most of the liquid has evaporated, stirring occasionally. Season to taste with salt and pepper.

5 Pot and cover in the usual way (see page 101).

Mixed Fruit Chutney

~

MAKES ABOUT 1.4 KG (3 LB)

225 g (8 oz) dried apricots
225 g (8 oz) stoned dried dates
350 g (12 oz) cooking apples, peeled and cored
1 medium onion, skinned
225 g (8 oz) bananas, peeled and sliced
225 g (8 oz) dark brown soft sugar
grated rind and juice of 1 lemon
5 ml (1 tsp) ground mixed spice
5 ml (1 tsp) ground ginger
5 ml (1 tsp) curry powder
5 ml (1 tsp) salt
450 ml (³/₄ pint) distilled or cider vinegar

~

Finely chop or mince the apricots, dates, apples and onion.

2 Put all the ingredients in a large heatproof bowl and mix them together well.

3 Microwave on HIGH for 25–30 minutes or until the mixture is thick and has no excess liquid. Stir frequently during cooking, taking particular care to stir more frequently during the last 10 minutes.

4 Pot and cover the chutney in the usual way (see page 101). Store for at least 2 months before eating.

Dried Herbs

~

fresh herbs, such as parsley, basil, rosemary, coriander

~

Strip the leaves of the herbs off their stems and arrange in a single layer on a piece of absorbent kitchen paper.

2 Microwave on HIGH for 1 minute. Turn the leaves over and re-position, then microwave for a further 1–1½ minutes or until the leaves are dry and will crumble when rubbed between your fingers.

3 Store in an airtight jar in a dark place.

Three Pepper Relish

~

MAKES ABOUT 350 G (12 OZ)

1 medium onion, skinned and chopped
2 red peppers, seeded and chopped
1 red chilli, seeded and chopped
30 ml (2 tbsp) vegetable oil
2 garlic cloves, skinned and thinly sliced
15 ml (1 tbsp) light brown soft sugar
30 ml (2 tbsp) lime juice
30 ml (2 tbsp) lime juice
15 ml (1 tbsp) hoisin sauce
15 ml (1 tbsp) paprika
pinch of salt

~

Put all the ingredients in a large heatproof bowl and mix thoroughly together.

2 Microwave on HIGH for 10–15 minutes or until the vegetables are soft, stirring occasionally.

3 Pot and cover the relish in the usual way (see page 101).

Sweetcorn Relish
~

MAKES ABOUT 700 G (1¹/₂ LB)

3 sweetcorn cobs
2 medium onions, skinned and chopped
1 small green pepper, seeded and chopped
15 ml (1 tbsp) wholegrain mustard
5 ml (1 tsp) ground turmeric
30 ml (2 tbsp) plain flour
100 g (4 oz) light brown soft sugar
300 ml (¹/₂ pint) white wine vinegar
pinch of salt
~

Remove the husks and silks from the corn cobs, then wrap immediately in greaseproof paper. Microwave on HIGH for 8–10 minutes or until tender, turning over halfway through cooking. Strip the corn from the cobs.

2 Put all the remaining ingredients in a large heatproof bowl and microwave on HIGH for 5–7 minutes or until boiling, stirring once.

3 Add the corn to the rest of the ingredients and continue to microwave on HIGH for 6–7 minutes or until slightly reduced and thickened.

4 Pot and cover the relish in the usual way (see page 101).

Pickled Cherries
~

MAKES ABOUT 450 G (1 LB)

450 g (1 lb) cherries
225 g (8 oz) sugar
300 ml (¹/₂ pint) white wine vinegar
4 black peppercorns
1 clove
1 bay leaf
pinch of salt
~

Put the cherries in a 450-g (1-lb) glass jar and sprinkle with the sugar.

2 Put the vinegar and remaining ingredients in a large heatproof bowl and microwave on HIGH for 6 minutes or until boiling rapidly. Allow to cool, then pour the vinegar and spices over the cherries. Leave to marinate for 24 hours.

3 The next day, strain the vinegar from the cherries into a medium heatproof bowl. Microwave the vinegar on HIGH for 5 minutes or until boiling. Continue to microwave on HIGH for 4 minutes until reduced slightly. Allow to cool, then return the cherries to the jar and pour over the cooled vinegar.

4 Cover the cherries in the usual way (see page 78). Store for at least 2 weeks before eating.

Sweet Indian Chutney
~

MAKES ABOUT 450 G (1 LB)

700 g (1¹/₂ lb) ripe tomatoes
25 g (1 oz) blanched almonds
100 g (4 oz) light brown soft sugar
4 garlic cloves, skinned and crushed
3 bay leaves
50 g (2 oz) sultanas
15 ml (1 tbsp) nigella seeds
2.5 ml (¹/₂ tsp) chilli powder
75 ml (3 fl oz) white wine vinegar
pinch of salt
~

Roughly chop the tomatoes and almonds and put in a large heatproof bowl. Add the remaining ingredients and microwave on high for 20 minutes or until slightly reduced and thickened.

2 Pot and cover in the usual way (see page 101).

Index

A

alcohol: drinks and liqueurs, 162–70
 fruits in, 7, 139–147
all-year-round chutney, 102
almonds: almond whisky mincemeat, 189
 plum and almond hooch, 146
 salted, 158
 storing, 152
anchovies: anchovy caper spread, 195
 salted, 160
 tapenade, 194
angelica, candied, 183
aniseed grapes in vodka, 147
apples: apple and onion pickle, 89
 apple and rose petal jelly, 47
 apple and tomato chutney, 106
 apple cheese, 74
 apple chutney, 107, 215
 apple ginger jam, 22
 apricot and apple chutney, 115
 aubergine and apple chutney, 103
 banana and apple spread, 214
 black butter, 71
 blackberry and apple jam, 17
 blender apple chutney, 107
 bottling, 133–4, 138
 cherry and apple jam, 28
 cranberry and apple jelly, 38
 crunchy harvest butter, 72
 currant and apple jelly, 40
 damson and apple jelly, 47
 four fruit processor marmalade, 58
 gooseberry and apple jam, 20
 honey and apple jelly, 48
 hot tomato and apple sauce, 123
 marrow and apple chutney, 104
 mint jelly, 36
 mulberry and apple jam, 17
 mulberry and apple jelly, 46
 orange and apple chutney, 110
 orange and apple jelly, 43
 pectin extract, 10
 pickled apples, 96
 plum and apple jam, 22
 plum and apple spread, 207
 rose geranium jelly, 37
 Somerset apple jam, 22
 storing, 151–2
 windfall marmalade, 63
apricots: apricot and apple chutney, 115
 apricot and cardamom spread, 207
 apricot and orange butter, 71
 apricot and orange mincemeat, 187
 apricot brandy, 163
 apricot jam, 25
 apricot liqueur, 168
 apricot, walnut and Cointreau
  mincemeat, 190
 apricots and prunes in brandy, 142
 bottling, 133–4, 138
 dried apricot jam, 25, 210
 marrow and apricot jam, 29
 spiced apricot and raisin chutney, 115
 sweet-sour apricots, 98
aubergines: aubergine and apple chutney,
 103
 aubergine and pepper chutney, 106

B

bananas: banana and apple spread, 214
 banana chutney, 113
 lychee and banana chutney, 114
 pickled bananas, 95
Bar-Le Duc, 31
basil: pesto, 194
beans, mixed pickled, 86
beef, potted, 202
beetroot: beetroot chutney, 105
 pickled beetroot, 79
 spiced beetroot relish, 118
 storing, 154
bilberries: bilberry jam, 18
 bilberry jelly, 40
black butter, 71
blackberries: blackberry and apple jam, 17
 blackberry cheese, 72
 blackberry jam, 19, 209
 blackberry jelly, 45
 blackberry liqueur, 166
 bottling, 133–4, 138
 bramble jelly, 45
 damson and blackberry cheese, 75
 elderberry and blackberry jam, 19
blackcurrants: Bar-Le Duc, 31
 blackcurrant and rosemary syrup, 171
 blackcurrant jam, 214
 blackcurrant jelly, 44
 bottling, 133–4, 138
 cassis, 167
 currant and apple jelly, 40
 currant and port jelly, 40
blueberries: blueberry bay jam, 16
 blueberry curd, 70
bottling, 130–9
bramble jelly, 45
brandy: apricot brandy, 163
 apricots and prunes in brandy, 142
 brandied cherries, 140
 brandied peaches, 141
 brandied pineapple, 141
 cherry brandy, 163
 peaches in strawberry caramel, 142
bread and butter pickle, 83
brining, 77
butter: Drambuie butter, 206
 sealing with, 193
 whisky butter, 206
butters, fruit, 65, 71–2
butterscotch: raspberry butterscotch sauce,
 206

C

cabbage: pickled red cabbage, 81
 sauerkraut, 159
candying, 178–84
capers: anchovy caper spread, 195
 salsa verde, 196
caramel: caramelled fruits, 182
 peaches in strawberry caramel, 142
cardamom: apricot and cardamom spread,
 207
carrots: carrot and raisin chutney, 215
 carrot jam, 30
 fresh carrot chutney, 201
 pickled carrots, 79
 spicy carrot mincemeat, 191
 storing, 150, 154
cassis, 167
cauliflower, pickled, 81
celeriac, storing, 154
celery: cucumber and celery relish, 119
 storing, 154
cheese: goats' cheeses in herb and saffron
 oil, 199

yogurt cheeses in oil, 199
cheeses, fruit, 65, 72–5
cherries: black cherry jam, 26
 bottling, 133–4, 138
 brandied cherries, 140
 cérises au vinaigre, 94
 cherry and apple jam, 28
 cherry and nut mincemeat, 187
 cherry and pineapple jam, 27
 cherry and redcurrant jam, 26
 cherry brandy, 163
 four-fruit jelly, 46
 loganberry and Morello cherry jam, 17
 pickled, 220
 sweet cherry chutney, 111
chestnuts: chestnuts in syrup, 146
 storing, 152
chicken: potted chicken with tarragon, 203
chillies: green chilli pickle, 91
 harissa, 194
 hot chilli vodka, 170
chunky vegetable relish, 116
chutneys, 101–15, 201–2, 215, 218–20
cider: black butter, 71
 sweet cider jelly, 44
cinnamon: redcurrant and cinnamon jelly,
 45
citric acid, 10, 13
citrus mincemeat, 189
citrus vodka, 170
clamps, storing root vegetables, 150–1
cobnuts, storing, 155
Cointreau: apricot, walnut and Cointreau
 mincemeat, 190
 orange slices in Cointreau, 143
conserves, 9, 31–2
cordials, 175
coriander: fresh coriander chutney, 201
 hazelnut and coriander pesto, 195
crab-apples: crab-apple butter, 72
 crab-apple jelly, 38
 spiced crab-apples, 98
cranberries: cranberry and apple jelly, 38
 cranberry chutney, 107
 cranberry jam, 20
 cranberry lemon cheese, 74
 sweet and sour cranberry sauce, 198
crunchy harvest butter, 72
crystallising, 179
cucumber: bread and butter pickle, 83
 cucumber and celery relish, 119
 pickled cucumbers, 79
 storing, 154
curds, fruit, 65–70, 210–11, 213
curing, 150
currants see blackcurrants; redcurrants

D

damsons: bottling, 133–4, 138
 damson and apple jelly, 47
 damson and blackberry cheese, 75
 damson cheese, 75
 damson chutney, 114
 damson jam, 21
dates: date and orange chutney, 114
 pickled dates, 99
 pineapple and date chutney, 111
diabetic marmalade, 59
dill pickle, mixed, 87
Drambuie butter, 206
dried fruit spread, 207
drinks, 162–75

drying, 7, 155–7

E
eggs, pickled, 92
elderberries: elderberry and blackberry jam, 19
    elderberry cordial, 175
    elderberry jelly, 40
    elderberry sauce, 198
elderflowers: elderflower cordial, 175
    elderflower gooseberry jam, 21
    gooseberry and elderflower curd, 70
    gooseberry and elderflower jelly, 39
Eliza Acton's mincemeat, 187
equipment: jams and conserves, 9
    pickling, 77

F
fat, sealing with, 193
figs: bottling, 133–4, 138
    fresh fig jam, 24
    green fig chutney, 110
    spiced fig jam, 25
    sweet and sour figs, 97
filberts, storing, 155
fish: salted, 160
    short-term preserves, 193, 203–5
flowers: crystallising, 179, 184
    drying, 157
four-fruit jelly, 46
four fruit processor marmalade, 58
freezing, 7
French beans, salting, 159
fructose, 11
fruit: in alcohol, 139–47
    bottling, 130–9
    butters and cheeses, 65, 71–5
    candying, 178–84
    chutneys and relishes, 101
    curds, 65–70
    drinks (non-alcoholic), 174–5
    drying, 156
    fruit sweetmeats, 183
    jams and conserves, 9–32
    jellies, 34–48
    liqueurs and alcoholic drinks, 162–70
    marmalades, 50–63
    mincemeats, 186–91
    pickling, 77
    syrups, 162, 171
    vinegars, 125, 126

G
gages, bottling, 133–4, 139
garden mint pickle, 87
garlic: herb and garlic oil, 127
    herb and garlic vinegar, 126
geranium jelly, 37
gherkins, pickled, 82
gin: orange gin, 165
    raspberry gin, 165
    redcurrant gin, 165
    sloe gin, 163
ginger: apple ginger jam, 22
    ginger and grapefruit jelly marmalade, 62
    ginger cordial, 175
    ginger marmalade, 55
    melon and ginger jam, 28
    pickled pears with ginger, 95
    rhubarb and ginger conserve, 32
    rhubarb and ginger jam, 28, 210
    three fruit and ginger marmalade, 56
glacé fruit, 179, 184
goats' cheeses in herb and saffron oil, 199
gooseberries: bottling, 133–4, 138
    elderflower gooseberry jam, 21
    gooseberry and apple jam, 20
    gooseberry and elderflower curd, 70
    gooseberry and elderflower jelly, 39
    gooseberry cheese, 75

gooseberry chutney, 107, 111
gooseberry jam, 210
gooseberry jelly, 39
gooseberry mint jelly, 39
raspberry and gooseberry jam, 15
redcurrant and gooseberry jelly, 45
grapefruit: four fruit processor marmalade, 58
    ginger and grapefruit jelly marmalade, 62
    grapefruit and tangerine jelly, 48
    grapefruit marmalade, 58
    lemon and grapefruit curd, 211
    three fruit curd, 67
    three fruit marmalade, 213
    windfall marmalade, 63
grapes: aniseed grapes in vodka, 147
    grape jelly, 39
greengages: greengage jam, 20
    spiced peaches with plums and greengages, 146
guava jelly, 42

H
harissa, 194
harvest preserve with port, 32
haw jelly, 42
hazelnuts: hazelnut and coriander pesto, 195
    salted, 158
    storing, 155
herbs: dried, 156–7, 219
    herb and garlic oil, 127
    herb and garlic vinegar, 126
    herb and saffron oil, 127
    herb jellies, 36
    herb spice, 158
    mixed dried herbs, 158
herrings, rollmop, 203
honey: honey and apple jelly, 48
    honey lemon curd, 66
    honey-pineapple jam, 27
    wholegrain mustard with honey, 199
horseradish vinegar, 126

I
Indian chutney: hot, 102
    sweet, 220
Indonesian vegetable pickle, 217

J
jams and conserves, 9–32, 209–11, 214
japonica jelly, 38
jars: bottling, 130
    for jams, 9, 12
    for pickles, 77
    sterilising in microwave ovens, 209
jellies, 33–48
Jerusalem artichokes: pickled, 82
    storing, 154

K
ketchups, 121–2, 124
kirsch conserve, raspberry, 31
kiwi conserve, 31
kohlrabi, storing, 154
kumquats: kumquat conserve, 32
    pickled satsumas and kumquats, 95

L
leaves, crystallising, 179, 184
leeks, storing, 154
lemon: cranberry lemon cheese, 74
    four fruit processor marmalade, 58
    honey lemon curd, 66
    lemon and grapefruit curd, 211
    lemon curd, 66, 213
    lemon marmalade, 57
    lemon pickle, 92
    lemon rhubarb marmalade, 59
    lemon shred marmalade, 57
    lemon squash, 174

orange and lemon pickle, 94
pear and lemon chutney, 108
pickled lemons, 92
sweet lemon pickle, 92
sweet orange and lemon marmalade, 56
three fruit curd, 67
three fruit marmalade, 213
limes: bitter lime jelly with Pernod, 48
    lime curd, 66, 210
    lime marmalade, 58
    lime pickle, 92
    rosemary and lime vinegar, 127
    sweet pickled limes, 93
liqueurs, 162, 166–70
loganberries: bottling, 133–4, 139
    loganberry and Morello cherry jam, 17
    loganberry jam, 14
    loganberry jelly, 44
low-sugar chutney, 115
lychee and banana chutney, 114

M
mangoes: fresh mango chutney, 201
    hot mango chutney, 110
    mango chutney, 215
    sweet mango chutney, 108
marmalades, 49–63, 211, 214
marrows: marrow and apple chutney, 104
    marrow and apricot jam, 29
    marrow and tomato chutney, 104
    pickled marrow, 81
    quince and marrow jam, 23
    storing, 154
meat, short-term preserves, 193, 202–4
medlar cheese, 75
melons: melon and ginger jam, 28
    pickled melon rind, 98
    sweet pickled fruit, 99
microwave preserves, 209–20
mincemeat, 186–91
mint: fresh mint chutney, 202
    garden mint pickle, 87
    gooseberry mint jelly, 39
    mint jelly, 36
    mint sauce, 122
    quick mint jelly, 43
    redcurrant mint jelly, 45
mixed dill pickle, 87
mixed fruit chutney, 106, 219
mixed fruit mincemeat, 191
mixed fruit and nut mincemeat, 186
mixed pickle, 82
mixed vegetable pickle, 85
mould, on jam, 12
mulberries: bottling, 133–4, 138
    mulberry and apple jam, 17
    mulberry and apple jelly, 46
mushrooms: mushroom ketchup, 124
    pickled mushrooms and shallots, 78
    preserved wild mushrooms, 196
mustard: mustard pickle, 90
    mustard relish, 118
    wholegrain mustard with honey, 199

N
nasturtium seeds, pickled, 99
nectarines, bottling, 133–4
nuts: mixed fruit and nut mincemeat, 186
    storing, 152, 155

O
oils, 122, 127
onions: apple and onion pickle, 89
    fresh onion relish, 202
    green tomato and onion pickle, 86
    pickled onions, 81
    pickled walnuts and onions, 91
    storing, 150, 154
    tomato and onion chutney, 103
oranges: apricot and orange butter, 71

apricot and orange mincemeat, 187
bitter chunky marmalade, 54
date and orange chutney, 114
diabetic marmalade, 59
four fruit processor marmalade, 58
ginger marmalade, 55
marmalades, 50–9
orange and apple chutney, 110
orange and apple jelly, 43
orange and lemon pickle, 94
orange and thyme jelly, 43
orange curd, 66
orange gin, 165
orange liqueur, 167
orange marmalade, 211
orange shred marmalade, 57
orange slices in Cointreau, 143
orange squash, 174
orange whisky, 166
orange wine, 170
Oxford marmalade, 54
pickled orange rings, 93
pressure-cooked marmalade, 55
quick Seville orange marmalade, 54
rhubarb and orange chutney, 112
Seville orange marmalade, 51–2
sweet orange and lemon marmalade, 56
three fruit and ginger marmalade, 56
three fruit curd, 67
three fruit marmalade, 214
Oxford marmalade, 54

P
pans: for pickling, 77
    preserving, 9
parsley: salsa verde, 196
parsnips, storing, 150, 154
peaches: bottling, 133–4, 138
    brandied peaches, 141
    peach and raspberry jam, 24
    peach brandy, 163
    peach chutney, 113
    peach jam, 23
    peaches in strawberry caramel, 142
    spiced peaches with plums and
        greengages, 146
    spiced pickled peaches, 94
peanut butter: satay sauce, 195
pears: bottling, 133–4, 138–9
    pears and lemon chutney, 108
    pear chutney, 113
    pear jam, 24
    pear sauce, 124
    pickled pears with ginger, 95
    storing, 151–2
    sweet pickled fruit, 99
pectin, 10, 11, 12–13, 50–1
peel, candied, 182
peppercorns: pepper vodka, 170
    spiced black pepper, 158
peppers: aubergine and pepper chutney, 106
    spiced pepper chutney, 105
    three pepper relish, 219
    tomato and red pepper chutney, 103
Pernod, bitter lime jelly with, 48
pesto, 194
    hazelnut and coriander, 195
petals, crystallising, 179, 184
piccalilli, 88
pickle sticks, 90
pickles, 76–99, 217, 220
pine nuts: pesto, 194
pineapple: bottling, 133–4, 139
    brandied pineapple, 141
    cherry and pineapple jam, 27
    honey-pineapple jam, 27
    pineapple and date chutney, 111
    pineapple liqueur, 167
plums: autumn plum chutney, 112
    bottling, 133–4, 139

pickled plums, 97
plum and almond hooch, 146
plum and apple jam, 22
plum and apple spread, 207
plum butter, 71
plum jam, 21
plum jelly, 46
plum sauce, 123
spiced peaches with plums and
    greengages, 146
sweet pickled fruit, 99
pork: rillettes de porc, 204
port: currant and port jelly, 40
    harvest preserve with port, 32
potatoes, storing, 155
preserving pans, 9
pressure cooking: bottling, 134, 135–6
    jams, 13
    jellies, 35
    marmalades, 51, 55
prunes: apricots and prunes in brandy, 142
    prune jam, 26
    prune liqueur, 166
    spiced prunes, 96
pumpkin chutney, 105
purées, bottling, 135, 136

Q
quinces: bottling, 139
    quince and marrow jam, 23
    quince cheese, 74
    quince jam, 23
    quince jelly, 35

R
raisins: carrot and raisin chutney, 215
    spiced apricot and raisin chutney, 115
raspberries: bottling, 133–4, 139
    four-fruit jelly, 46
    harvest preserve with port, 32
    light set raspberry jam, 14
    peach and raspberry jam, 24
    raspberry and gooseberry jam, 15
    raspberry and redcurrant jam, 15
    raspberry and butterscotch sauce, 206
    raspberry curd, 70
    raspberry gin, 165
    raspberry jam, 14, 209
    raspberry jelly, 44
    raspberry kirsch conserve, 31
    uncooked freezer jam, 18
red cabbage, pickled, 81
redcurrants: Bar-Le Duc, 31
    bottling, 133–4, 139
    cherry and redcurrant jam, 26
    currant and apple jelly, 40
    currant and port jelly, 40
    four-fruit jelly, 46
    harvest preserve with port, 32
    raspberry and redcurrant jam, 15
    redcurrant and cinnamon jelly, 45
    redcurrant and gooseberry jelly, 45
    redcurrant gin, 165
    redcurrant mint jelly, 45
    redcurrant wine, 170
refrigeration, 7
relishes, 101, 116–19, 202, 219–20
rhubarb: bottling, 133–4, 139
    lemon rhubarb marmalade, 59
    rhubarb and ginger conserve, 32
    rhubarb and ginger jam, 28, 210
    rhubarb and orange chutney, 112
rillettes de porc, 204
rollmop herrings, 203
root vegetables, storing, 150–1
rose geranium jelly, 37
rose petals: apple and rose petal jelly, 47
    rose petal jam, 27
rose water cordial, 175
rosehips: rosehip jelly, 41

rosehip syrup, 171
rosemary: blackcurrant and rosemary syrup,
    171
    rosemary and lime vinegar, 127
rowanberry jelly, 42
rum: plum and almond hooch, 146
    rumtopf, 143
runner beans: runner bean relish, 116
    salting, 159

S
saffron: herb and saffron oil, 127
salsa di noci, 196
salsa verde, 196
salsify, storing, 155
salt: brining, 77
    salting, 7, 150, 158–60
satay sauce, 195
satsumas and kumquats, pickled, 95
sauces, 121–4, 195–8
sauerkraut, 159
set, for testing for, 11–12
Seville orange marmalade, 51–4
shallots: pickled mushrooms and shallots, 78
    storing, 155
short-term preserves, 193–205
shrimps, potted, 205
sloes: sloe gin, 163
    sloe jelly, 47
smoking, 7, 150
soft fruits in wine, 144
Somerset apple jam, 22
spice, herb, 158
spiced apricot and raisin chutney, 115
spiced beetroot relish, 118
spiced black pepper, 158
spiced candied peel, 182
spiced crab-apples, 98
spiced fig jam, 25
spiced peaches with plums and greengages,
    146
spiced pepper chutney, 105
spiced pickled peaches, 94
spiced prunes, 96
spiced summer fruit vinegar, 126
spiced vinegar, 127
sprats, salted, 160
spreads, 207, 214
squashes, 174
sterilising, 7
    bottled fruit, 131–2
    jars in microwaves, 209
    sauces and ketchups, 121–2
storing, 150–5
    apples and pears, 151–2
    bottled fruit, 136
    candied fruit, 179
    cheeses, 65
    chutneys and relishes, 101
    curds, 65
    fruit syrups, 162
    jams and conserves, 12
    mincemeat, 186
    nuts, 152–5
    pickles, 78
    root vegetables, 150–1
    sauces and ketchups, 122
strawberries: bottling, 139
    crushed strawberry jam, 211
    four-fruit jelly, 46
    harvest preserve with port, 32
    peaches in strawberry caramel, 142
    sparkling strawberry water, 174
    strawberry conserve, 31
    strawberry jam, 14
    summer fruit jam, 14
    uncooked freezer jam, 18
sugar, 7
    candying and crystallising, 178–9
    jams and conserves, 10–11

jelly-making, 34–5
   marmalades, 51
   sugar syrup, 130
summer fruit jam, 14
summer fruits in vodka, 147
summer pickle, 83
swedes, storing, 155
sweet and sour cranberry sauce, 198
sweet and sour figs, 97
sweet Indian chutney, 220
sweet mixed vegetable chutney, 102
sweet pickled fruit, 99
sweet-sour apricots, 98
sweet spiced vinegar, 126
sweetcorn relish, 119, 120
sweetmeats, fruit, 183
syrups: for bottling, 130
   candying fruit, 178, 179
   fruit syrups, 162, 171

T

tangerines: grapefruit and tangerine jelly, 48
   tangerine curd, 67
   tangerine jelly marmalade, 62
tapenade, 194
tarragon, potted chicken with, 203
tartaric acid, 10
temperature, jams and conserves, 11
testing for a set, 11–12
three fruit and ginger marmalade, 56
three fruit curd, 67
three fruit marmalade, 213
thyme: orange and thyme jelly, 43
tomatoes: apple and tomato chutney, 106

bottling, 135, 136
bottling juice, 139
drying, 156
green tomato and onion pickle, 86
green tomato chutney, 104
green tomato marmalade, 63
green tomato sauce, 122
hot and spicy tomato chutney, 218
hot tomato and apple sauce, 123
hot Wellington sauce, 123
marrow and tomato chutney, 104
rosy tomato jam, 30
storing, 155
sweet green tomato pickle, 86
tomato and onion chutney, 103
tomato and red pepper chutney, 103
tomato chutney, 218
tomato ketchup, 124
tomato relish, 119
turnips, storing, 155

U

ugli fruit curd, 67
uncooked freezer jam, 18

V

vegetables: chutneys and relishes, 101–19
   drying, 156
   pickling, 77–99
   storing root vegetables, 150–1, 154–5
vinegar, 7
   chutneys and relishes, 101
   flavoured, 122, 125–7
   for pickles, 77

preserving fish in, 193
vodka: aniseed grapes in vodka, 147
   citrus vodka, 170
   hot chilli vodka, 170
   pepper vodka, 170
   summer fruits in vodka, 147

W

walnuts: apricot, walnut and Cointreau
   mincemeat, 190
   cherry and nut mincemeat, 187
   pickled walnuts, 91
   pickled walnuts and onions, 91
   salsa di noci, 196
   storing, 152
Wellington sauce, hot, 123
Whisky: almond whisky mincemeat, 189
   orange whisky, 166
   whisky butter, 206
   whisky marmalade, 52
windfall marmalade, 63
wine: orange wine, 170
   redcurrant wine, 170
   soft fruits in, 144

Y

yogurt cheeses in oil, 199
Yorkshire ketchup, 124

Z

zahter seasoning, 198